A Life In Folklore
helen creighton

Other books by Helen Creighton

Songs and Ballads from Nova Scotia, 1932, J. M. Dent
& Sons, Toronto, and 1966, General Publishing
Company Ltd., Toronto.
Twelve Folksongs from Nova Scotia, (with Doreen
Senior), 1940, Novello & Company, Ltd., London.
Published under the auspices of the National Council
of Education of Canada.
Folklore of Lunenburg County, 1950, National
Museum of Canada, Ottawa.
Traditional Songs from Nova Scotia, (with Doreen
Senior), 1950, The Ryerson Press, Toronto.
Bluenose Ghosts, 1957, The Ryerson Press, Toronto.
Reprinted 1974.
Maritime Folk Songs, 1961, The Ryerson Press,
Toronto. Paperback edition, 1972, McGraw-Hill
Ryerson, Toronto.
Eight Folktales from Miramichi, (with Edward D.
Ives), 1962, *Northeast Folklore,* IV, University of
Maine, Orono.
Gaelic Songs in Nova Scotia, (with Calum MacLeod),
1964, National Museum of Canada, Ottawa.
Bluenose Magic, 1968, The Ryerson Press, Toronto.
Reprinted 1970.
Folksongs from Southern New Brunswick, 1971,
Canadian Centre for Folk Culture Studies, National
Museum of Man, Ottawa.

A Life In Folklore
helen creighton

by Helen Creighton

McGRAW-HILL RYERSON LIMITED

Toronto   Montreal   New York   London

HELEN CREIGHTON: A Life in Folklore

ISBN 0-07-082241-7

Printed and bound in Canada

1 2 3 4 5 6 7 8 9 10 JD 4 3 2 1 0 9 8 7 6 5

For Lisa my great-grandniece,
and all my other nieces and nephews to whom
she suggested I dedicate this book.

Foreword

Now that I am considered a pioneer, young people come to interview me, usually with a tape recorder tactfully concealed. When sufficient rapport has been established they slip it out and ask permission to use it. When I tell them that I collected folk songs long before there was any such recording device they look at me as though I came from a different world, as indeed it was. What time in history has seen more changes than the last seventy-five years? What were the singers like who kept folk songs alive down through the centuries and why had they sung them? Who were the collectors who discovered them and how did they work? What other folklore did they find? Ghosts? Witches? Superstitions?

There are few women whose whole adult life has been spent collecting folklore. One of the most interesting things about it has been the variety of material and of people. One week I might be in a humble cottage and the next in a palace of a former king. The subject has opened many doors. I would like you to come with me through those doors before age plays tricks with my memory. A grant from the Canada Council, which I gratefully acknowledge, has made the writing of this book possible. Here then is my story.

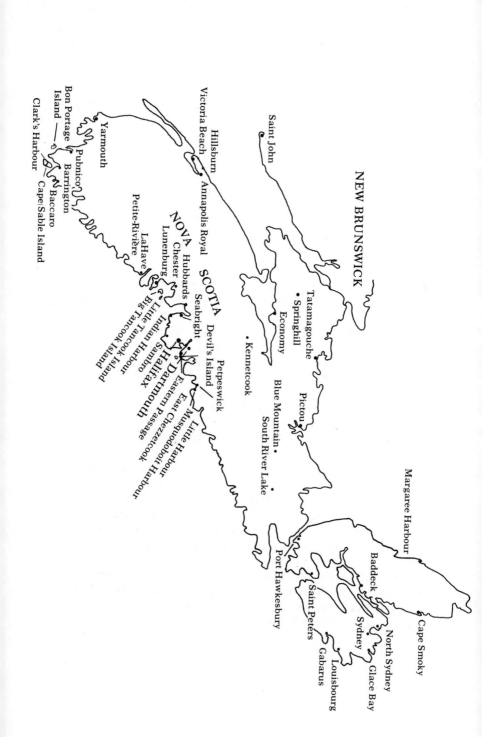

A Life In Folklore
helen creighton

Chapter I

Was it prophetic that I was born with a caul? This thin membranous tissue that sometimes covers the face of a newborn baby is universally known in folklore, and folklore was to become my life's work. The most common belief is that the fortunate infant will never be drowned (sailors used to buy cauls for protection) and will inherit second sight, or at least a sixth sense, and this is true in a slight degree in my case.

I learned the most comforting of many old beliefs about cauls in the 1950s when I visited Mrs. Charles Ritchie in Annapolis Royal after hearing that she could foresee the future. We made friends quickly, and after a while I said, "Mrs. Ritchie, were you born with a caul?" "Yes I was," she said, "but how did you know?" I told her it came to me by the way she looked at things. She then told me a person so born need never worry. Things would always work out for them, and this has been true for me. Today in hospital births I doubt if anybody pays attention to this magic veil, but on September 5, 1899, when I appeared, the doctor carefully preserved my caul (on a piece of foolscap paper), and presented it to my mother in the custom of the day. I must have been ten or twelve when it was shown to me and I thought the whole business ridiculous. Like my contemporaries, I had no idea how babies were born and I suppose if I ever asked I was put off with evasive answers—which seems incredible in these days. Mother wisely put it aside for a few years, and now it is one of my most cherished possessions. I also had the cord three times round my neck; if that has a meaning I have never heard of it.

I am the sixth generation of our family which now runs to the ninth. We began in North America when the Honourable Edward Cornwallis sailed up Halifax Harbour in 1749 to found the city of that name. One of his passengers was James Creighton, a lad of sixteen. He must have been a spirited youth, for legend has it he was the first ashore. We've traced him back to Glastonbury, Somerset, but it is believed the family is of Scottish origin. His land grant was Citadel Hill, once a fortification, now an historic site, later exchanged for $3500, two houses and a large tract of land in the north end which for a time was known as Creighton's Fields. One of the houses was Grenadier Fort, given him, according to an old newspaper clipping, by his friend the Duke of Kent, and this is where he lived. James' daughter Lucy married Captain Thomas Maynard of the Royal Navy and that is how the parallel streets of Creighton and Maynard got their names. He also gave the Maynard name to a lake he owned in Dartmouth which was part of a huge property extending from Maitland Street to the Nova Scotia Hospital on the waterfront and back as far as Oathill Lake. With the Creightons owning so much of the south end of Dartmouth and the Albros (the name of my paternal grandmother) so much of the north end, it used to be said that a wind from the north was an Albro wind, and from the south a Creighton wind. James Creighton's son, James junior, gradually sold most of the land except for "Brooklands" on the northwest corner of Pleasant Street and the Old Ferry Road where he built the family homestead, thought to be the oldest estate in the town.

Another property stayed with us for a much longer period. Mary, another daughter of the first James, married Captain James Crichton, also in the Royal Navy, and

when, in 1810, they presented her father with a grandson, George Augustus Seymour, James Creighton deeded
200 of his 210 acres to the boy in trust. Twice Creightons
married Crichtons, which is awkward because the names
are so similar. Twice they married Grassies, and twice
they married Albros. And to add further to the confusion,
a Creighton married a Creighton. According to our town
historian, the late Dr. John Martin, part of this property
on the western side of what is now Lake Banook was a
vast forest, a favourite hunting ground for the Duke of
Kent. I had always heard that George Crichton's
daughter, Anne, held her head a bit high because of her
brush with royalty and there may have been others of
royal blood serving here with the navy who were entertained at "The Brae". My cousin Isabel who is our family
historian, told me that Queen Victoria had sent her photograph to Anne and that when Prince Louis of Battenberg
was here he called on her. When all the Crichtons moved
away, mostly to the New England states, my family ad-
ministered what property was left. The last was disposed
of by my brother, Paul, as late as the 1940s, just before
the boom in property began. The name is perpetuated in
Crichton Avenue and Crichton Park Road and School.
Our two names were pronounced the same at one time,
"Cryton," and in England to this day we are always addressed as Crichton. It takes a little getting used to, as
we are accustomed to the sound of "Crayton."

The Albro family did business on both sides of Halifax Harbour. The name originally was Aldborough and
was later changed to Albro' and eventually the apos-
trophe was dropped. It is pronounced Allbro. Neither the
family itself nor the Nova Scotia Archives have any record
of the origin of this family, but presumably they are of
English stock. We know that they played an important
part in the settlement of Rhode Island, particularly in
the Newport, Portsmouth and Kingston areas. The first
record is of a John Albro who was granted a lot in 1639.
He went from corporal in 1644 to major in 1681, and

3

was a member of the Council for Rhode Island. His descendants, Samuel and William, were among the pre-Loyalist Rhode Island settlers who were given grants of land in Hants County, Nova Scotia, in 1761. Either this Samuel or his son later moved to Halifax and Samuel became prominent in the business life of Halifax and in freemasonry. His business was mostly on the Dartmouth side where he became a justice of the peace, a road overseer, commissioner of streets, and the proprietor of a tannery which shipped leather to Montreal. He also had a nail mill which was capable of turning out two tons of nails a day. The mill was run with water from a lake which still bears the Albro name.

Samuel's brother John lived on Hollis Street in Halifax where he owned two fine stone Georgian buildings with a carriage way between them. These eventually became the Queen Hotel Annex. One house was occupied by John and the other by his nephew and business associate, Edward, who was also connected with the Dartmouth tannery. One or both houses were there in 1819 according to an old Halifax newspaper (date unknown). It states that John conducted a hardware business in the lower flat and, in the custom of that day, lived upstairs. The newspaper says "The upper flats are finely furnished and the rooms have corniced ceilings and centrepieces. Obviously intended for gracious living, the upstairs rooms are spacious with attractive carved fireplaces embellished with decorative ironwork and marble," and so on. This was not the only place in which John did business, for he had a number of other properties in Halifax. He served in the army; Volume 17 of the Collections of the Nova Scotia Historical Society has a picture of Lieutenant Colonel John Albro (1764-1839) of the 4th Halifax Regiment. He was also Master of the Grand Lodge of Masons, and for a time a member of the Nova Scotia Assembly for the Halifax Township.

My particular interest lies in Edward. During the American Civil War, Halifax merchants flourished as agents for the Southerners, and they also speculated in gold. Profits from these activities resulted in a number of large houses being built, among them Edward's residence, Pine Hill, which in 1897 became the site of Pine Hill College. Perhaps he needed more spacious rooms to display the three portraits painted in 1854 in London by an artist named Herrick noted for portraits in oil. They are of Edward, his wife Elizabeth (Aunt Bess) and their son John. As John says in a letter to my father asking if he would like to have them, they were part of the Albro extravagance. They are handsome with beautiful ornamental gilt frames and originally cost fifty pounds each. They hang in my sitting room today and as Edward looks down on me I like his eyes which I find kind and with a sense of humour, and others speak of feeling comfortable in his presence. It is a strong face. Dr. D. P. Varma, however, who specializes in tales of Dracula and other horror stories, shivered when he looked at him and was so affected that he mentioned it to his English class at Dalhousie University the next morning. Edward must have had a stubborn streak because when his son John wanted a career in the army his father wouldn't hear of it. I remember my father saying that great-uncle Edward remained in sail too long which accounted for the loss of most of his business. Perhaps it was this inflexibility that conveyed itself to Dr. Varma. I have never heard anything but good of Uncle Edward—I am sure his spirit doesn't haunt the house, and Miss Marjorie Lavers of the Nova Scotia College of Art and Design who is restoring the painting for me says the eyes are beautiful. She too finds them kind and is very happy in his presence.

One more word about John. When he was a boy his mother died and in time his father married a widow with a daughter near John's age. Eventually they too married and when the wedding party came out of St. Paul's Church, the group of townsfolk waiting outside shook their scandalized heads, not realizing that there was no blood relationship. One woman was heard to say,

"Ain't it awful the things they're allowed to do these days!" My father always chuckled when he told it.

My brother Mac, third in our family, insists with relish that there was a pirate in our background although he can't remember who told him so. No one else living ever heard of this. We did however have a sea captain, my paternal grandfather, Thomas Colton Creighton whose nature was anything but piratical, judging by the diary he kept while on a three and one-half-year whaling voyage to the South Pacific at the age of seventeen, and another kept by his Aunt Eliza to bring him up to date on his return. After my cousin Isabel had typed his dairy, she summed him up as having humour, a cheerful disposition, a sense of duty, and a firm belief in God. He would need these qualities because in all those years away the ship only received mail once. Many years later, in 1862, he sailed on the topsail schooner *Beauty* taking Frank, one of his five sons with him. This was a Creighton and Grassie barque with a red house flag crossed white diagonally. The Albros also had a shipping flag for their firm with a white flag bordered in blue. There was a severe storm off the coast at the time of my grandfather's expected return and the ship was never heard of again. For years my grandmother, Ann, scanned the harbour, and if she heard that a schooner had come to port she sent one of her boys to make enquiries. Trade in those days was largely with the West Indies and consisted of lumber, staves and hoops for making barrels, salt cod-fish and mackerel. On the return voyage they brought back sugar, rum and molasses. On the voyage on which my grandfather was lost they were returning from Puerto Rico.

My father was five at the time. He remembered his father being chased by his mother through the house in fun and also his being kissed good-bye, but he doesn't remember their move after the loss, from a tall house on Brunswick Street in Halifax to the Albro homestead at Turtle Grove, just north of the present Angus L. Mac-

Donald Bridge. It stood where the Roman Catholic School is now by a stream of running water, and here in their younger days his mother and her sisters had often entertained their friends in the navy. It was not far to the Dockyard by water, and on summer evenings many boats rowed around the warships to hear the sailors in the forecastles singing. At nine o'clock the boatswain's whistle would blow and everybody would call good-night. Sometimes there were five or six big frigates with three masts and yards on all the masts. It was a pretty sight when somebody important was coming, my father said, and the sailors would race up and man the yards, five or six on some and three or four on others. Sometimes the ship's band would play. This would not be advertised as a concert but would just happen, and it was saved for a time when the sails were set. As a small boy he was often teased, and he recalled the bigger boys telling him that the shaft of light that goes down into the water from street lamps was used by fish at the bottom of the harbour when they wanted to come to the top!

One of the big events in my father's boyhood was the occasional arrival of a beautiful coach drawn by two horses with a coachman and footmen in livery. This signalled the visit of the Halifax Albros, laden with gifts. My grandmother was probably given quite a large sum of money by her father who ran the tannery, but before my father had reached the age of fourteen it was necessary for him to stop school and help support the family. He was errand boy and clerk for several years but this was not the life he wanted, so he took a bookkeeping course, studying morning, afternoon and evening, and at eighteen established his own business, C. E. Creighton, commission merchant and food broker. In 1883, following his marriage, he opened a branch in Toronto, but after one winter returned to Halifax. Many years later, in 1910 or 11, he was joined by my brother Paul and eventually they added Paul's son, C. Jacob, making three generations in the firm at one time. It became Creightons

Limited and under that name has expanded under the guidance of my nephew Jake. It has had its ups and downs and once in the early days it hit rock bottom, a calamity which took some years to overcome. The family has never been wealthy, but has always been able to live comfortably.

In 1879 my mother came from Kentville to visit her cousin Daisy deWolfe at Mount Amelia, an estate at the top of the Old Ferry Road. Daisy's husband, T. A. S. deWolfe, was huge, weighing three hundred pounds. He owned gold mines from which I suppose he made his money. The Old Ferry Road at that time was little more than a lane, but a beautiful and romantic one bordered with trees. Many of those at the lower part were willows with low branches which made a lovely place to stop and rest. A babbling brook ran beside the road and always seemed to be full of water. I expect much of my parents' courting was done as they walked up and down this lovely road. There were Albro cousins living in Kentville at this time and they were greatly amused at the sudden interest my father took in them before his wedding in 1883, causing him to visit them more often than he had ever done before.

My mother was a Terry, a name traced back to Roman lictors. *The Terry Families*, (compiled and published by Stephen Terry, A. M., Member of the Connecticut Historical Society, Hartford, Connecticut, 1887), states that the name among the early Franks was Thierry. They were said to be Romans, then French, and then three brothers settled in Wales, Ireland and England, and we are of the English branch. The name was found in the roll of Battle Abbey (England) A.D. 1066. Samuel Terry came to Springfield, Massachusettes in 1650 and in the late seventeen hundreds his descendant, Captain John Terry, came to Cornwallis, Nova Scotia where he had a grant of 3,000 acres, presumably awarded in recognition of his services in the Fourth Regiment in the Louisburg Expedition. Here too I am of the sixth generation.

A story is told of my Grandmother Terry who in today's parlance would, I suppose, be called unflappable. Some person, or persons, apparently decided to put her to the test. This happened late one afternoon when she and my grandfather were awaiting the serving of the evening meal. My grandmother was sitting beside a window that looked out upon the street when she saw a man and his wife, friends of long standing, approaching the house. When the door was answered they had the appearance of people who expect to be invited in. They were no sooner seated than another couple arrived and then a third. Without showing the least surprise Grandma excused herself for a moment and explained to her faithful retainer, Rebecca, that company had arrived unexpectedly. In those days most people had dinner at midday, and the evening meal, known as Tea, was more easily prepared. As quickly as it could be done without showing undue haste, the table was set and a meal prepared. My grandmother never knew who had done this to her, and the guests never knew that she hadn't invited them. I never saw my grandfather, who may have died before I was born, but I remember my grandmother who looked not unlike Queen Victoria and was somewhat formidable to a small child. My mother must have been quite pretty as a young girl with light brown hair and hazel eyes. She was of medium height. My father was slightly taller, had darker hair and eyes that were blue. Looking back, I can see that mother would have met Grandma Terry's dilemma with equal poise, but I can't imagine anybody wanting to place her in such a position.

When my eldest brother was a small boy he was taken to Kentville to visit. Letters came with messages for dear little Paul. After hearing them read he looked around at the assembled family and remarked complacently, "Everybody loves me!" Truer words were never spoken and they proved true for the whole of his life. Always loveable, a man of action, astute in business and a very present help in time of trouble, this was our Paul.

Next came my sister Lilian, the unfortunate one of the family. A normal child for her first ten years, she suffered brain damage when a board fell off a tree when she was swinging and as a result she became epileptic. Today an operation would have repaired the damage, but these skills had yet to be developed. Her mental growth showed little development, yet she had quite a sense of humour and would have been warm-hearted and probably domestically inclined. We know her brothers must have been fond of her because the attic has recently revealed letters they wrote to her on their early trips away from home. Their tone was affectionate.

My brother Mac (Thomas McCully) could well have a book to himself and indeed has considered writing his own autobiography. Blessed with considerable charm, good judgement and initiative, he followed the pattern of other new Dalhousie graduates in medicine and left for London to do post-graduate work. When the First World War came he was, we think, the first Canadian to enlist and the first on active service, sailing as Surgeon on H.M.S. *Argonaut*. He held many posts of responsibility. Then after a few years spent in Mexico following the war, he decided to attempt the impossible—to set up a practice in London's elite West End, something it was thought no Canadian could do. When our present Queen was a child living at 145 Picadilly, he often attended her and her sister Princess Margaret and later when they moved to Buckingham Palace he had many patients on the staff there. When Mac was eighty-four a Cambridge oarsman was taken sick and needed a doctor to fit him for the race the next day. It was to Mac that he came. When I asked him about it he said, "Oh yes. He had a stomach ache. He raced and they won."

My brothers were all fond of sports, but none quite as much as Syd (Sydney). He was a Civil Engineer and worked with Nova Scotia's Department of Highways until age forced his retirement. Although he did well at his vocation, when I think of him I think mainly of his enjoyment of games both indoors and out. He loved family games around a table and when outdoor games became too strenuous he was still able to bowl. At the age of eighty-four he drove to Halifax and back from Montreal for his summer holiday but, as his wife Winnie said, they won't do that again. But it gives some idea of his spirit.

Terry was next above me and I think it was for the way we held our fists as infants that mother dubbed us her Pigeon Pair. As a child I can remember Terry and his great friend Jack Carson laughing merrily at jokes in magazines. Terry always loved jokes and had a new one up his sleeve to the end of his days. His great sorrow was the loss of Jack in the First Great War, a sorrow so profound that he felt it impossible to continue his university training without him. Had he done so, Terry would probably have gone into the Church which he loved and served all his life in various ways. It was a proud day when, shortly before he died, he presented me with a photograph of himself in cassock and surplice as lay reader and oddly enough said, "I wanted you to have it when I die," having no such thing in mind for the immediate future. His death within two months was due to a motor accident. After a few unsettled years following the first war, including a period in my father's business and insurance in Toronto, Terry returned to Halifax in 1934 as Supervisor for Excelsior Life.

I would never suggest that the Creighton's geese were all swans (my mother was full of these old sayings), but all through my life I have heard of kindnesses done by one brother or another. They came by it honestly—because my parents were the same.

I was born in a double house on Portland Street, facing Hawthorne. Everybody was born at home in those days. Hawthorne was a short street with woods between the school and the next parallel street. I can remember coming home from a picnic one night when I was no more than four and having to climb a steep bank on Prince Albert Road to reach a path through the woods.

But I was not afraid of the dark, for wasn't one small hand clasped in my father's while he carried a lantern in the other? I mentioned this to Terry one day and he looked surprised; this was also one of his cherished recollections.

In December of 1903 I nearly died of pneumonia but by Christmas was sufficiently recovered to be carried downstairs to receive my gifts from under the gayly decorated and candle-lit tree, but I was not strong enough to lead the procession that paraded through the house before dinner with horns blowing in preparation for the culminating events of the day, the dinner and the opening of our gifts. We began our day by opening our stockings which hung on bedposts. These were not our own little stockings but men's great long woolen ones that could be stuffed to the top. There was always an apple at the heel and an orange at the toe, or was it the other way around? There was also a lump of coal for a joke, nuts, raisins, a toy or two, and at the top a tin horn or other noise-making instrument with which we could greet the day. After breakfast we went as a family to church, saw our friends' presents, ate lightly at noon so we wouldn't spoil our appetite for the turkey dinner at six. Turkeys were a real treat then because that enjoyment was reserved for only the most festive occasions. After all this was over we opened our gifts—such forbearance! During the day we could look at the gifts on and under the tree and if there were skates and the lakes were frozen they might be given us earlier. We loved the suspense. A few weeks later at Sunday School I heard the teacher, Miss Hamilton, say, "And now we thank Thee for one little girl who was very sick and has been restored to us." Suddenly I realized the whole class was giving thanks for my recovery. I can still remember the awe of that first occasion when I was singled out in public.

On New Year's Eve my brothers sometimes had a party when they would dance on a five-ply Brussels carpet purchased at a Dockyard sale in 1905—my mother's pride and joy. We were still dancing on it in 1933. At midnight they would go outside with guns to fire the New Year in, a custom prevalent all through the province then. On New Year's afternoon the gentlemen of the town called on the ladies who had entertained them during the year. In our house they were served sandwiches, fruit cake, Moir's pound cake and possibly blueberry or some other wine. Or was it raspberry vinegar, a non-alcoholic drink that was much more palatable than its name would imply? If we had tea or coffee I don't remember them. In some houses they were served port wine, coffee, sandwiches and fruit cake, and ambrosia made of sliced orange and cocoanut which stood in syrup and was eaten with a fork. This was a pleasant if somewhat formal occasion and preparations were made well ahead. When the first war was over and my brother Terry returned, he began his rounds as his father had done before him and was chagrined to find that nobody expected him. New Year's calling was a casualty of war.

Six for me was an important number. I was last in a family of six and my sixth birthday is the only one I remember. It began a memorable year. Hidden in my birthday cake were a five-cent piece signifying wealth, a ring for the first to be married, and a button we all tried to avoid lest we end up an old maid, as unmarried women were contemptuously called in those days.

We were spending the day at our camp which I shall mention later and when Joan VanBuskirk got the money it slipped through her fingers and disappeared down a crack in the floor, a calamity in days when five-cent pieces were hard to come by. One alone would buy five Mott's chocolate bars, the best I've ever tasted, and made right here in the town. We had a hail storm that day. Stones as big as robins' eggs fell and were held in our hands wonderingly. On that day too I was allowed to row our big boat with two oars, no mean feat in that cumbersome craft, and probably when one oar hit the water the other was still in the air. My father made an occasion of it to show I had reached a milestone.

The previous year we had moved to another comfortable house on Portland Street, now Hart Day's Furnishings Limited, where I grew up. Beside the house we had a croquet lawn and at the back a flower and kitchen garden. There was also a greenhouse for starting plants and vegetables and here grapes and roses were grown. My parents did most of the gardening which they loved. In later years I noted my father's hands as he worked in the soft earth, they were both gentle and firm, indicative, I thought, of his character.

Dartmouth in those days was as nice a place for growing up as I can imagine. Life was freer and less inhibited than in Halifax. The ferry, which Haligonians looked upon as a fearful means of transportation, was to us a social club, and crossings were anticipated with eagerness. No matter what the weather, men and women, boys and girls paced the upper deck to breathe the pure fresh air, even though they might already have walked a mile or two from home. When automobiles came in, the person in the car next to yours was probably a friend and you would visit back and forth. For those young people who got their schooling at the Halifax County Academy, the ferry trips were sheer delight, and many a boot was finished its lacing and the last touches given to a lesson during the fifteen minute crossing. This went on until the Second World War when the population expanded and strangers sat where friends had sat before. Now most of us travel by an impersonal bridge. Today's ferries are small and no longer take cars, and you may easily cross without a friendly word to anyone.

The ferries also took us to McNab's Island for our Sunday School picnics when we paraded from the Parish Hall with a band to lead us and sailed down the harbour to a glorious day on the island's beaches and playing grounds. There were quantities of food upon which it seemed we were expected to gorge outrageously, the band played most of the day and there were races with prizes. Then tired and happy we would take the long trip back and Miss Hamilton would tell us about the stars and make us aware for the first time that the dots of light in the heavens were part of a great galaxy and that some even had names.

Another annual trip took us to Cow Bay ten miles away. Two or three families with children would hire a horse-drawn wagon filled with straw to sit upon. The beach was beautiful, the breakers tremendous, and the water bitterly cold, but we never seemed to mind. More prolonged enjoyment however came from "Camp Retreat" at the head of what is now Lake Banook. It was then known as First Lake, the first in a chain of waterways that continues through Nova Scotia to the Bay of Fundy. It is just over three quarters of a mile in length, and an opening called The Tittle took us to Second Lake, now Lake Micmac, a mile and a quarter long, and thence to the Locks where we loved to picnic. Long before I was born my parents, with Crichton cousins, decided to pitch tents there largely because my father had digestive troubles and it was thought the outdoor living might help him. That meant rowing down the lake in the morning, walking a good mile to the ferry where of course he paced the deck while crossing the harbour, and in the evening reversing the process. On top of that there would be wood to cut for the evening's bonfire. This proved so therapeutic that at the end of the first summer my brother Sydney said to him, "Father, where is the box of pills you used to carry around with you all the time?" He realized then that the cure was working, and camping became an annual event. The bonfire was probably my first memory. I can recall Terry and me being put to bed early and trying to keep our eyes open as we watched the older members of the family and their friends sitting beside the fragrant burning wood talking and singing. After we were fast asleep there would be hot buttered toast and coffee made over the wood embers, so delectable that years afterwards when these young people had homes of their own they would come home to visit and tell my mother what it had meant to them.

Terry and I usually went to Sunday School together but one day I had to go alone because he wasn't well. I can remember him lying on a couch breathing heavily. Soon after, our beloved family physician, Dr. Cunningham, arrived to see my father but the moment he saw Terry he said, "What's the matter with that boy?" Diptheria has a peculiar odour which he was quick to detect. A placard was put up beside the front door with an order that no one must come in or go out, and I was dispatched to my Uncle Grassie's for the time of quarantine. (When the illness was smallpox a yellow flag was erected and sometimes a watchman stood on guard in a temporary shelter outside.)

This happened to be the time of my parents' silver wedding anniversary, so I went to the house that day and handed in a five-cent piece. Mother treasured it for years; it was my all, and I was eight.

When I was nine the founder of the Dalhousie Law School, Dean Weldon, decided to spend his retirement in Dartmouth. He bought "The Brae" from Miss Anne Crichton. It was at the top of a hill now known as Cleveland Crescent, and he settled there with his large family. His daughter Lil and I became chums and we were together day and often night, for their house and ours were always open to friends. This is the scene of my happiest childhood memories, and as I look back, winter seems to have brought the greatest joy. A long avenue bordered with trees led from "The Brae" to the Notting property, now "Oakwood," and thence to Lake Banook. We coasted there on sleigh and toboggan with no fear of traffic for it was virtually nonexistent. Up and down the hills—what energy we expended! Then in warmer weather, Lil and I would climb our favourite tree with book in hand and snuggle down, each in our selected crook and read to one another. Girls' books were not for us. It was adventure we wanted, and we got it mainly through Henty and Ballantyne, and when we were lucky enough to get a copy, that unsurpassed book for boys of all ages, *Chums*.

It was my grief that I was born a girl. A boy would grow up to have the adventures we read about so avidly, and might even become an Arctic explorer or a midshipman like those we saw when British ships came to Halifax. To both of us in time life proved adventurous enough, for Lil became a wife and mother of nine children, and I a pioneer in the folklore of the Maritime Provinces.

My mother could never understand why two girls could play together happily but would invariably quarrel when a third one came along. To break this, she decided on a novel experiment: to take twelve of us, at the ages of twelve and thirteen, to camp for a whole week one summer. Her friends thought she had lost her senses, but my mother was very good with children and, having six of her own, she had no fears. By this time our tents had been discarded and the camp consisted of a cabin with three square rooms, the centre one divided into a kitchen at the back and a dining room open on the east side, so that all meals, rain or shine, could be eaten out of doors. My mother slept alone in the sitting room while my father wisely elected to sleep in town that week. So did our nearest neighbor after the first night when our tongues never stopped, for my mother thought we might as well get all-night talking out of our systems and after that we would settle down. As she anticipated, there were no quarrels and we all loved it so much that this annual excusion continued for the next five years.

There were two conventional beds, one a huge feather bed given the two who would do the next day's chores on the assumption that they would need a good night's rest. The other was a straw tick hard as a rock. What we loved most was a bed of spruce tips on the floor made by my father. Eight of us nestled down side by side, breathing in the sweet aroma of conifers while we slept. We could all swim, row boats and paddle canoes, and some of us sailed. At that time molasses came in huge puncheons from the West Indies, and there was nothing better to munch on after school than a slice of homemade bread and molasses. Our brothers managed to get a few of these puncheons and had them sawn in half to make unwieldy tubs that were tricky to paddle. We had to use a special stroke or we would go round and round, and we had to balance properly or we would get a ducking. I used to anchor Terry's in the Cove and curl up for hours with a book. Often on Saturdays in summer my father would take us sailing in his boat and in the evenings we would line our canoes in a row and sing, unaccompanied, the popular songs of the day.

How we loved our lakes, and with all the activity it is strange there were not more accidents. One however had a strange forerunner which I learned about in the sixties from Edith Stevens who would have been about fourteen at the time. Her family too had a camp a little further up from ours on Second Lake (Lake Micmac). It would be about 1912 when they had guests for the day. It had been a beautiful day and by early evening the lake was calm and there was promise of a gorgeous sunset. Since their camp was on the west side of the lake the best place to see it was from the water, so she took a cousin with her and set out in her canoe, headed towards the Owl's Nest, an island at the upper end of the lake. At the same time her father took other guests in his boat and they went to the same island but on the other side. Edith rested her paddle and with no sound but the gentle lapping of the water beneath them, they drifted along enjoying the beauty of the evening. Suddenly she was startled to see her father rowing his boat frantically around the tip of the island. When he saw her he called out, "Are you all right?" "Yes," she replied and wondered why he was so agitated. As their crafts came together he explained that all in the boat had distinctly heard a call for help, and the sound came from her direction. There was nobody else who might be in trouble; indeed there was no other boat or canoe in sight. They decided they must have been wrong, but by then the peace of the evening was shattered. And well it might have been if they had known what was to come.

A few days later a tremendous storm came up and the placid water was whipped to fury. Two young people, Nell Burton and Percy Simmonds, had gone to the Owl's Nest and were caught by the weather. In those days it would have been unthinkable for them to stay on the island over night unchaperoned, so they set off for shore and had only gone a short distance when their canoe capsized. Women playing bridge in a camp on the shore thought they heard a call for help, but the rain was so heavy and the wind so loud and the call was not repeated so they decided they had imagined it.

Knowing nothing of this, Mr. Stevens took his boat the next morning and rowed across the lake to Graham's farm for his daily order of milk, and it was he who found the upturned canoe. When this was reported along with word that the young couple were missing, men went to the lake and grappled for the bodies. They were found in the spot where you will have supposed, the spot where Edith and her cousin had been the night when the cries for help were heard.

We at our camp were dubbed "The Infants" by Edith Stevens and her contemporaries who, being two or three years older, we called "The Grandmothers." Their chaperone was an aunt of the two Sterns girls who, like my mother, took them camping for nothing more than to give them a memory of outdoor life they would never forget. Indeed they never have forgotten. Most of them are real grandmothers now, and still look back on those days ecstatically. Today, just across the Cove on what we called Pine Point, a YM-YWCA building has been erected. Does this generation enjoy the Natal Day regattas as much as we did when we sometimes raced with the boys in paddling and knew all the contestants well? When evening came we took our decorated boats and canoes in a procession with Chinese lanterns giving light and many of us were in costume. Can the expanded Dartmouth relish such simple but never-to-be-forgotten pleasures of life as we did before that August afternoon in 1914 when my father arrived with an expression of fear and incredulity on his face to tell us war had been declared? What would become of the world, and what of his four sons, my older brothers?

"The Grandmothers" were contemporaries of as fine a group of young men as this town has ever known. In their early teens, or perhaps a little before that, these boys established a club and because they had a spot to themselves in the woods they called it the Robin Hood Club. My brother Terry, being plump and jolly and able to say grace before meals, was given the name Friar Tuck. Each year they held a banquet at our house and a friend and I were allowed to wait on table providing we got out of hearing the moment the speeches began. They reached young manhood during the First Great War as it was called then, and all served in the armed forces. Three were killed. "The Grandmothers" started a Chapter of the Imperial Order of the Daughters of the Empire while the boys were away and in their honour called it the Robin Hood Chapter. Years later their daughters also started one and called it the Maid Marian Chapter. Visitors coming here today wonder what Robin Hood had to do with a peaceful Order like the I.O.D.E., and one evening when I spoke to the Maid Marian Chapter I found that some of the members who had come here recently were unaware of the history of their name. A composite picture of these boys is in the Dartmouth Heritage Museum and it is good to know that their presence here will never be forgotten.

To most children the burning of their school means little more than a change of classrooms. All through our childhood we loved fires, and in a town where structures were nearly all of wood and fire equipment was horse-drawn and consequently slow, a fire would make such headway that the whole town would gather for the spectacle. We watched the tower of Greenvale School collapse with a feeling akin to awe but behind the excitement we were really not too happy. School was a way of life, we all made pretty good marks and we enjoyed it. We soon found ourselves crowded into a wooden building downtown known as Central School, and my parents felt this too could be a fire trap. This fact helped my mother carry out a cherished ambition: to give me a taste of life in a boarding school. Consequently April, 1914 saw me going as a day scholar to the Halifax Ladies College, escorted by Annie Carson whose family were friends and who was to graduate that year. The next year I lived in and came home for weekends. Fifty years later when visiting Dartmouth, Annie asked if I remembered a conversation we'd had about our ambitions on one of our walks to school and reminded me that I had said, "When I grow up I want to write a book. If I could write only one book I would be so happy."

Writing however had already begun, sparked by a series of contests in the *Montreal Star*, a newspaper to which a number of families subscribed. At that time it had a children's page with prizes of a gunmetal watch or a fountain pen. I think I won one of each, which is surprising considering the quality of one masterpiece which ended:

> But what of the kiddies?
> Fred lectured them badly
> And they marched up to bed
> So exceedingly sadly.

Actually I had begun even before that, for a story in a neat up and down hand about a little girl who wanted a pony was written for a school assignment at the age of ten. For years when we made out our Christmas list of things we wanted, I had headed mine with "Pony." All I had at this point was a tricycle and nobody would trade a pony for that. In the story, of course, the little girl got her pony.

I must have been about ten when I realized that my

jaw was too prominent and that my lower teeth were further forward than my upper ones, and that it was the reverse with everybody else. There were no orthodontists then. Nobody had ever mentioned this defect, but as I became aware of it I set about correcting it. I have no idea how long it took, but every night after I was in bed I would work my jaw to bring the lower teeth to where they ought to be. It must have been gradual since nobody seemed to notice the change this made in my appearance. My mother often said I was the most persistent child she had ever known, and I suppose this proves it. Looking back, it seems quite remarkable.

In those days I was known as Nellie in honour of mother's dear friend Miss Nellie Dustan. I loved her but detested the name. Again my mother came to my rescue and suggested that when I changed my school I could also use the name with which I had been christened, and Helen I became forthwith. Today the occasional childhood friend calls me Nell or Nellie and I rather enjoy this reminder of the past.

While the Dartmouth Schools were excellent in many ways, Miss Findlay and Mr. Stapleton were not trained properly in languages and could only do their best. I enjoyed H.L.C. as we called my new school but was so far behind in these classes that for years after graduating I would dream that I was going to Mrs. Trueman, our scholarly headmistress, for Latin and didn't know my lesson. There were many highlights such as the *feeds* that followed the arrival of parcels when we would cover every crack of door and transom lest staff be suspicious and we would devour the contents in fearful glee, listening all the while for footsteps of the mistress on duty. She probably knew and made a little extra noise to warn us so we could put lights out and stop breathing until she passed. There were *crushes* we had on older girls picked out as our Ideal. But the greatest highlight was the French play, "La Grammaire," put on in costume in our graduation year. A unit from McGill University on its way to war thrilled our romantic hearts by coming to see us and at the end gave their college yell. We realized sixty dollars for the Red Cross, a magnificent sum in those days. We were used to seeing troops on parade before embarkation and were allowed to stand behind the great iron fence and cheer them. For our graduation my brother Mac had a crêpe de Chine dress made for me in England and it fitted. I was as proud of that as I was of graduating, and it was a complete surprise.

I learned later that Mrs. Trueman was disappointed that I didn't go on to university. In those days there were no guidance counselors and a teacher would hesitate to advise unless asked. Instead I got involved in war work and took lessons in piano, domestic science and elocution. One evening as I was reciting "To be or not to be," with all the fervour of youthful heart and soul I burst into tears. I was tired out, and this was the beginning of the ill health which has plagued me ever since. After a life which had included swimming across Lake Micmac and back without stopping, a silly thing to do really, paddling Lake Banook with Terry in seven and a half minutes, steering my toboggan down the steep wooden slide on the Newcastle Street slope, a feat many men shrank from doing, I was told that life must be more or less sedentary because my heart was affected. I sat around for months and couldn't get my energy back, and when I asked my doctor if I could swim he thought for a moment and said, "In half the drowning accidents the victims are dead before they start for the bottom," so that finished that. One day I heard father say to mother, "The little girl doesn't seem to be getting any better. What would you think of a trip to the West Indies?" I wasn't supposed to hear this conversation but I called out, "Yes father, yes."

These were delightful trips enjoyed by many Haligonians and others, and two such trips had saved my father's life after pneumonia in 1910. Small passenger boats sailed from Halifax every two weeks, if I remember rightly. After Bermuda and St. Kitts they visited a different island every day. Mother suggested that for this cruise I put my hair up and go as a young lady making it my début. She went with me and we stopped off in Trinidad to visit our cousins, the Tod Creightons while the ship went on to Demerara. We picked it up again on its return. There were three army officers on board who had been wounded, and were convalescing. Two had artificial limbs, the first to come to the West Indian islands, and at night when they were removed and stood in a corner of their cabins the young stewards thought they were magic and were terrified of them. We were gone for six weeks, but even after this therapy, when I returned I was still listless. However too many things were happening too fast for me to remain inactive indefinitely. For instance we had the Halifax Explosion.

On December 6th, 1917 at approximately nine o'clock in the morning I was awakened by what seemed to be a heavy blast. Doris Davis, whom I had met on my West Indies trip, was staying with me. We sat up and saw towards the northwest a great ball of fire in the sky. Then came a terrific explosion. Was it the sixth sense inherited with my caul, my guardian angel, or what that caused me to shout, "Duck, Doris, duck," so that we quickly slipped under the bedclothes? Glass from four windows and plaster from the ceiling descended upon us and part of the window casing with the nails down was imbedded where my head had rested on my pillow. Like everybody else we thought a bomb had fallen and fled to the cellar. Every step was over broken glass but miraculously our bare feet didn't get a scratch. Mother had a slight abrasion over one eye, otherwise we were untouched. She was anxious about my father who had gone to Halifax, for by now we knew there had been a great explosion. Doris and I volunteered to find him. We dressed hastily, shaking tiny fragments of glass from our shoes for it had penetrated everywhere. Then we ran to the ferry. Dartmouth ferries have a remarkable record and not even this calamity stopped them although blood and broken glass were everywhere.

My father loved a spectacle and like other commuters that morning had been watching the great columns of smoke billowing from the burning *Mont Blanc.* Her cargo of munitions had ignited after a collision with the Belgian Relief Ship *Imo.* Father declared afterwards he was the only one on the ferry deck left standing, but it is unlikely he had any idea what he did. From the habit of a lifetime he made his way to his office on Bedford Row, and when we found him a teen-aged boy was helping him clear away the rubble of plaster and broken glass.

Then word came to run south, that another explosion would follow ten times worse than the first. Father wouldn't budge, but promised to leave shortly and insisted that Doris and I go on. We knew mother would worry, but daren't return by ferry and instead followed the crowd to the Gorsebrook Golf Links at the edge of town. Here sick people were lying out of doors wrapped in blankets against the cold and everybody was in a state of bewilderment. Before long we heard that the crisis had passed; ammunition at the Halifax Dockyard was under control. Back at father's office we learned that he had gone to Citadel Hill, the worst possible place if another explosion had happened, and had met there a Presbyterian minister clutching his one remaining child by the hand. His wife and other children were dead. I can picture them, both dazed, and trying to help one another. On the return trip we talked to two men from the *Niobe,* our one naval ship stationed in Halifax and docked close to the scene of the explosion. One had been blown from the ship to the jetty, but fortunately was unhurt.

By the time we arrived home, I realized that though I had been caught up in the general excitement, it was now time to consider others. Consequently I got the car out and started downtown to offer help wherever needed, but there was so much glass on the street that in no time

I had a flat tire. Three men helped, and by the time it was changed a distraught Mr. McAulay asked if I would take his family to his contractor's shelter in Halifax. They had been at Tufts Cove where the destruction was as devastating as in the north end of Halifax, and he had only been able to get them this far. One daughter had pneumonia so we stopped at Dr. Dickson's office but he had heard that one of his north-end patients was dying and had left in a hurry. A nurse was dressing a woman's face. She was fortunate because many people with cuts could get no attention and for the rest of their lives carried streaks where falling soot had mingled with blood in their wounds. I delivered Mrs. McAulay and the children while he searched for bedding, and on the way back I had the good luck to see my brother Sydney who had brought a company of engineers in from McNab's Island where he was stationed. They were putting tents up on the Commons, and I was able to tell him we were safe.

On the return ferry I took on another assignment. A mother and child were being taken by horse-drawn cart to the Nova Scotia Hospital on the Dartmouth side, probably because Halifax hospitals were filled to overflowing. There was no room for the sailor accompanying her and the child on the cart where the woman was lying flat. I was asked if I could drive them and first take the mother to see a doctor. Dr. Dickson assured us the mother would live so I drove slowly to the hospital with the team following. There were a number of discharged patients standing in the hospital doorway so I was given a young man whose face and head were bandaged from the nose up, a mother and infant and a girl about fourteen badly cut, and a man in agony because in addition to his own wounds, his wife and child were missing, and he was now in the care of two soldiers. After delivering the man with the bandaged head at Thistle Street, I had to go to North Dartmouth. All along Windmill Road, buildings were burning, and all the north end of Halifax, seen clearly across the harbour, was either in flames or smouldering. As we neared Tufts Cove I saw that spruce trees had fallen across the road and wondered if I would be able to take the mother and child all the way. Mercifully there were no more flat tires and it was a great relief when we came to a little green one-story house and they were home safely. By now darkness had fallen and the only illumination came from infrequent car lights and burning buildings. On the way back I was glad to take soldiers in who had been doing rescue work all day; they filled the car and stood on the running boards outside and hung on. The young girl was still with me because the Fairbanks Street house where she had been staying had been abandoned, and I said we would put her up for the night.

Tired out, I was thankful to return home. Father and mother had been hanging grey camp blankets at the windows all day against the cold and otherwise making the house habitable. But the girl didn't want our hospitality and begged to be taken to her home in Eastern Passage, and father, who loved to drive, thought he would like the six-mile trip. Doris went with him. Time went by and they failed to return. We were filled with anxiety aggravated by the fact that we had no telephone communication. Eventually they arrived by taxi. There had been another flat tire and father had been unable to cope with it. We were touched by the appearance of Mr. Ellsworth Smith, our carpenter, who dropped in to make sure we were all right for the night. We had lost one hundred and six panes of glass. This would include the small panes into which windows were often divided, the winter's double windows, and perhaps some of the panes from the greenhouse. Much of the plaster had fallen and chimneys were damaged. Picture frames were studded with tiny fragments of glass, and to this day we are finding pieces of glass that ooze up from the soil. Some fifteen hundred people were killed and six thousand wounded by the explosion. The world was shocked because heretofore it was our men who went to battle who were killed. Now for the first time women and children, the aged and infirm, were victims in their own homes.

Fortunately for me, though not for other people, it snowed the next day and I could rest with a clear conscience. Then we heard that volunteers were needed in Halifax, and the next day Doris and I offered our services to City Hall. We were soon off on a house-to-house canvass, and at noon theatre players at the Academy of Music gave us a welcome meal. That afternoon as we were coming off duty we got a ride on a horse-drawn wagon where we met a young woman who had lost everything. Wearing little under her coat and with nothing on her feet but rubbers, she was in search of clothing for her children. We took her to the Green Lantern Building where we got outfits for her as well as the children, and then to Colwell's store to get thawed out. I can still see her patient selfless face—we thought her a noble character.

One regret stays with me. As I was sitting in the car one day waiting for the ferry, a man approached with a sheet of paper in his hand with a song on it about the explosion. He wanted to sell it to us. I took one look and saw a line which read, "There lies a little baby's hand and there an old man's head." I gave it back in a hurry and we laughed at anything so gruesome. Little did I know the time would come when I would scour the land for someone with a song of the explosion. I found one in 1933 and another twenty years later, but I have never come across that ballad sheet, or indeed any other. Words (and music) which may be the very ones I rejected in 1917 are in my *Maritime Folk Songs*,* taken down from two singers so many years later.

We were to go through the same thing just after the Second World War (July 18, 1945) when ammunition at the Armament Depot on the Dartmouth side of the har-

Maritime Folk Songs.(Toronto: The Ryerson Press, 1961).

bour ignited. Joan Gregson, later famous for her acting at Neptune Theatre and on the CBC, was sitting with me on our doorstep. She had been our neighbor for years and was visiting me before moving to another part of the town. Again there was an explosion, but on a much smaller scale, and this was followed by other small explosions. Recalling our former experience, I had no wish to be caught indoors, but went in long enough to get my radio and a long extension cord to connect it. This would keep us informed about what was happening. Joan's mother joined us soon afterwards and then my niece, Kathleen, phoned to know if I would drive her and her children to Eastern Passage. By this time many were leaving town. As I drove back I wondered what I was returning to, and when I got to my own street people from the north end had already arrived that far. We stayed in town largely because Mrs. Gregson (Lorna) belonged to the St. John Ambulance Corps and felt she must stay on call.

All evening we heard putt putt as small shells exploded. Occasionally these explosions were severe but not too alarming. Cars went in a steady procession away from town. At midnight Lorna and Joan were so hungry they went inside, but had just opened the refrigerator door when there came a heavy blast and the door was ripped from their hands, a few blinds were ripped from their rollers and they had a taste of what could happen if a larger explosion followed. We had talked of leaving, but there was always Lorna's sense of duty. At twelve-thirty came the heaviest blast thus far, and with it an official ordering everybody out of town. Lorna capitulated and I went inside and called to the two navy couples now living upstairs, "We're going. We'd love to take you with us but we're going anyway."

Hamilton Gosse, bless him, called down, "We'll stick together." I thought his wife Gretchen, a very new mother, would never get the baby's food assembled, and the Morrows had retired for the night and had to be aroused. They had never been through an explosion and didn't realize the danger. Eight of us finally left in my car. I had locked the front door of the house but left all my possessions behind. It is odd how little they mean at a time like this. We had no trouble finding shelter ten miles down the road because our navy boys were Dems (demolition) officers and had access to another ammunition depot! We soon bedded down, but at four-thirty there was the heaviest explosion of the lot and we lay there expecting to return to a town in ruins. In the morning I drove Lorna and "the boys" back to town so they could report to their various work areas and was astonished to find the house still standing. The glass in the front door with its leaded panes was stove in and chimneys were affected, but there was little other damage. People in England and other war-torn countries who went through this sort of thing nightly, would take this in their stride. For those of us with the 1917 explosion still vivid in memory, the atmosphere seemed fraught with danger, and we were glad to see the end of it.

When hospital ships began bringing wounded soldiers home from the First World War, my father along with other men in business and various societies established a Halifax Citizens Reception Committee. From then until all troops were returned representatives met every ship and handed out gifts—an apple, cigarettes and matches, the daily paper, a card saying "Welcome Gallant Boys"—and their letters were posted free. Here we realized the difference between cheering men on their embarkation, and receiving them back crippled and broken. Edna Davidson and I, as daughters of members, were given the privilege of helping, and I scampered about so much from one sphere of duty to another that Miss Annie Bullock of the Immigration Service dubbed me "The King's Messenger."

Father and I loved being there when a ship was docking with everybody aboard shouting and cheering. Then as the ship nosed its way in beside Pier 2, the band broke out and played *O Canada*. Suddenly every man realized his dream had come true and he was really here, home at last. There would come a breathless silence like nothing I have ever known. It lasted perhaps a full minute. Then the tension was released and the great cheers that rose to the topmasts and beyond rent the air with joy. We could never experience this too often and each time it happened it was as breathtaking as if we had never heard it before.

It was exciting to grow up beside wartime Halifax where I went for many social events, and there were always young men for dances and picnics. I remember one night taking several Fijian soldiers of English stock canoeing on the Dartmouth Lakes when they were enroute overseas, and when we got into deep water they gave the war cry of Fijian natives. What nervous Dartmouth natives thought I never knew. There was a restaurant in Halifax called the Tally Ho, and some of us served there to raise money for the Mayflower Chapter of the Daughters of the Empire, our heads covered with becoming starched veils to distinguish us as volunteers. Here Halifax youth and beauty dropped in for tea, and it was a fine place to keep up with local gossip. There were canteens where women gave servicemen the nearest thing possible to a touch of home, and it was "the thing" to devote your time and energy here.

A United States warship, *The Old Colony* spent the early months of 1918 in the Dartmouth Cove, and her officers made our house a second home. They always came laden with gifts, and two with serious romantic intent. The house rang with laughter as we sought to turn our thoughts from the ever-present war, and occasionally a love-sick youth would pour out his heart to mother about the girl he had left behind. Through them I met young women stationed here to drive ambulances for the American Red Cross. (It must have been about the same time that I saw my first aircraft. I was in Halifax and saw a man climb a telephone pole to get a closer look.)

These American girls and I became friends, and I was green with envy. I could drive a car, so why shouldn't I join up? I enquired everywhere but was told I was too young to go overseas. Then I heard that the Royal Flying Corps in Toronto had girl drivers, and applied, fortified with a recommendation from our lieutenant governor, the Honourable MacCallum Grant. I was successful. My mother was still giving us our annual week at camp and all the girls helped to get me off putting in last minute stitches and helping wherever possible. In late August, with father and mother to see me settled, I went on my first adventure outside Nova Scotia where I would be on my own.

I wish I could feel again the wonder of the moment in Montreal when we stepped outside old Bonaventure Station and looked at the great Canadian Pacific Station above. How could man have erected anything so vast? With mouth agape I took in the marvels of my first big city, and when we sat in the lounge of the Windsor Hotel, we saw automobiles larger and more luxurious than we were to see in Halifax for many years. In Toronto I lived in a house where most of the guests were young war workers. Boarding places could be most pleasant and much more friendly than today's impersonal apartment buildings. Physical surroundings have always been much more important to me than they probably should be. My lodging had to be the best of its kind in Toronto, and it was.

My classification was Civilian Subordinate and I was issued with a man's greatcoat with a black badge on the shoulder which declared in white letters that I belonged to The Royal Flying Corps. For my five-foot height, it was ridiculously oversized but the jaunty little khaki glengarry-type hat was becoming enough. The ambulance was so big and I so small that one day, when I passed a curb on which Mother was standing, she heard two girls laughing. The ambulance was there and it was moving, but where was the driver? Mainly I drove one officer from house to office and back and forth through the day, averaging sixty miles, but while he was in his office I had little to do. I often came off duty at the same time as Augusta Jarvis, daughter of Mr. and Mrs. Amaelius Jarvis, and she frequently took me to their home for dinner. I loved the atmosphere of this gracious home, and her parents and family always made me welcome. Another friend was Dorothy Milner, daughter of a prominent doctor. She later served on the staff of the Extension Department of the University of Toronto. It was in the Jarvis car that I rode up and down Yonge Street on the night of the Armistice, shouting and cheering as they did all over Canada.

At this stage I was a small-town girl with no comprehension of what *sophisticated* meant. Right was right and wrong was wrong and there was no middle course. I was expected to behave myself and it never occurred to me to do otherwise. Toronto, of course, was different, I was unknown and one day when an officer found me sitting in my car with airmen draped over the hood and running board, he jumped to the worst possible conclusions. I was told I would have to go home. Yes, and in disgrace. With all the fanfare that had attended my enlistment, I couldn't do it, and I was not allowed to explain or be given a second chance. I was devastated. I had noticed that our drivers fell into three distinct categories: those from the old families, the nouveau riche, and the toughs, and it was interesting to see how they reacted to my dilemma. The toughs were sympathetic but would have talked back to the horrid-minded old So-and-So; the noveaux riches would have accepted the judgement and gone unhappily home, but the old family girls realized the importance of a good name and that it must be preserved at all costs. Again, as when I enlisted, I was to see how influence in the right place can work wonders. It was Mrs. Jarvis who intervened and in no time my slate was clean. However the nasty business took its toll and after an otherwise marvelous three months I resigned, finishing up a little wiser, but still far from mature.

I had always been a great reader, and a photograph

at the age of thirteen shows me sitting with a large book in hand, possibly Dickens, then my favourite author. Now while I rested from strenuous Toronto, I again read a lot. This could go on just so long, and one evening I thought, "What am I doing reading about other peoples' adventures when I should be having my own?" I put the book down, and reading has taken a second place ever since. Moreover something new was waiting.

Chapter 2

In July of 1920 Dr. F. W. Woodbury telephoned to say that money left over from the Halifax (Explosion) Relief Fund was being used by the Red Cross to send two public health caravans through the province. Each would have three ambulances, a truck with moving picture equipment and a touring car for doctors and nurses who would take professional services to outlying districts. They needed one more driver; would I join them? My immediate response was "no" because I was looking forward to a lazy summer with tennis and picnics, and the last thing I wanted was to drive an ambulance again. My "no" couldn't have been convincing because the morning paper a few days later told about the trip and featured me as a driver. Few girls drove in 1920, so this had news value, and throughout the tour they made good use of that fact.

What a scramble to get ready for a whole summer in two days! On the morning of the twelfth I saw for the first time the monstrosity I was to drive, a Chevrolet much used by the United States army, high, narrow, and heavy to manipulate, and when I ground my gears before an assembled crowd I was mortified. It was pouring rain, but the whole personnel formed up at the Parade in Halifax and Dean Llwyd pronounced a blessing. Moving pictures were taken, and I was told I'd be "heroine of the movies." There were stills of each car with its occupants, and many people watched our departure. With me were a spare driver, Henry Davidson (Davy) from Bridgewater, and a young reporter from the Halifax *Herald*, Rita Chisholm Frame, two excellent companions. Roads were little better than country paths and to make good time was to go twenty miles an hour. Every town we visited had its Mayor and Aldermen out to welcome us, and often a picture of the drivers preceded us declaring, "The beautiful girl in the centre is—." Gross exaggeration, but fine publicity!

Our first big hazard was Economy Mountain, and I found the touring car at the top awaiting me. After that, nobody gave me a thought, concluding that if I could surmount that elevation under its road conditions, I could go anywhere. With the confidence of youth, I agreed.

Our first clinic was at Five Islands, and Dr. Ritchie asked me to be dental assistant for the day. I watched him extract teeth without anaesthetic and without tears and from that time I was his right hand man. I even extracted a tooth myself once, much to the old patient's delight. So many tonsils were removed and later disposed of by our two Boy Scouts that somebody wrote:

Tonsils and adenoids removed here by Schwartz,
To be had on request packed in gills, pints, or quarts.

Or, when Dr. Sam McLennan substituted as surgeon:

T is for tonsils removed here by Sam,
He wades in blood knee-deep and don't give a—.

Days were hard for all. At Advocate, for instance, in one day, three doctors saw one hundred and thirty-three patients under primitive conditions. (Nova Scotia has changed a lot since then.) In a way that happens to me sometimes, I knew that in going from Pictou to Blue Mountain I would get lost, and I even had a map drawn to prevent it. As the road grew more wooded and desolate and we were deciding to turn around and go back, the engine boiled, the battery caught fire, and Will Chase, a young interne who was taking Davy's place for the day, had to walk ten miles for help. The thirty-five-mile trip from Port Hawkesbury to St. Peters took eight hours as one car after another broke down or slid into the ditch. The Smoky Mountain trip, considered today an easy part of the Cabot Trail, took twenty-four hours. As a Halifax paper described it: "Cape Smoky (is) a narrow tortuous road with a ten-mile grade on either side, culminating in the fog-encircled mountain towering over a thousand feet above the sea. Never before in history has this passage been made by a motor truck, and the slightest fault in mechanism or in steering gear would have meant instant death to the occupants of the truck which passed along within but a few inches of the precipice." Think of the risk, with all three ambulances being castoffs that were always breaking down. Being a girl I was not allowed to drive the dangerous mountain road but had to hand my ambulance over to Davy for that trip while I, to my indignation, was taken the safe way by boat. Whoever planned the trip could not have realized the danger, and of course it had to be faced again when we returned.

To make the most of our time, we were up one morning at 3:45 and another at 5:15. Again I passed Dr. Ritchie the instruments he needed, gave impromptu talks to children on the care of teeth, and often drove patients to their homes. One mother after seeing her four children through tonsilectomies asked a nurse where the driver was. Appalled at seeing me, the mother said, "Are you going to drive this car all by yourself?" and when I nodded cheerfully she moaned, "Oh my!"

At Baddeck we were invited to the home of Dr. and Mrs. Alexander Graham Bell and shown his great inventions. I missed this because I was watching a boy's tonsils being removed on somebody's kitchen table, and I didn't know about the invitation. I did, however, meet Mrs. Bell on the main street and was struck with the metallic quality of her voice, unaware then that she had been a deaf mute and that this had led indirectly to her husband's invention of the telephone.

At Margaree we had to keep some patients overnight. I'd had an easy day while doctors and nurses had worked constantly and I agreed to sit up. Will Chase was taking duty in the one-room schoolhouse; the father of one child was there and the mother of another. In the evenings Dr. Doull lectured and showed pictures about tuberculosis, a great scourge at that time. Men the worse for liquor had caused a disturbance and been sent away, but Will felt they would return, which they did just after everyone was quieted down. On their third visit they got inside the porch and woke the patients, but I went among them pretending nothing was amiss and mentally dramatizing the event: the courageous nurse in danger showing no fear. The father already had me on a pinnacle. Didn't I drive that huge ambulance, and hadn't I turned it in a space no bigger than itself? The look on his face was enough to turn any young head. In time it was quiet again and we sat on straight-backed chairs and tried to get some rest. Then from underneath the floor boards came the one sound that paralyzes me, and I jumped on the nearest table. I will never forget the look of disillusion on the father's face. "Just a woman, no braver than any other, afraid of a mouse."

This was the only Red Cross Caravan Nova Scotia ever had. We had lost one life, but through no error of the surgeon's. We had also saved one by virtue of being on hand at the time of an accident. I've thought since of the carefree way I drove children over bumpy roads after tonsilectomies, not realizing that this might start a hemorrhage. In all, we gave two hundred and twenty-one public health talks, had forty-one meetings with moving pictures, held twenty clinics, treated nine hundred and twenty-seven dental patients, examined six hundred and fifteen tuberculosis patients, operated on one hundred and seventy-two patients, and gave advice on throat and general illnesses to six hundred and fifty-two patients, making two thousand three hundred and sixty-six in all.

At the end of August, the two caravans returned for a great reception. It lasted for two hours, and twenty-seven choirs sang as our vehicles took their positions. Lieutenant Governor Grant, Major-General Foster and others spoke, the band played and the Rev. Dr. Clark pronounced the invocation. It seemed somehow superficial, perhaps because we were too tired, had seen too many people in need, and didn't feel one bit heroic, although perhaps we were. Few of us got paid more than food and lodging, and we all worked our heads off. Yet we had been a happy group, and Doctors Ritchie and Schwartz became my dentist and eye specialist as long afterwards as they were in practice.

In the days when I grew up, it was assumed a girl would marry and set up her own home, probably with a maid to wait on her. If not, she would live with her parents and do volunteer work or enjoy the social round. The former hadn't happened, and the latter had never appealed to me as a way of life, so I looked now for a place where I could be useful. Social Service seemed the answer, and that meant training at the University of Toronto. Three of us went from Halifax and were billeted at St. Christopher House, a settlement house still functioning today. Along with our university courses, we helped in the settlement's clubs and learned something of urban poverty.

A memorable event of the Toronto session took place when I went one day with another student, Helen Griffin, to her brother Frank's fraternity house when an initiation was taking place. Two students dressed as mother and baby were to go to the corner of Bloor and Yonge Streets where the baby in his carriage was to cry loudly. Years later Helen said, "Do you know who that baby was? It was Dr. Best," co-discoverer of insulin. In 1961 I related this incident to his son Henry at an International Folk Music conference in Quebec and thus established a very pleasant and unexpected friendship with him and later, his charming wife whom he brought to visit me one day in Dartmouth.

Mac, my second oldest brother, was always surprising me and shortly after Christmas wrote to me in Toronto to say that he was sailing from London for Mexico by way of New York and if I would meet him there he would pay all the expenses for my trip. On enquiry I found his ship would dock the following morning and that an overnight train would get me there on time. I sent two telegrams, one to Mrs. Wolcott Robbins who had been one of my American Red Cross friends in Halifax, and one to Mac, but there was no one at the station in New York to meet me. Then I saw a lace jabot over an ample bosom and recognized Mrs. Ellsworth whose husband had been head of Imperial Oil in Dartmouth. With her help I telephoned Mrs. Robbins who immediately fetched me and we reached the dock as Mac was going through Customs.

These were fabulous days in New York with a generous brother, and one day we lunched with a Canadian known as Klondike Boyle. I believe he was on a quick trip to the United States, and Mac considered himself lucky to meet him there. He told me that Colonel Boyle was the only person with influence over Prince Carol of Rumania and that he was trying to persuade him to marry Princess Helene of Greece to prevent Rumania from going Communist. Little did I think the day would come when I would belong to the International Folk Music Council and be housed at a convention in the summer palaces of Rumania's former kings, and that our meetings would be in the palace Carol had built, not for his Princess whom he did marry in 1921, but for the successor in his affections, Madame Lupescu.

I returned to the University and by February my strength was exhausted. Helen Griffin (now Dingman) was staying with her aunt, Mrs. Hartley Dewart, wife of a former head of the Liberal Party in Ontario, and she took me home with her. I was soon ensconced in a four poster bed the canopied top of which had a gold star edged in black in its centre. Mr. Dewart's mother was having her ninetieth birthday and one of her ninety roses was slipped out and put by my bed. I'm sure the dear lady never missed it and I needed cheering, for the doctors said Social Service was too strenuous a life for me. At the end of a month I gave in, and father fetched me home along with another of the Halifax trio, who alas died the following September. Mina was a tall beautiful girl and called me "Wee 'Un." We wrote one another daily as long as she could hold a pen.

Doubt and uncertainty followed my return home. What form would life take now? As I grew stronger and drove father back and forth to the ferry, I felt compassion for girls without understanding parents to shelter them. One day I drove a girl home whom I knew came from a poor family, and when I let her out she said enviously, "My, it must be lovely to be you with nothing to do all day but drive around in a car." I gasped, realizing how little we know of another person's heart and from that moment have never envied anybody.

As Social Worker, I made use of my Toronto training at the Halifax Infants Home where I had to interview unmarried mothers and sometimes the man responsible. I also conferred with the Stipendiary Magistrate on the proper handling of various cases. I did my best but was much too immature, and anyhow Miss Sibella Barrington, the superintendent, didn't really need me. I've often wondered what happened to little Helen, named in my honour after I had arranged her adoption.

When I was twenty-two Mac invited me to visit him in Mexico where he was practicing medicine. Mother had always taken my leave-takings in her stride, but when she saw my diminutive figure alone on the train at the start of so long a journey she suffered one of the worst days of her life. It meant the train to Yarmouth, boat to Boston, train to New York, boat to Havana and Veracruz and train to Mexico City. In New York, at the consul's office, I had my first experience of the head-to-toe look a Mexican man gave a woman, and was frightened. After a few months in Mexico if I were not looked at that way I wondered what was the matter with me.

This was one of my happiest years ever. Mac and his wife shared a house with an Englishman whose wife was on a London visit. Never have I sat around a jollier dining table nor enjoyed such sparkling wit. Our friends were in the English and Canadian set and we had few worries because if you let yourself start, there were so many things to fear that you would never stop.

Two events of that wonderful year stand out. One was the fiesta held annually on the sixteenth of September to commemorate the GRITO, the start of the 1810 Revolution. Mac had invitations to the National Palace which meant driving through crowds that had been merry-making for three days. No provision was made for traffic, so we literally tooted our way through the mob. At the Palace, guests were gathering on the second floor and, like them, we stepped out on a balcony. The crowded Zócalo, a great city square, lay below us. Many men wore blue trousers, pink shirts, and sombreros and, as protection against the chill night air, a serape in brilliant greens, reds, and yellows that slipped over the head. Women wore either vivid colours or black and often lovely mantillas over their dark hair.

When President Obregon arrived, visiting ambassadors were presented to him; then at five minutes to eleven on the dot he stepped out on the balcony. Mac said, "Watch! You'll never see anything like this anywhere else in the world." The Cathedral bell tolled as it had when signalling the beginning of the Revolution, and instantly every man in that great crowded square fired off his repeating revolver. It was quickly over, then we and other guests were taken to a great dining hall where, if memory serves me, we partook of a banquet standing up. On the way home five men in a car passed us, each with a revolver, fortunately empty.

It added spice to life to drive Mac's car when young motor-cops would come dashing up to the girl at the wheel. A friendly smile with, "No entiendo Espanol," a little flirting with the eyes and away they went. There were dances and picnics, but after four light-hearted months the altitude proved too high for my health. It was too soon to go home. One day Mac discovered an advertisement for a teacher at the American School at Guadalajara and suggested I apply.

"I'm not qualified," I objected.

"That doesn't matter," he said. "You'd see more of the country and the altitude is lower there." So I wrote, and along with the credentials I could supply, I listed those I couldn't. This honesty got me the job and I taught six girls, all half-Mexican and half either English, Scottish, or American. I didn't send the requested photograph because hair was just starting to be cut, and mine was short and curled to the nines. Skirts too were short and when I arrived, Miss Walsh, the Principal, took me for a new eighth grade pupil. By keeping one lesson ahead nobody guessed how much I had forgotten. Fortunately for me two slow learners kept the bright ones back. I got paid in silver dollars poured into a cotton square once a month, and walking home on those days I looked fearfully for bandits.

When I had left, a Mexico City newspaper, regretting my departure, said

"Miss Creighton is a welcome addition to the colony and since she is petite and an excellent dancer, it is needless to say that the Thursday nights at the American Club are much enlivened. To which could be added that while without doubt she is a distinct gain to Guadalajara, her loss is felt in society circles here."

I wish I had danced that well but since my heart murmur had been discovered, I was afraid to let go. Nevertheless dances in Mexico were memorable, and I managed nicely by dancing only the first half of every number. Our young men were tall and they would encircle me, bend their knees to meet my level and call "Fourth floor please." They called this game "Elevator."

What a happy time youth can be! In Guadalajara, my pupils were tall too and loved to take pictures with the little teacher in the centre. In class we kept a formal relationship, but with lessons over we were more like girls together. I cherish quite lovely poetry written to me by the Howard girls. It was a rewarding six months. However I knew I wouldn't want this for my life's work. I thought I'd been teaching first year high school but the Howards told me twenty-five years later in Washington that it had been the second year, and one girl had been prepared well enough to enter the University of California. Ena Howard and I still exchange greetings at Christmas.

It was my Mexican experience that started me writing, for I'd been to a bullfight and thought Canadians might like to read about it. I signed my article with my Mexico City nickname, "Golliwog," and the story came out in the *Toronto Daily Star* captioned, "Canadian Girl Witnesses Bullfight in Mexico." The other stories that followed were published in a United Church paper.

In those happy days I should have been looking for a husband, but life was too exciting to settle down and anyhow no young man could stand comparison with Mac. At the end of the school year I packed the mementos kind friends had given me and this time returned home well and happy. Then I began to write seriously, favouring poetry, so-called. To father my poems were masterpieces and one:

> I am a Nova Scotian with the vagrant gypsy blood
> A-flowing and a-coursing through my veins

he carried with him for the rest of his life. I also wrote for children and had written a book-length story called *The Tale of the Golliwogs*. Fortuitously, when this was finished, Radio Station C.H.N.S. was set up in Halifax and two of the men read bedtime stories to children. Sensing an opening and having my own story on hand, I applied for that job and got it.

44

In 1926 I was "Aunt Helen," the first station "aunt" in Halifax and probably in Canada. I read from my book, made woolen golliwogs for those who wrote in, wrote all the dialogue for the half-hour show, found the music, and was paid, by the *Herald and Mail*, two dollars a broadcast. Major Borrett, director, and Cecil Landry, technician, were often worked into the dialogue, and many times I had children sing on the air, probably another Canadian first.

It was on the strength of this creative effort that I was invited to join the Canadian Authors Association. I shall never forget my first meeting, presided over by Dr. Archibald MacMechan, a distinguished professor and gentleman of the Old School. Submissions were read anonymously and we were expected to make comments. When the professorial finger pointed at me I ventured a thought which I suspected wasn't very good, and was withered with an "Oh!" Then he explained what was wrong with it. The next story was badly written and I thought, "Oh no you don't; I'm not being caught twice," and this time I kept silent. The next day I met a member who said, "Helen, I enjoyed your story so much last night." *My* story? By my not commenting, they thought I'd written it. Fortunately this didn't discourage me, because membership in this organization has several times put me on my proper course.

I enjoyed being station "aunt" but after I'd finished "The Golliwogs" and several episodes of another story, my ideas began to peter out. Then someone whispered that members of the Authors Association could get free transportation to the national convention in Ottawa in June. I got a radio replacement and went off with Juanita and Helen O'Connor at whose house I had attended my first meeting, thinking that if I were to be a writer this was a golden opportunity. We stayed with Miss Claribel and Miss Winnifred Smith, who were in a transition stage between running a school and taking paying guests, and they used us as an experiment to see if they would like this new way of life. A speech by Mrs. Madge MacBeth made a lasting impression. She spoke of writers waiting for an inspiration and said, "A writer must be inspired every morning at nine o'clock." How true. That year the unfinished Peace Tower was open for inspection, the top ascended by ladder. We talked to the carilloneur, Percival Price, whom I later wrote up in Toronto's *Saturday Night*. (In 1966 we met again at a Montreal meeting of the Canadian Folk Music Society.) At the Ottawa convention we were often escorted by McClelland and Stewart's Donald French who liked the Halifax contingent and wrote:

Where do we go from here?

When I arrive at the Golden Gate
A weary traveller grave and sedate
And St. Peter greets, "Ah, here you are;
Did you come C.N. or C.P.R.?
And now that you're here and not in—well,
Pray think a moment and quickly tell,
To what part of Heaven do you wish to go?"
My dear St. Peter, how can you ax?
Of *course* I'm going to Halifax.

Here I met Mr. Douglas MacKay of the Parliamentary Press Galley and his wife Alice, both writers, and it occurred to me that if I stayed in Ottawa for a year they might oversee what I did in the field of articles, show me the markets which were plentiful then, and share the profits. They agreed to all but the last. The ideas were my own, and the MacKays added or deleted and the articles written under their direction sold easily.

Here too my health improved and I was less nervous and tense but didn't realize why. My sister Lilian was thirteen years my senior, and as I have said, at the age of ten a board had fallen from a tree and hit her head when she was swinging, causing her to become epileptic. I have a recurring dream which probably goes back to the seizures she had in church. In this dream I am doing something undignified or it might be the minister or someone in the congregation. Suddenly I realize we are in church. I have always been fond of Lil and tried to smooth her path as she strove to keep up with the rest of our lively family, but with such compassion for her, living so closely was much harder on me than any of us realized. Being separated was probably why I felt so well in Ottawa.

Living opposite the National Museum and Art Gallery, I found many things to write about, and I was there when the West Coast artist Emily Carr had her first exciting exhibition. Friends saw that I went to all important events and got me a seat in the Reserve Gallery at the House. They also arranged for my presentation to the Governor General and Viscountess Willingdon at their Drawing Room, the great social event of the year. I had the honour of a long conversation with Lord Willingdon and have a delightful memory of a grey-haired lady in a white fur coat over a long white gown, wearing her veil and feathers as we all did (or was it just those being presented who wore the feathers?). She was standing in one of the Gothic entrances of the Parliament Buildings with a light full upon her and a background of snow to complete the picture.

The year went quickly, and by now I had published articles and stories in all the big Canadian magazines. The next Authors' convention would be in Calgary and Banff, transportation was again available, so why not go? Then stimulated by the start I'd made in writing, I returned once more to my family.

Chapter 3

In Ottawa when looking for things to write about, my thoughts had often turned towards home. At that time *Saturday Night* in Toronto was a large weekly paper and it usually carried a feature article on the front page of the third section. There people read my story about Margaret Floyer, a mysterious Englishwoman exiled in Dartmouth in the early days of the settlement where she lived in comfort but without family or friends. There too they read about two little girls lost in the woods near Dartmouth when picking early mayflowers. Toronto women toyed with the idea of erecting a memorial for them. The older child in death looked distressed but the younger child, cradled in her arms, had apparently died in peace. Their grave and the Floyer home were on the six-mile trip we teen-agers sometimes walked, and we had always stopped to reflect upon them. I felt there must be an endless source of equally fascinating stories in familiar places, but when I got home I found that things that seemed romantic from a distance now looked commonplace and dull. Yet I must go on; who could advise me?

Why I selected Dr. Henry Munro, Superintendent of Education, I can't remember, but on a late spring day in 1928 I called on him. We talked of many things and then he showed me a book just off the press, *Sea Songs and Ballads from Nova Scotia* compiled by Dr. W. Roy Mackenzie from Nova Scotia's north shore. It contained one hundred and sixty-two songs with copious scholarly notes and forty-two melodies. Dr. Munro held it proudly in his hands and suggested I might do for the rest of the province what Dr. Mackenzie had done for the River John and Tatamagouche areas. "If you could find only one ballad," he said, "your fortune would be made." It was eventually, but not with money. At that time I didn't know what a folk song was. At school we sang the "Mapul Leaf our Emblum dear" and other patriotic songs which, incidentally, we loved. He suggested I take the volume home and study it, and what happened next seems more than fortuitous.

A few evenings later I was invited to a picnic at Eastern Passage at the entrance of Halifax Harbour. As the evening shadows lengthened we strolled along the beautiful sandy beach, leaving a small bonfire to burn itself out. On our return we found a villager, Mike Matthews, standing beside it, and in that easy way one does in the country, we began to talk. The stillness of the night, the long twilight, and the gentle murmur of waves lapping the shore turned our thoughts to earlier days and I said, "Has treasure ever been found along this shore?"

"Yes," he said, "a boy came to a farmer one day with a penny in his hand and when the farmer rubbed it he saw it was a double loon. That's what they call a gold piece. He asked the boy where he got it and then sent him on an errand. As soon as he was out of sight, the farmer dug, and that family has lived comfortably ever since. It isn't always safe to dig because there's usually a body buried with the treasure, but the old people will tell you about that."

"What else do they say?"

"Did you ever hear of oxen talking? No? Well, there was an old man living down here who had an ox team. (I had often seen this man distinguished by his white beard and sturdy team.) One Christmas Eve he went in his barn to see if it was true that the oxen talked then.

He heard them say, 'This time tomorrow we'll be drawing wood to make our master's coffin,' and he was so frightened that he died. Now they're fed at noon on Christmas Eve and no one goes near them till daylight." We laughed, but I learned later of an identical experience reported by Sister Mary Fraser from Cape Breton, and read a similar tale from Brittany. Legend says that all animals talked once but they gossiped so much that speech was taken from them except for this one hour. You may listen, but what you hear will probably result in your death. Mike wasn't through.

"Yes," he continued. "They'll tell you stories and sing you songs as well."

"What kind of songs?"

"Pirate songs," he said. Well, if the stories were too incredible, I could write about men who still sang pirate songs, so I asked Mike where to go. "To the end of the land (now Hartlan's Point)," he said. I asked him to advise the Hartlans of my coming, little realizing that a great new door had been opened and that the Eastern Passage road had become my path of destiny. I sometimes meet Mike and say, "You started all this," and he nods with pleasure.

A few days later with Helen O'Connor, my friend from the Authors Association, I called on Mr. Thomas Osborne whose name Mike had given me, and learned that his wife was the singer there and that she would write down some words. We were to return many times. Further along, the Hartlan road was so full of ruts we had to make the last half mile on foot. In a clearing at the top of a wooded hill we saw a cluster of houses with an abandoned house in the centre. Mrs. Enos Hartlan, on whom we called, knew me because she sometimes brought market produce to our house in Dartmouth. She was an eager talker and answered questions readily, but here it was the men who sang, and in daytime they weren't available. As we were leaving, she saw our eyes wander towards the abandoned house and explained, "That's our

Ghost House. I've been in that house and heard the ghost knocking at the door. Yes, and I've heard it come down the steps while we were sitting there. Ferdinand lives in a new piece he built on, but nobody lives in the old part now." She, and later the men, always spoke of it as one would speak of a prized possession.

The Hartlan's dwelling was small and built of wood like nearly all of our houses then. The only entrance we ever used led into the kitchen and there I did all my work, turning the kitchen table into a temporary desk. The interesting thing about this room was the board with nine German letters that was placed above the entrance to keep witches out. There were ten letters in the English translation which meant, "And the Word was made flesh and dwelt among us." (John 1:14) Enos, who I am sure never practised witchcraft, but who firmly believed in it, explained in all seriousness that a witch could go over the board but not under it. Since there was no open window above the board, they were now protected. I was puzzled for years to know how I could use the Hartlans' stories of witchcraft without holding them up to ridicule. In time I found a place for them in my *Folklore of Lunenburg County** because it was with other Germans there that the family had settled before coming to South East Passage. Their other stories of witchcraft are in my book *Bluenose Magic,*** and their tales of the supernatural are in *Bluenose Ghosts.**** Their folklore came largely from their German uncle, they told me. Their mother was English, and I suppose it was from her and from visiting seafaring men that they learned their songs, many of which are in my folk song books.

As we were leaving from our first visit, we met Mr. Enos's brother, Richard. He had a large moustache and

*Folklore of Lunenburg County. (Ottawa: National Museum of Canada, 1950).
**Bluenose Magic. (Toronto: The Ryerson Press, 1968).
***Bluenose Ghosts. (Toronto: The Ryerson Press, 1957).

rosy cheeks that fairly glowed when he smiled. We said
we were looking for pirate songs, and he agreed to ob-
lige us on our next visit. A few evenings later, Dr. Stanley
Walker, later President of the University of King's College, drove with us, and it must have been our high spirits
that lifted the car over the sandy part where it was usually mired. From the Hartlans' bluff we gazed upon Halifax
Harbour on one side, the red cliffs of Lawrencetown to
the eastward, and then the open sea. Mr. Enos answered
our knock; he was a small man with bright blue eyes,
wispy greying hair and a grey moustache, and he greeted
us with old world courtesy. Being naturally direct I said,
"I hear you sing old songs down here."

He agreed. "We don't sing nothin' else. I used to be
a pretty singer. I could sing all day and all night and all
the next day and never sing the same song twice. You see
them stars in the sky? As many stars as there are up there
is as many songs as I used to sing, but now me teeth is
gone and me voice is rusty. But come in, come in." Then
he told about the Ghost House, that it had been built from
wrecks, which was risky as the drowned seamen might
still be in the wood. He explained that persistent distur-
bances had forced the family to build smaller houses on
the periphery of their property. Eventually I brought the
conversation back to songs.

It was a pity Mrs. Hartlan was out, for men sing
more willingly and freely with their wives' support. There
was much clearing of the throat and repeated regrets
that "the bats" had got into it, but he finally started with
his tune pitched much too high, a common practice
among folk singers. The tune of "When I Was a Young
Man I Took Delight in Love," a song I've never taken
down since nor found in any book, wandered all over the
scale and I wondered how I would ever get it down. Words
were no problem, for I could write a quick longhand but
the dots which Dr. Walker suggested putting on paper
signified nothing when I got home. In other visits I got
words but was still puzzling about the music when one

52

day my father and I drove Judge Murray home. This was a delight, for he was a great wit and always left us laughing. Besides, he knew the area, and we told him what I was discovering. He said he had a little melodeon, or hand organ, on which I could work out the tunes and, with a twinkle we missed, that it had been used in services with the Micmac Indians. We learned later that actually his revered father had hymns played on it to be sung at his bedside during his final illness. It filled the bill, and all the tunes in my first published collection were worked out on this instrument.

I don't know how I did it with no training except piano playing and a little theory of music. It was made no easier by everybody crowding around. A trained musician needs no instrument, but for me it was this or nothing. Before long, tunes were shaping up and my head got a bit too big. Wasn't I clever? I couldn't get to Mr. Hartlan fast enough. By then we were meeting at the Osborne house to which Mr. Hartlan walked a mile or two, so that my car wouldn't get stuck in the sand where the road was low. The room was full, and all were anxious to hear the singing. I said, "Mr. Hartlan, would you like to hear 'The Turkish Lady'?"

He nodded and looked pleased and everybody sat a little straighter. As I played he seemed delighted, and if I'd had any sense I'd have left it there. Instead I said, "Do you like it?"

"Yes," he replied with complete honesty. "It's a fine tune, a fine tune, but it's not 'The Turkish Lady'." He was right, of course. By continued repetition and tramping about our drawing room to get the time right I eventually mastered it, but at that point I had needed taking down a peg.

Should I go on now with children's stories and magazine articles, try my hand at fiction, or make this my vocation? Then I remembered the Dominion Graphologist's reading of my handwriting in Ottawa and the observation, "You are the investigative researcher type." Was this right? Even with my inexperience in folk music, I knew these were good songs and sensed they should be written down.

My parents' advice tipped the scales, which was astonishing, for songs seemed unlikely to bring monetary returns for years, if ever. Nor was either parent particularly musical, yet we all felt there was something here I should pursue. Perhaps my fight against ill health had something to do with it, for I'd had another near-breakdown a year or two earlier due to what was then called a disappointment in love. Perhaps my vanity suffered as much as my heart, for I'd been much indulged. After the first shock, I saw how easy it would be to grow bitter and let my tongue say hurtful things, but that would make me a nasty waspish spinster. I made myself become more considerate of others and tried to turn my thoughts outward. I knew deep down that that marriage might not have worked, so I accepted the grief and kept my eye open for guidance towards what my life should be. Over the long months as I grew spiritually, my physical strength diminished. Then when I needed it most, a visiting heart specialist came to Halifax and was called in consultation. Perhaps my parents told him why I was so dispirited. I must have been a pathetic sight because years afterwards he told me he had never been so sorry for anybody in his life. Mercifully he asked no questions, but said, "Find some occupation you enjoy and work at it. When you get tired, stop and rest; then get up and go at it again." The wound hurt for years, but the struggle was over and I realized later it is not so much what life does to you that matters but the way you take it. The new interest therefore must have seemed providential to my parents who stood staunchly behind me, and for years my father would willingly walk home from the ferry if I needed the family car. With their encouragement, the graphologist's estimate, the doctor's advice and the feeling that this was my job, I decided to concentrate on folk songs.

Besides their songs, the Hartlans gave me my first instruction in folklore and I couldn't have had better

Terry and Helen.

Helen at age four.

The Creighton family.
Back Row: Sydney, Lilian,
Mac, Paul, Mother.
Front Row: Helen, Father,
Terry.

Helen, a graduate of
Halifax Ladies' College,
in 1916.

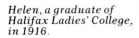

Royal Flying Corps, World War I.

Helen Creighton and Rita Chisholm Frame, Red Cross Caravan, 1920.

Presented to the Governor General, 1927.

Doreen Senior.

teachers, for their beliefs were so much a part of their lives. They told how pirates would souse (intoxicate) a man and bury him with a treasure so he would act as its guardian ghost. Enos would always end with, "Yes, I've heard men say that around these parts not once but a dozen times," and when at home I would repeat one of his old sayings like, "It's enough to charm the heart of a wheelbarrow and make a shovel dance," Father would match it with, "to set all the handbarrows talking and all the wheelbarrows laughing," which was the way he knew it.

Richard Hartlan loved to spin tales. He would say, "If it's a lie I'll tell you, and if it's the truth." When he talked of ghosts and witches, pirates and wrecks, he would look solemn and his eyes would grow round with the marvel of it all. A tall tale or song of exaggeration he would dub a foolishness song, and his face would light up as he looked for our response. Fortunately, I wrote everything down, mainly I think because it seemed to please them, but also because I hoped that some day I would see a way to use it, which of course I did.

One of the most lovely songs in my whole collection, "When I Was in My Prime," a variant of the English "Seeds of Love," came from Enos, and I never hear it now without thinking of him. Richard's greatest pride was in "The *Flying Cloud*." He remembered seventeen double verses. I later had a disc made for him, and for the rest of his life he would play it over every second Sunday. One evening father gave me a cigar for Enos and I made the mistake of presenting it before the singing began. He smoked it till it burnt his fingers and then finished the stub in his pipe and by that time the evening was over. Above all, Enos loved to have his picture taken and would stand stiffly like a soldier on duty. I soon discovered that all men like to be photographed, and to come back on my next trip with a few prints for their private use was much more reward than paltry dollars, which they never expected anyhow.

As I worked along this shore, people said time and

again, "You should go to Devil's Island and get Ben Henneberry to sing. That's where you'd get the songs," and I would look seaward towards the island at the mouth of Halifax Harbour near the Dartmouth side where there wasn't a tree to be seen. There were two lighthouses and a number of dwellings. I asked how I could get there.

"Just go to the end of the land and holler," Enos advised, so on a fine summer day in June, 1928, again with Helen O'Connor, I drove to the end of the land. Mr. Nieforth said I could leave my car at his farm as often as I liked and for as long as I liked, but a "holler" would never have sufficed. We were seen, and a boat came across the half mile to fetch us. Finding that we wished to visit the island they helped us over the seaweed-covered rocks and we scrambled aboard. The day was calm and the waves gentle, but I was to cross later just after a hurricane when the sea was so turbulent that we all got soaking wet before we started. Perhaps that first day was an omen that the island would always treat me kindly.

A number of women and childhen were on the wharf, all friendly and anxious to help. When we said we were looking for Mr. Henneberry to sing for us, old "Aunt Jane" linked her arm in mine and took charge. He was not at home so she concluded he had gone fishing. Mrs. Faulkner, wife of the lightkeeper, recognized my name as the "Aunt Helen" who had told bedtime stories on radio to her children, and for years they called me by that name, until one day Mr. Henneberry shocked his family by just saying Helen. Now Mrs. Faulkner took us to meet her husband, a kind, gentle man who took us proudly up the lighthouse steps and explained the function of the great beacon at the top. Before long I learned that Mr. Faulkner also sang the old songs and soon we were settled in their hospitable living room in the lightkeeper's dwelling beside the lighthouse listening to "The Farmer's Curst Wife" whom the devil took to hell where she was such a nuisance he brought her back again. It has a whistling chorus which in some places is sung to words instead, probably because some old timers hadn't enough teeth to make a whistle. After a while, Mr. Ben's son Edmund walked in. He and a Faulkner son, Ken, were friends, and years later they recorded the most ancient ballad in my collection, "The False Knight upon the Road," with Ken playing a fiddle accompaniment. On this first visit the song came timidly because Edmund was shy, and he sang unaccompanied, the usual way in Nova Scotia.

Devil's Island is one mile in circumference and never more than eleven feet above sea level. At that time there were seventeen houses there, fourteen of which were occupied. The inhabitants were of English, Irish and Welsh descent and the Henneberrys, whose name was predominant, probably came with Alexander McNutt early in the nineteenth century when he brought 300 Irish settlers over. Fishing was their occupation and they found their catch in waters near at hand. They also had a government lifeboat of which Mr. Ben was coxswain. They told me there had been trees there once, but they had been cut down to make lobster traps and to fill various household needs. Houses were made of wood and were small but comfortable, with the kitchen the focal point. The Faulkners had the largest house since it was government-owned, and it stood between the two lighthouses facing the open sea. Mrs. Faulkner was a fine looking woman with beautiful brown eyes and she was an excellent housekeeper. They all loved company and in all subsequent visits to the island I was always made to feel welcome. The island is deserted now because in the Second World War the government discouraged them from living in this vulnerable position.

By early evening on the day of our first visit to the island, we were still at the Faulkner's, nourished by home-made bread, strawberry jam, and tea. We had despaired of seeing Mr. Ben. We strolled slowly along the narrow footpath to the boats. On such a night most people had wandered towards the little harbour formed by two breakwaters and were watching the sun setting over Citadel

Hill, ten miles away in Halifax. Some men sat on a log, and I inquired if one might be Mr. Ben. A short stocky man stood up and I asked if he would sing. He agreed readily and began the long sad tale of the children lost in the woods near Dartmouth whose story I had written for Toronto's *Saturday Night*. The others had heard it many times, yet hung on every word as the familiar voice floated over the still night air. Then more joined us, moving quietly lest they disrupt the poignant tale. Like wraiths they slipped between fish houses and sat on barrels, lobster pots, or wherever they could find a perch, and sometimes Aunt Jane's high quavering voice would join the singer's. They were torn between sympathy for the lost children and pride in their singer. Then Mr. Gordon Young sang about the Ghostly Sailors who, when the boat that rammed their vessel next sailed over the spot where they had drowned, had come aboard and taken over.

It seemed unreal, this setting so near home, yet so remote. It was like stepping into a different world, and we were loathe to leave, but the sun had set now and we still had to go ashore and find our car. When the boatmen left us alone on the mainland in pitch darkness, we realized we were in territory peopled with Enos Hartlan's ghosts and witches. Helen and I held hands and made our way over rough terrain and stunted growth as best we could. It was a happy moment when the car came into sight and the engine purred to my command. Starry-eyed and full of news we finally burst in upon my parents and told the adventures of our day.

Other daytime trips were profitable but I realized that if I wanted songs I must go to the island and stay, so a few weeks later I asked Mrs. Faulkner if she would board me. Then came one of the most strenuous weeks I've ever spent. I was given a bedroom downstairs at the front of the house while the rest of the family slept upstairs, and my coverlet was from a warship, H.M.S. *Dauntless*, I think. The islanders had retrieved some items after a part of the ship's cargo had to be jettisoned. It was perhaps as well that the Faulkners' dwelling was not a part of the lighthouse as it was in many cases, because I learned many years later that the lighthouse was haunted. With such a kind host and hostess I had nothing to fear.

In the morning, Mr. Ben, so called to distinguish him from all the other Henneberrys, would sing while mending his nets, and I would sit in the door of his fishhouse with the melodeon at my side. It had a wooden case with leather handle, but was too heavy to carry, so I pushed it in the Faulkners' wheelbarrow. In the afternoon the children sang their fathers' songs, and it was strange to hear from them of Villikens and his Dinah, and how he "kissed her cold corpus a thousand times o'er." Later, at his home, Mr. Ben would sing for another hour songs learned when fishing off Newfoundland's banks, or from sailors shipwrecked on their island. Mrs. Henneberry would give what encouragement she could. One afternoon he sang the whole seventy-eight verses of "The Courtship of Willie Riley" at one sitting. I shifted from one hand to the other, trying to keep up with the words.

After the briefest rest, I would hear the latch lift as the first evening visitor arrived. Mr. Ben would come at seven, and as long as he was there nobody would sing because he had taught them most of the songs they knew, so they felt the songs were his. The singers were never interrupted except to help if a word or line was forgotten. If the tempo was too quick to write down all the words at the first singing, I would get the opening line of each new verse and fill in later because in repeating, a whole verse might be left out. Then came the tune and everybody helped. They felt that what I was doing was important, but if their songs were being preserved, they wanted them to be right. I realized this a few months later when Mrs. Faulkner called to know if she, Ken, and Lawrence Henneberry could come to hear a talk the newspaper said I would give at our house to the Authors Association describing my collecting work. When it was over they looked troubled so I said, "Is something wrong?"

"It's 'The *Mary L. MacKay*,' " they said. "It goes with more of a swing." I worked it out with them and discovered it should have been in two-quarter time and not six-eighths. That settled, they departed happily.

During my stay on the island, Mr. Ben would leave soon after nine, and before I could begin with someone else, Mr. Faulkner sometimes turned the radio on. Why? To make me take a rest. The younger men would sing then and it was usually three a.m. before the last one left. A modern collector with tape recorder could never imagine such a day. Added to the transcription of songs in a room jammed with people, it was necessary to keep the singer interested so he wouldn't weary of repeating a phrase over and over again. I soon learned how to put tails on the music dots and to divide the notes in bars, and the instrument must have been in better shape than it is to-day. The results were far from perfect, but this was a lot better than not doing it at all. Then one day a year or so later, I wondered if a dictaphone might help, and tried one out on the Hartlans where I got twenty-six songs at a sitting that might have yielded six before. The Devil's Island week had given me one hundred songs, and I am amazed because years later, with a tape recorder, I thought I'd done well to complete ninety in that time.

They used to say on the Island, "You ought to come at Christmas; that's when you'd get the songs. We dance in the lighthouse from Christmas to New Year," but I sensed there would be drinking which would mean muddled thinking and songs begun but never finished. There were other trips, and sometimes Mr. and Mrs. Henneberry would come to our house where he would sing into the dictaphone. Later I got him on disc recordings, but his diction was so bad due to a facial deformity, that I often needed help to make out his words. Fortunately his son Edmund knew them all and many years later with the words before him recorded them in the longest session I've ever had. The clock struck one shortly after we began and when it struck eleven that night we were still recording. The willingness to share in those early days and the kindness all the Islanders showed was so heart-warming that I wanted to do something in return, something personal they would have to remember. My parents and I finally hit upon an idea. We invited six of them for evening dinner and we did it up in style. We enjoyed it, and I think they did too.

By the end of a year I had a sizeable collection, and Mr. Murray Gibbon, Chief Publicity Agent for the Canadian Pacific Railways who was then putting on folk festivals in western Canada, paid me sixty dollars for ten pirate songs. I took the rest to Dr. Archibald MacMechan, head of the English Department at Dalhousie University. He had been President of the Canadian Authors Association when I joined them. As he read, he grew excited and sent for Dr. McOdrum, a young professor who had just taken his Ph.D. in ballads in Scotland. Both assured me I had some rare treasures, but what should my next step be? To publish anything comparable to the Mackenzie book would mean scholarly notes far beyond my capabilities, so Dr. MacMechan asked Dr. McOdrum if he would do them and he readily agreed. Unfortunately he was going through an unsettled period due to the death of his wife, and the promise was never fulfilled. For years I held this against him until I realized he had actually done me a service because Mr. Murray Gibbon and Dr. Marius Barbeau of the National Museum urged me to do it myself. How this was to be accomplished I had no idea, but in 1931 I went to Queen's University where Dr. McOdrum was teaching, retrieved the manuscript, and, with no definite purpose in mind, went to Toronto.

Again it seemed more than fortuitous that a day or two later at a matinée I espied Dr. E. A. Hardy, then the National President of the Authors Association, in the lobby, and I wasted no time in telling him my problem.

He suggested Mr. Stewart Wallace, University of Toronto Librarian, as the person to advise me, and he in turn sent me to Dr. John Robins, professor of English at Victoria College. Dr. Robins had himself made a collection of ballads but had lost them by fire. Instead of nursing bitterness at his bad luck, he rejoiced to have another collection to work on and immediately secured an unused room at the College and brought all his private folk song library there. Then he showed me how to go through every book and read every word of every published folk song and ballad available and, when I found a variant of any song in my collection, or an outstanding line or phrase that would be comparable, to make a note of it. He also arranged for me to use the Toronto Public Library. Every few days we would go over what I had done and he would give encouragement where deserved, and straighten out inevitable mistakes. When I thanked him he would wave such thoughts aside, although he knew even better than I how much I needed him.

With the scholarly notes looked after, there still remained the problem of music. Soon after my collecting began, I had met Mr. Campbell McInnes when he had brought a girls' chorus to Halifax, and I had wondered then if I would ever find music to enchant others as theirs had enchanted me. He had advised me to consult Dr. Healey Willan at the Toronto Conservatory of Music, so I went to see him. I suppose it was my eagerness and complete sincerity that did it, combined with my good fortune in looking like his sister! He examined my feeble efforts and agreed to straighten them out with Mr. McInnes to help him and Sir Ernest MacMillan as well. It took a few months longer than they anticipated, but eventually it was finished and the manuscript sent off to a publisher who had expressed an interest, J. M. Dent & Sons.

Back home in Dartmouth, February eleventh, 1932, was a red letter day for me. It began with a luncheon invitation from Lieutenant Governor and Mrs. Covert in honour of His Excellency the Governor General, Lord Bessborough. This was a tribute to the position I was achieving as a writer. A much greater excitement, however, was the arrival of the express at noon with the parcel I'd been waiting for, my books at last. I would have liked to wait for Father to share the opening of the parcel with Mother and me, but I couldn't contain myself that long. I wasn't prepared for anything so beautifully executed. As I held a copy in my hands I felt as a mother must when she holds her first child in her arms. Jacket and end papers had been drawn by Reginald Knowles of "Everyman's Library" fame who wrote that he had styled them out of the quaint woodcuts that adorned the old broadside ballad sheets. In fact the cover was made to look like old lace or tapestry, and the dust jacket was designed to bring out the feeling of woodcuts. He had studied the text, for the drawings show the devil coming to the man at the plough as in "The Farmer's Curst Wife." "The Bold Pedlar and Robin Hood" are there, "The Miller and His Three Sons" and so forth.

Reviews were kind. The *Toronto Evening Telegram*, under the initials C.H.J.S., wrote, "The book is beautifully prepared and (has) ample footnotes following each selection, elucidating the meaning and explaining the sources, or comparing the Nova Scotia variants with the originals from the old lands. One excellent line-drawing by R. Wilcox of the boats and fish stores and nets and gear on Devil's Island, supplies alike a frontispiece and a key to the spirit of the collection. The latter is pleasantly emphasized by Reginald L. Knowles' end-papers, filled with knights and sailors and ships and shepherdesses and doves and devils and drummer-boys and all the motley company who gallop through these hundred and a half songs." Publication of this de luxe edition was made possible by my good friend Dr. Munro who ordered two hundred and fifty copies for Nova Scotia schools. Many were given to musicians and other dignitaries as a memento of their visit to our province. Thirty-five years later, it was reprinted by the Dover Publishing Company of New York at their request.

On the Sunday of the week my book was published,

we launched it with a christening party. Entertaining was easy then, and we invited thirty-three guests, personal and literary friends. I had already said thank-you in church that morning and all the hymns seemed appropriate to the occasion. The big thrill came when it was announced at the party that Mr. Gilbert Hart would sing "The *Mary L. MacKay*," and Mr. Chesley Allen called out, "What page and number?" It made it seem so real.

By now we were living in a much larger house purchased in 1919 from my cousin Graham and his wife. The house commanded a magnificent view of Halifax Harbour for ten miles to the open sea. Ours was a happy home and a truly Christian one. My father was a great Bible student and taught a Bible class for twenty-five years. He nearly gave up once, but on a walk beside Sullivan's Pond he had a vision which told him to go on. He used to say there were many things he couldn't understand in the Bible but that the nearer he could live to the teaching of Christ, the better he would be. This was his standard and example. We all went to church on Sunday morning, to Sunday School in the afternoon and often, of our own choice, to the evening service. Occasionally we stayed at camp on Sunday but always had a short service conducted under the trees by my father. In later years we have all found comfort, strength, and courage within the sacred walls that we could find nowhere else. There is something about getting down on your knees and praying that is therapeutic even if you are uncertain where your prayers go; but they are heard, for I have often had directives when praying. I've always begun my day with a short prayer and I start my nightly prayer with a thank you for all the blessings of the day. Then I think of special blessings and marvel that there are always so many. Or, on one of those dreadful days there is always something, even if it has been only a bright star in the sky, which has startled me with its beauty.

In addition to my collecting, I had become Halifax correspondent for *Mayfair*, then a prestigious society

magazine published in Toronto. I had dramatic ambitions
and took part in a play at St. James Church, Dartmouth,
which was later repeated in Halifax. In Ottawa I had
auditioned for their Little Theatre but didn't quite make
it. Four times a day I drove father to and from the ferry
and spent many an afternoon driving mother and her
friends to their bridge games and teas. There were trips
to Devil's Island and Eastern Passage for more songs,
and many visits to my brother Paul's house to comfort
him and his five children following the death of his wife.
I wrote short stories and a book which I coudn't sell, and
in June heard a chorus of 1300 school children sing
"Caroline and Her Young Sailor Bold" from my collection. This good idea had come from Mr. B. C. Silver, then
Director of School Music. Yes, from 1300 young throats
the pleasant music floated over the summer air, and if
there was a little extra wallop to my heart beat, it is little
wonder.

For years the Nova Scotia Summer School had been
bringing interesting people here, and one day I was invited to meet a new teacher, Miss Doreen Senior of the
English Folk Song and Dance Society. She liked people
and they liked her to such an extent that whenever I
met one of her old summer school students in later years,
they would always ask about her. She was a musician
with the gift of perfect pitch and she had an interest in
folk music. Her schedule was heavy, but she had abun-
dant energy. We talked about English folk songs, what I
had found here and my problems with music. I asked if
she would like to go collecting with me, but made it clear
that as far as money was concerned it was a gamble,
since I had none to offer. She was too interested to let
this deter her, and, after a few more meetings, when our
friendship had ripened, we decided to spend the two weeks
at the end of her term, before she returned to England,
on a collecting trip.

Books on collecting usually said that folk songs
were found in remote areas where people had no outside

interests and were forced to entertain themselves. With this in mind we chose Cape Breton, and named the family car Cecil in honour of the great English collector Cecil Sharp, whose work we tried to emulate. We set out on August 15th, 1932, full of high spirits and a sense of adventure. We were both in our early thirties. This might be called the Year of the Giggles, so merrily did we ride.

Cape Breton Island, except for the steel plant and the mining towns in the Sydney area, was largely rural in 1932, and on my summer trips I found it so beautiful I wondered why I ever spent that season anywhere else. There are hills and valleys, the Great Bras d'Or Lakes in the centre, and small farms everywhere. The coast is dotted with fishing villages, and the main occupations then were farming, fishing and mining. Transportation in those days was poor, so that many people lived fairly isolated lives, especially in winter.

The extent of their isolation is seen in the story of a Cape Bretoner who was asked if he had ever been off the island. "No," he replied, "but I once knew a man who had slept with a man who had been to Truro," a mainland town. In such circumstances they indeed had to make their own entertainment, or do without, and it is upon such ground that folklore flourishes, and that is why we expected so much.

The trip from Dartmouth to Antigonish is beautiful but was wooded for much of the way, and I learned later that the deep green of the conifers gave Doreen a feeling of claustrophobia. Crossing the Canso Strait with a touring car was much easier than with the cumbersome ambulance I had driven on the Caravan trip when I had to back it on a scow so I could arrive facing in the right direction and get a run up the steep hill on the Cape Breton side. It was late when we reached Port Hawkesbury, and we got a room at the Farquahar House run by a Scotswoman, Miss Mary McMaster, known to all who travelled this road. We had planned to picnic whenever possible, with Doreen looking after the cuisine, and we went to a house to buy milk. The good lady would take no money, so our first experience of Cape Breton hospitality was a gracious one. When we realized we had no water for making tea, I went to another house where the owner was enjoying the summer twilight in his garden comfortably relaxing on the seat of an old motor car. While I asked where we were likely to find songs, Doreen prepared our meal. An evening star appeared followed by the moon at the full. Stretched on a beach and munching leisurely we felt that life was good.

Pleasant though it was here, we decided to go on, and our road skirted the beautiful Bras d'Or Lakes. We stopped at a farm in Malagawatch to enquire about songs and were astonished when the young woman who greeted us was a Mrs. Rose who had come over from Scotland on the same boat as Doreen. All along the way we made enquiries and got names, but following them up was disappointing. A teacher at the Indian school was three miles away haying. At Whycocomagh our good lead was out too, and so it went. But we were young and the day was fine so we decided to go on to Baddeck. I love driving in the early evening when the shadows lengthen and all is still after a busy day. Dr. MacMillan, whom we had hoped to see, was out too, so I decided to look up Benny McAskill who had been in Dartmouth in the first war as a young soldier and who had often gone to our picnics and dances. Here it was arranged that we sleep at the Philip MacLeod's. They had a most comfortable house and sometimes took tourists for the pleasure of meeting them. We had a sumptuous meal and then established temporary residence at the MacLeod's, after which we talked our heads off to our gracious hostess. Then she and her son went out, and when Mr. MacLeod came home he found us in possession. We asked about singers, and without hesitation he said what we had been hearing everywhere, that we should go to Mr. D. B. MacLeod at Briton Cove, a farmer who also had a small store and was the Big Man of the district. We also learned that songs in Cape Breton were in French or Gaelic. I have since taken many down in English, but these were the main ethnic sources. With Margery Kennedy Fraser's Hebridean collection in mind and so many people in agreement, we asked him how to get to Briton Cove.

It is little wonder we overslept after the long drive over dirt roads and our disappointment at not finding singers, and it was a temptation to linger at the McAskill's over an enormous breakfast. It was eleven before we got away and an hour or so later we called at a farmhouse.

Perhaps the worst hazard in visiting strange farms in remote places is being confronted with people who have mental disorders, and we even encountered an occasional case of severe physical deformity. People get used to these unfortunates in their midst and don't realize the shock they give a stranger. That was our experience this day. Although such people are usually harmless, you can't take your safety for granted.

We were tempted to make many calls en route but allowed ourselves only one. Mr. Will Ross of St. Ann's was in his aunt's hay field and we were advised to turn back, climb a steep hill, and talk to him there. Many Cape Breton farms are on steep hillsides, and a man would need a strong heart to work them. Mine wasn't strong, and by the time we reached him I was thankful to stretch out on the warm grass and let Doreen do the talking. Indeed there was no need of any words in this idyllic setting overlooking the Bay and the peaceful farms nearby with their crops soon to be harvested.

Mr. Ross knew no songs, but he was full of stories of manitous, Indian myths, and French warfare. As I rested I worried because we were nearing the end of the third day and had not found a single song. Also I knew that even the best leads can be disappointing, and Mr. D. B. MacLeod might not even be home. Would his be a house where we could stay comfortably, would they have room for us, and would it be clean? I thought of forbidding houses I'd been in and how I marked the worst ones "fine day" houses, those I could visit when the weather was fine and we could work outside. I've been in houses so sealed up against draughts that it seemed the air hadn't been changed for thirty years. I had learned to take my own sandwiches along. I and any friend with me enjoyed eating outside. In daylight you can skirt around these difficulties but arriving at night we would have no choice of where to stay.

Today cars skip over Kelly's Mountain in no time, but the road then was rough and narrow. There were miles without a house in sight. Doreen was finding the conifers depressing. When we finally got to lower ground and the lovely panorama of Cape Breton's countryside unfolded before our weary eyes, our spirits rose, even though the nagging uncertainty persisted. This was suddenly dispelled as we drew up at D.B's farm. Mr. MacLeod came to the gate himself to meet us looking so good and clean and gracious that we greeted him with a burst of laughter and I said, "You'd never guess what we've come for!"

"Looking for husbands?" he suggested, and that set us off again.

How needlessly we had feared. The MacLeods kept a spotless tourist home and their homemade food and home-grown vegetables and fruit were a traveller's dream. Late though it was, we were given a good meal, and though we talked of songs enough to know they existed here, we made no attempt to collect. I doubt if our eyes would have stayed open had we tried.

The following days were delightful, for Mr. MacLeod sang whenever he had a free moment. Doreen had little difficulty with music, and could put the notes directly on paper, but I needed help with the words. Most were in Gaelic which many could speak but few could write. Fortunately Mr. MacLeod was one of the few.

Even today an occasional church service there is held in Gaelic. We felt this was something we should experience. We nearly disgraced ourselves when near the end of the service Mrs. MacLeod asked if I had understood any of it.

"One word," I whispered.

"What was that?"

"Collection," I said, supressing a giggle. Somehow the minister had conveyed its meaning. The music was led by precentors who sat facing the congregation and everyone joined in with tremendous enthusiasm. Afterwards these people from their far-flung farms talked with their friends on the grounds outside the church and caught up with the gossip of the day.

Malcolm Angus MacLeod, from another farm family of MacLeods, sang for us on this trip and again twenty years later when I had the pleasure of recording him. In those days, when Doreen put their notes on paper and sang them back they looked at her in wonder, for they had never met such an accomplished musician before. And how kind they were. A neighbour, Mrs. McInnes, posed beside her spinning wheel, gave us blackberries and cream, kissed us when we left and gave us her blessing. In later interviews on my work, more has been made of an amusing incident here than it deserved, but at the time it caused great merriment. A tall, lean bewhiskered man came to the MacLeod's one day and tried to flirt with me. He said if I'd come back he'd shave his whiskers off and get a new eye. We had our picture taken standing in the middle of the road together and if he had any serious intentions, which I doubt, they were lost in the general fun of the occasion. Reporters writing me up are so anxious to find a romantic note that they give the impression that such things often happened. They could, of course, for old men are vulnerable, but a young girl travelling alone, as I so often did, would be silly to flirt unless she wanted that kind of attention. I developed a friendly attitude and was so intent upon my quest that there was no doubt what I was there for. Anyhow I didn't invite attentions and that is probably why I got off with so little trouble, just enough to add a little spice to life.

We loved to watch D. B. MacLeod with his grandson, and indeed all his family, for this was a happy home. A story goes that somebody came to his store for lobsters and biscuits and he said, "I just picked the lobsters out of the ocean so there'll be no charge for them, but the biscuits came out of the store so they'll be ten cents." In time he became Sergeant-at-Arms in the Provincial Legislature and died much later full of years and beloved by all who knew him. Some of the songs gathered in this area are in my *Gaelic Songs in Nova Scotia.**

On our return we stopped, as everybody else did, at the grave of giant Angus McAskill, a man of noble frame whose height reached seven feet nine inches, and who had toured in Barnum and Bailey's Circus. In Sydney we were invited to Framboise to meet the bard who had written what is almost the Island's national anthem, "Oran do Cheap Breatainn" (Cape Breton Is the Land of My Love). Unfortunately time was running out and we had promised to return to Baddeck. Again the Philip MacLeods put us up, and in the morning when we were filling up Cecil from the gas tank, a lad came on the run, waving a dollar bill which he hastened to return to us. We had overpaid his mother by giving her two dollars for bed and breakfast when she had asked only one. That was in 1932.

Doreen sang a lot as we drove. She knew so many English folk songs that I was continually learning about my craft. There were few silent moments as we chatted in unison with the roads' bumps, but, when we left Cape Breton and thought of all the kindness we'd received, we were thoughtful. We'd have been more thoughtful if we'd known how many good singers we were passing by.

We had stretched our trip to the limit, and Doreen had a boat to catch. It was long after dark on the last possible day when we arrived home. The next day, exhausted but happy, we parted on the deck of the "Westmoreland," Doreen with a week at sea in which to recover,

Gaelic Songs in Nova Scotia. With Calum MacLeod. (Ottawa: National Museum of Canada, 1964).

and I to a long period of early nights and long rest periods, a price I paid willingly. However I managed to get a little collecting in, including a visit to a widower named Alex. He had a large family and his mother-in-law was keeping house for him. He didn't know the song I wanted but knew someone who did, so I asked if he would go there with me and show me the way. He hesitated, so his mother-in-law said, "Why don't you go with Miss Creighton, Alex? Maybe people will think she's your financy, but that don't make no difference."

Chapter 4

I don't know who dreamed it up or how long it took to plan, but in 1933, seventy Canadian authors toured England and Scotland. Our national secretary, Mr. Howard Angus Kennedy, was a man of great vigour and charm. His daughter, Mrs. Barrett, who lived in London, travelled with us as guide and, I believe, made all the preliminary arrangements. This was no ordinary tour; the only difficulty was that it took great endurance to keep up with the pace. We not only did everything a tourist does, but we were entertained by many a mayor and corporation. In each of the places we visited we met whatever authors of note were residing there. It was an opportunity of a lifetime.

Our tour began immediately after our annual convention, held that year in Quebec, and on the afternoon of July first when we sailed away on the *Empress of Britain*, French folk singers saluted us from the pier. There were hundreds of people on the dock and the hillsides. I had a friend in C.P.R. Publicity who arranged everything for my comfort—including his tie to complete my boy's costume for the play on board that evening, written by the late Mrs. G. K. MacIntosh of Halifax. The ship had printed programs saying, "Touring Members of the Canadian Authors Association Cordially Invite You to a Performance this Evening of 'Britannia at Home.'"

73

After the play, Mr. Murray Gibbon demonstrated what he called gramo-poems; his theory was that words written to fit classical music would form new rhythms in poetry. Then to my surprise and delight a baritone from the ship's orchestra sang "Green Bushes" from my folk song collection, harmonized by the pianist for the occasion.

We had four national presidents in our group as well as Ralph Connor (Rev. Charles Gordon of Winnipeg), who was then at the height of his popularity and turned out to be the only Canadian author in our group the English people knew.

At the Sunday service on board, he preached an able sermon and we were proud of him. On July fourth we put on a play written by our member, George Palmer. Now and again Sir Charles G. D. Roberts (then Dr. Roberts) read poetry to us in a quiet gentle way endearing himself in a manner I hadn't thought possible as I hadn't particularly liked him before. Dr. W. G. Lighthall of Montreal also read to us, but Ralph Connor was able to mix very little as he had a publisher's deadline to meet. Dr. E. A. Hardy had a birthday on our last day aboard so the chef made a cake for the occasion. Dr. Hardy blushed crimson when it was brought in and to the orchestra's accompaniment, we sang that he was "a jolly good fellow."

Our arrival proved that our planners thought us worthy of nothing but the best, for we were welcomed at an early hour by the Mayor of Southampton. He was resplendent with his gold chain of office, and was accompanied by his wife and daughter. Before the day was over we were to be welcomed by two more mayors. Six cameramen came on board to photograph us and I have a copy of the *Southern Daily Echo* with a large picture of our group.

The itinerary was arranged to take in visits to the homes of Britain's great authors and we travelled by bus. Through the narrow streets of Southampton and the New Forest to Wimborne Minster and Bere Regis (the Kings-bere of *Tess of the D'Urbervilles*) and Puddletown (Weatherbury of *Far from the Madding Crowd*), we came finally to Dorchester ("Casterbridge") and the home of Thomas Hardy. His widow received us, and for many this was the first English home we had ever visited. It was small, but filled with interesting antiques, and we loved it. We walked through the garden and thought of the tales that had been worked out here, and then drove to his birthplace and place of burial where his heart lies in the grave with his first wife; his ashes are in Westminster Abbey. If I had known what I do now of the distress it often causes the departed to have their parts separated after death, I would have worried, but at that time I hadn't delved into the supernatural. We were given a small booklet entitled, "A Short Tour of the Near Hardy Country Prepared for the Visit to Dorchester of the Canadian Authors on July 7th, 1933."

At Dorchester we had our first English tea and our hosts at the Guildhall were the Mayor and Corporation. Many English people had been invited to meet us and they couldn't have been more friendly. Here we met H. M. Tomlinson whom I described in my diary as "very shy and unassuming."

The evening reception at Salisbury's Guildhall gave us the jolliest mayor of the three we met that day. I also met and talked with the Earl of Pembroke and his countess, little knowing that after the coronation of King George VI, the chair the Earl had occupied during the ceremony (I presume it was the same one) would be given by him to my brother Mac, who shipped it home to mother. It has had a place of honour in our house ever since. The Mayor told us that the roses used at the reception were from his garden. They were placed on a table banked with maple leaves from his own trees, and set on a Union Jack. He said that when he had once wanted a good shade tree his gardener had advised, "If you want something sturdy, solid, and full of sap, plant a maple." What pleased us most was that while we thoroughly enjoyed our hosts, they also seemed genuinely to enjoy us.

At Salisbury the next day the Dean himself took us around the Cathedral. Among other things, we stood fascinated beside the tomb of St. Swithin of whom we think every July fifteenth, hoping that it won't rain that day, and thus, according to legend, for forty days thereafter. We visited Stonehenge and Winchester where we were guests of the Headmaster, Rev. H. T. P. Williams at Winchester College, the oldest Public School in England, and he himself showed us the school. We were reminded that Jane Austen had died at Winchester. Driving through Alresford we were made aware of Mary Mitford (*Our Village*), at Farnham of Swift's "Stella," at Guildford of C. L. Dodgson (Lewis Carroll), and reminded that this was where he had told Alice his immortal story. We spoke of Keats at Burford Bridge where he wrote his "Ode to a Nightingale." Fortunately there was no evening entertainment, and in London the comfortable, old-fashioned very English hotel, "The Kingsley", embraced us.

On Sunday morning we attended a service at Westminster Abbey and later drove to Hampstead and stopped at the home of Keats, where we saw the old house with its garden and museum. The outstanding event of the day was tea with Lady Pentland whose parents, Lord and Lady Aberdeen, were highly regarded in Canada where her father had served as Governor General and her mother had, among other services, established the Victorian Order of Nurses. The Right Honourable R. B. Bennett, Prime Minister of Canada, received with them, and when I was introduced he surprised me by saying, "I was just telling Lady Pentland about your book of songs and ballads." My day was made. Mrs. Nevanson, sister of the late Cecil Sharp, was there and when I told her I called my car Cecil in honour of her illustrious brother, I felt she wasn't too complimented. Other guests were Sir James Marriott, Sir George and Lady McLaren Brown, His Excellency the High Commissioner of Canada, Howard Ferguson and his wife, and delegates to the Economic Conference from India. When more chairs were needed, Lady Pentland didn't call a busy butler but went to the garage herself, and Marjorie Tozer and I helped her carry them out.

As we were about to leave, Lady Aberdeen returned from Denmark looking full of years but still vigorous. As a memento we were given heather on a card autographed by Lord Aberdeen and sent down from Scotland, and on our departure our hostess, her daughter, and guests walked to the buses to see us off and waved as we drew away. On the way back, Priestley's house was pointed out and Galsworthy's, and we toured the beautiful estate known as "Kenwood." Then we visited two houses Charles Dickens had lived in, and here my mind is a blank. Since I was a great Dickens fan, I couldn't have forgotten such a visit, so I must have succumbed to fatigue for I didn't even mention it in my diary while Laura Carten in her column "Farmer Smith" in the Halifax *Herald* described it in detail.

On Monday a great depression came over me as we strolled through the Tower of London. It was as though I were shouldering the sufferings of victims whose misery still lingered there. It was a relief to go on to the Mansion House, official residence of the Lord Mayor. Arriving ahead of time we saw two beautiful coaches drive up, the first drawn by four horses, the second by two. The coachmen wore gorgeous livery and high hats over powdered wigs. Sir Percy Greenaway was Lord Mayor in 1933, and he descended robed in red; sheriffs in purple robes descended from the other carriage.

After signing the Visitors' Book we were received by a distinguished line: the Lord Mayor, the Lady Mayoress and their daughter, and then a little man who looked vaguely familiar. As I went along the line to Lord Dunsany and Viscount Cecil I heard a voice behind me say, "And you are Mr. Kipling?" I stopped short. My favourite author, the one I most wanted to meet, and I hadn't recognized him.

There was music in the great hall, and the speakers

sat in a semi-circle, with five members of the press between them and us. The Lord Mayor, nicknamed Mr. Pickwick, spoke first and was followed by Viscount Cecil, a large man with broad shoulders who struck a serious note with his theme "Service." He was as interesting to watch as to listen to for his eyes were penetrating and his fingers never still. Later he listened with rapt attention to all the other speakers. Lord Dunsany seemed nervous at first, but probably wasn't, and he gave a humourous talk. He looked immensely tall to me, had a heavy brown moustache and enormous feet. He spoke with a slight lisp and many people liked him best. Sir Richard Lodge, brother of Sir Oliver, and President of the Royal Society, also took the light approach and talked largely about professors in politics. Then Ernest Raymond, popular author of the day, spoke on the England he loved, and we loved this tanned man with his cheerful outlook. Ralph Connor spoke for Canada. It was a good speech, but any speech at that point would have seemed long.

As we left this room I found myself beside Mr. and Mrs. Kipling, and heard him say, "Hurry, we're going to eat!" Mr. Kipling was distinguished by great bushy eyebrows that stuck out like brushes, and Mrs. Kipling chatted constantly. They seldom appeared at any public function, yet we were to have them again on Wednesday. Mrs. Kipling explained that the display of gold plate on a table was put there especially for us; usually it was kept behind glass on shelves built for that purpose. I lingered as long as possible beside the Kiplings but also talked to Ernest Raymond and Sir Richard Lodge and with my tea enjoyed cake brought by the daughter of the house. The Prime Minister of Canada was there and our High Commissioner, and other prominent Canadians residing in England, also Dean Inge, Miss Rose Macaulay, Mr. Sean O'Casey, Sir Max Pemberton, Mr. F. Brett Young, and many others.

An incident occurred here that helped me in writing an article for the *Atlantic Advocate* in 1965. Mr. Kipling had wished to speak to a Halifax delegate and when Miss Laura Carten was presented he enquired for his friend, Dr. J. G. MacDougall, a Halifax surgeon, and asked her to give him his love. Yes, love was the word he used. A deep friendship had grown up between them because the doctor had attended Mrs. Kipling when she had an appendectomy while travelling in the West Indies. The correspondence between them, now in the beautiful Kipling Room at Dalhousie University, bespeaks his undying appreciation.

At a reception at the Lyceum Club our hostesses had pinned on their dresses bouquets of maple leaves in our honour. This was an exclusive club where more of England's great writers had been invited to meet and address us. Katherine Hale (Mrs. John Garvin) responded for the Canadians, and I expect we all wondered what we had done to deserve all this.

The next day, Tuesday, we visited the house where Milton wrote *Paradise Lost* and *Paradise Regained*, and then to Oxford and lunch at Rhodes House. Here to meet us were John Buchan, Poet Laureate John Masefield, and Sir Gilbert Murray. Rev. Father Knox, large, witty without a smile, blue of eye, felt he had a connection with Canada by virtue of being nephew to Miss Knox, first principal of Havergal School, Toronto. Dr. E. A. Hardy spoke well for us, and students took us to the various colleges and served tea.

At Westminster Abbey the Dean was our guide. We were guests of the Royal Society of Literature for luncheon at Claridge's, a gala affair, and I was placed near the head table with members of the English press. Few of us had ever seen a toastmaster in scarlet jacket, and we thrilled when he announced, "My lords and ladies, I pray silence for the President, the most Honourable, the Marquis of Crewe, Knight of the Order of the Garter," and so on. Mr. Kipling was dwarfed by much bigger men and, there being no microphone then, we had to strain to hear him. Mr. G. K. Chesterton referred to himself as no newspaper man in the United States sense, for who could imagine him sliding through a skylight to get a story? Sir Henry Newbolt was the final speaker, and Dr. Lighthall and Charles G. D. Roberts spoke for us.

We were then hurried through the Houses of Parliament to be on time for tea at Number 10 Downing Street as guests of the Prime Minister, Mr. Ramsay MacDonald. I had quite a chat with his daughter Ishbel who mingled and served tea as any of us would do when entertaining at home. Our president, Ralph Connor, was a personal friend of the MacDonalds and their house guest while in London. As we went up the stairway we could pause to look at photographs of former prime ministers, and I liked this arrangement so much that I have used it in my own house for pictures that appeal to me. The afternoon ended with a visit to Canada House where the display of books had my *Songs and Ballads from Nova Scotia** in the front row.

The evening had its comical side. Like citizens of any maturing country, we were sensitive, and after Ian Hay, John Drinkwater and St. John Ervine had spoken, the latter had the whole delegation lined up before him. He had stated that we had no theatre and ought to write our own plays, not knowing that the Little Theatre movement was then in full swing. I don't know who looked after John Drinkwater, but I had read Ian Hay's books and had him all to myself. P. G. Wodehouse was also there but left immediately after the speeches. We were able to tell W. W. Jacobs that a Halifax group was about to produce one of his plays.

The stamina needed for all this! On Thursday morning at Windsor Castle I thought my limbs would refuse their office. The Royal Librarian himself showed us through his domain but I was so tired I could see little of the castle's splendour. Fortunately I rested all afternoon,

*Songs and Ballads from Nova Scotia. (Toronto: J. M. Dent & Sons, 1932).

for that evening proved the most dramatic of our trip, with George Bernard Shaw as guest speaker. The Forum Club in London, foremost club for women interested in the arts, was the scene of this reception. This was a full dress affair, a large orchestra played for us, everybody seemed to talk non-stop, and among the English authors somebody pointed out Elinor Glyn, one of the first avant garde writers, whose books were the talk of two continents.

There was an atmosphere of expectation, but time went on and the guest speaker failed to show up. Several people, including Mr. Wickham Steed, gave impromptu addresses, and Katherine Hale answered for us. Finally it was suggested we have refreshment before, instead of after, his speech. Some had finished and were about to leave when word came that the great man had arrived. We got up immediately, and I was lucky enough to meet him at the foot of the stairs and heard him mutter, "Disgraceful hour to be going anywhere. I've been at a dinner party." It was then ten forty-five.

We took our places quickly and Mrs. Barrett introduced him. He was immaculately dressed in tails and white tie and began by saying, "Ladies and gentlemen, you have all come this evening to see me. Well here I am; take a good look." He thrust his hands behind his coattails and pirouetted like a manikin with no apology for being late. We laughed and applauded. Then while smiling genially, he set out to abuse us like a naughty boy seeing how far he can go before being sent home. He'd never heard of a Canadian author. He didn't know there were any. Nobody in England ever read a Canadian book. There were chiding cries of "Hear, hear, Mr. Shaw," but he went on. Canadians, huh! He'd been on a steamer filled with Canadians and couldn't tell the difference between them and Americans because there wasn't any. (I'd enjoyed it up to this point because it was so obviously an act, but he continued.) He'd like to know what Canadians thought of England and of him but he had no desire to visit so wild and uncivilized a country lest he be mobbed or blindly idolized. He then asked if we'd had enough and when we clapped feebly he said the applause wasn't loud enough so we clapped a little louder and he said, "There, that's better; now is the time an experienced speaker stops," and he sat down. The whole thing didn't take ten minutes, if that long.

The Club's president looked mortified and said, "Is there any Canadian in the audience capable of replying to Mr. Shaw?" Ralph Connor nodded negatively and so did Charles G. D. Roberts. The atmosphere was tense when our beloved national secretary made his way from the back of the hall and mounted the platform. In a well-modulated voice, in contrast to Mr. Shaw's which was strident and high-pitched, Mr. Kennedy said, "The sword of Damocles has been hanging over my head all day until I have no brains left." Then turning to Mr. Shaw and bowing low he continued, "And I am sure Mr. Shaw will agree that I have no brains left when I say that I enjoyed his speech." We all sat a little straighter. "I am sure we all agree with Mr. Shaw when he says he knows nothing whatever about Canadians or Canadian books. He says he has never been to Canada and he is afraid if he did come that he would be either mobbed or blindly idolized. Let me assure Mr. Shaw that nothing of the kind could possibly happen in Canada, but that he would be treated as a distinguished British citizen." As he stepped down there was tremendous applause and when he passed the speaker he put out his hand and said, "We trust Mr. Shaw your foreshadowed trip may soon become a reality." I suspect by the way he threw back his head and laughed that Mr. Shaw enjoyed Mr. Kennedy's reply as much as the rest of us, but in a more dignified way, because when we got back to our hotel we formed a circle around Mr. Kennedy and danced in his honour.

Added to London's overwhelming hospitality we were given honorary membership privileges by the Royal Empire Society, the Forum Club, the Overseas Club and, I think, the Lyceum Club. Luncheon menus had all been printed in our honour. That of the Royal Society of Literature had its crest in gold and was printed and edged in gold.

From sheer exhaustion I had to skip some items including a tour of Canterbury Cathedral where Dean Hewlett Johnson was our host, and a tour of Stratford-on-Avon. However I managed to see *The Merchant of Venice* and *Macbeth* when we were guests of the Director, Sir Archibald Flower and Lady Flower. At tea in their garden the following day we met Maurice Colbourne and many Shakesperian actors, and that year we all received Christmas cards from our host and hostess. This kept up until the war, probably to those who acknowledged them. Little did we think then that war would come and we would be the givers for, when food was rationed, many of us sent parcels to the Flowers.

We saw Windermere and Ruskin's home; Rydal Mount, Wordsworth's home; and Abbotsford, Sir Walter Scott's home where the pipes played thrilling music in the valley. Later we paid a visit to Stevenson's home and that of Robert Burns on the river Ayr. When we visited Edinburgh Castle, the Nova Scotia group performed a little ceremony in memory of Charles I who had created Baronets of Nova Scotia, and had also given us our flag. For the investiture he had declared a piece of ground in front of the castle Nova Scotian soil. Miss Laura Carten thought this link with Scotland should be made an historic occasion and had brought with her a silk flag measuring one and one-half yards in length. All ten members stepped forward as it was presented to the Lord Provost and later at his luncheon, four of us were photographed with him, each holding a corner of the flag. I believe it is still in Edinburgh Castle as a memento of our visit.

Looking back I marvel at the founders of our association, for they must have rated it highly or they would never have planned a trip of such magnitude. The past presidents with us were Mr. John Murray Gibbon, Montreal; Dr. W. T. Allison, Winnipeg; Dr. Charles G. D. Roberts, Toronto; and Dr. W. D. Lighthall, Montreal.

Other prominent members of an earlier day were Mr. Justice Surveyer, Montreal and Mr. B. K. Sandwell, Toronto, both scholarly men. Occasionally the association talks of repeating this venture, but life is different now and we would never be given such personal deference again.

When the tour was over I joined my brother Mac in London for a few days. Ever since Mexico I had looked forward to visiting him there and meeting his friends in the West End where he lived. These dreams gave me grandiose ideas which prevented my settling down to life in Canada. A lengthy visit was impossible then, however, for we were booked on the *Empress of Britain* and must be home in time for our parents' golden wedding anniversary. The English trip had been one of mother's dreams for me and it was her gift.

"Evergreen," so called for the evergreen trees that used to surround it, was built in 1867 and had been our home for thirteen years. It was a perfect house for entertaining for its rooms were large and could easily accommodate the many friends who called. The drawing room had two mantlepieces, one of grey marble and the other hand-carved in wood. The latter is now at the Dartmouth Heritage Museum. Receptions had great spreads in those days, so much so that a Haligonian once remarked that at a tea in Dartmouth she met nine Mrs. Creightons and had ten kinds of cake. Our whole family with children and grandchildren were in attendance.

Mother wore a beige lace gown I had brought back from London. She was short, a little plump and had a clear skin and high colour and with her hazel eyes and white hair she looked both pretty and motherly. She stood beside my father who was of medium height. His hair too was white and so were his moustache and Vandyke beard. His eyes were blue and his manner formal but warm and gracious, and both loved dispensing hospitality. In the evening an orchestra provided music for dancing. All in all it was a grand occasion, and the last we would have as a family. Mother had showed symptoms of diabetes, but we kept the diagnosis from her until the festivities were over. For the next eight years I gave her insulin because arteriosclerosis had also set in and she couldn't use the needle herself. Unhappily her outlook and disposition changed and, like many an elderly person in such circumstances, she turned against those who lived closest to her, my father and me. My letters from England, tender and full of love, show how deep the bond had been between us. I remained active in my own affairs but now the needs of the family came first. That, of course, included the care of my sister Lilian.

This did not prevent a trip at the end of Doreen's 1933 summer school session. We thought we might drive to Ecum Secum on the eastern shore and work back, but on second thought decided to begin near home and work towards Ecum Secum which, of course, we never reached. I wanted Doreen to meet Mr. Thomas Young, the postman at West Petpeswick, whom I'd visited on an earlier trip with mother. His house was on a low hillside overlooking Petpeswick Harbour, a sheltered inlet about seven miles long. There were green islands between this and the eastern shore, and I was to find this whole district a collector's paradise. Mr. Young was tall with a yellow beard and he usually wore a broad-brimmed hat and carried a long stick like a shepherd's staff. I had words taken down on my earlier visit and in no time he was singing and Doreen was transcribing his tunes.

At lunch time we left him to have our picnic and also to give him a rest, but even at eighty-three he felt no need of rest and soon came to look for us. We invited him to join us but he seemed to feel this would be an intrusion so we packed up and went back to the house where he sang until his voice grew husky and his tunes confused. It was still early in the afternoon, so we secured a lodging for the night at Musquodoboit Harbour and then drove down Petpeswick's eastern shore to Martinique Beach. After a good rest and another picnic we returned, and just in time too because Mr. Young had given us up and as we entered his front door he was going out the back. Whatever he had in mind was put aside and again he sang until his voice grew husky. Fortunately we had asked James Young, a neighbor, to join us, and he took over until the older man's bedtime, which was early, as he got up every morning at four-thirty to carry the mail.

The next day we called on Mr. James Young and found him painting his house with a mixture of oil and ochre. He left it to sing for us all morning. Mr. Thomas Young sang all afternoon. Our picnic lunch was eaten under lowering skies. For our evening meal we sat in the pouring rain and enjoyed feeling it on our weary brows. However a little of that was enough and we soon set out for the home of Mrs. Dennis Greenough at the top of a steep hill, and there we tucked our feet in her oven and dried wet stockings and shoes. "Why didn't you use our kitchen?" she enquired, even though she had never met us before. "You're perfectly welcome to it."

Here we got the best-known song in my whole collection, although it was thirty years before it became famous. Doreen and I had been so steeped in the English tradition that we didn't realize anything locally composed could have that much value, and anyhow Doreen didn't consider it a folk song. "The Nova Scotia Song" or "Farewell to Nova Scotia" combines the pull of the sea with the nostalgia sailors feel towards home. The beautiful tune is in a minor key with changes from four-quarter to six-quarter rhythm and back again. Neighbors added to Mrs. Greenough's words so I made a composite version for *Traditional Songs from Nova Scotia*.* Since then I've found one singer in King's and another in Colchester County whose tunes were practically the same, and a friend knew the song when a child in Cape Breton. It was known best however in the area we were now working because it had been taught in their schools at the turn of

Traditional Songs from Nova Scotia. With Doreen Senior, (Toronto: The Ryerson Press, 1950).

Ben Henneberry of Devil's
Island (in the early '30s).

Mr. and Mrs. Dennis
Smith, Chezzetcook.

Helen, Dean of
Women, King's
College, 1940.

Helen with Peter
Chiasson, Grand Étang
(early '50s).

Ben and Edmund Henneberry making cod liver oil.

Recording Mr. Jack Turple, Upper Kennetcook (1952).

With Dr. and Mrs. W. Roy Mackenzie ('50s).

Angus "The Ridge" MacDonald, South River Lake.

the century. A letter from western Canada tells of a similar song in Scotland called "Auld Scotia," but I've never found it in any book. Whether original or adapted it fits our mood and countryside.

On many later trips to West Petpeswick one of my most pleasant contacts was with the Berton Youngs. Mr. Young was of slight build, quiet and gentle and must have been full of fun before this sad period when he was losing his sight. He had sailed on schooners as mate for twenty-five years and had composed a song about sealing which is in my *Maritime Folk Songs*. His wife was the daughter of Mr. Thomas Young, and with all she had heard from husband and father, she could often supply missing words. A sample of Mr. Young's chin music, or diddling, sung when no instrument was available to make music, is on my record, *Maritime Folk Songs*, issued by Folkways.* He said, "We'd get a bunch to meet of an evening, five or six fellers and three or four women and they'd say, 'Let's have a couple of sets. . . . Here, you go to work and give us a little chin music,' and one old feller'd set down on the floor and haul his legs up and put his elbows on his knees and his chin on them under his jaw, and he'd set there and sing for hours."

The Youngs, and there are many in the Petpeswicks, are, according to Mr. Thomas Young, of French descent and his parents spoke French between themselves. There is no trace of it now, and all their songs are of British origin. Mr. Clergy, on the east side, whom you'll meet later, is also a connection, and said his name originally was Clergie and that his Acadian ancestors came there at the time of the expulsion. His father, Charlie, was a noted singer. I was to find songs everywhere and in the three days Doreen and I spent on the west side, we took down forty-six.

Looking back to the home front now, I realized that

Maritime Folk Songs. (New York: Folkways Records & Service Corporation, Ethnic Folkways Library Album # FE 4307, 1962).

I had got out of the way of playing games. They had been a delightful pastime from tiddly-winks on to games that were suitable for our age. In my thirties I particularly enjoyed a two-table bridge club. Those were days of gracious living when all eight of us took our turn as hostess and each house had its maid in uniform to wait on us. Other games came and went, but at home and with friends, bridge was the favourite. I also played golf, sometimes with father, but more often with friends, and I loved being out of doors with congenial companions. I applied here and there without success for grants to carry on my work, and continued a series for children which I had begun in 1931 in *Church Work*. This largely gratuitous service went on for five years. Any picnic trip over the next few years was directed towards a place where there might be singers, but I had less free time now due to mother's condition. Yet for one who has always had to consider her health, just to look at my diary makes me gasp. As a friend said, "Helen, when you go to bed at night you can say, 'There hasn't been one thing today I might have done that I haven't done,'" and that was about it. Added to this variety of interests, much time was spent on the songs Doreen and I had collected, and I was always dabbling at writing of one kind or another.

The telephone has brought all kinds of unexpected delights, none more surprising than a call one summer afternoon in 1936. Miss Rosalind Rieman from New York was travelling with a Pennsylvania Dutch friend, Miss Helen Oppenlander. They had gone to the park at Grand Pré but were disappointed to find this pastoral setting of Longfellow's poem *Evangeline* too formal, and they had asked if anything had been done here in folklore. When they were shown my book they decided to come to Halifax. Following the first flurry of excitement little of great interest had resulted from its publication, so, after a short conversation, I agreed to meet them that evening. During the next few days I drove them over the territory I had covered, had them meet some of the singers, showed them

88

Devil's Island, and entertained them at home. Rosalind was interested in folk arts, singing games and folk music, and Helen had an executive position with the Girl Scouts of America. Our brief hours passed all too quickly, and as I made the most of every minute I had little idea this visit would mark a turning point. It was therefore a complete surprise when they said, "Would you consider coming to New York to give lectures?"

"New York?" The thought had never entered my head. I hesitated a moment and then said I would but only if paid, thinking that now I might get something back for my father. They assured me this would be done, and we wondered what this might mean. Finally word came of four outstanding assignments, none of which paid a cent.

I said to father, "What do I do now?"

He thought a moment and then observed, "If you don't go you'll be no further ahead; if you do, there's no telling what may come of it." Wise man, for this was the beginning of a ball that started rolling and has never stopped. In the custom of the day for writers and lecturers, I applied to the Furness Withy Steamship Company and was given a complimentary passage in return for mentioning their line in my talks. My new friends lived together and offered hospitality so that while the talks were spread over most of a month, the cost to me was slight. It probably cost them more than I realized. The world is said to be divided between givers and takers; there is no doubt where they fitted.

I had prepared my talks carefully and had typed headings so I wouldn't have to read every word. I had already done some public speaking which paid off now with experience in facing an audience. Experience in radio was also a help for I wasn't put off by the sound of my voice and I knew how to time a speech. Illustrations were the biggest worry because songs need to be sung. However a Welsh tenor and madrigal singer, Mr. Ben Davis, supplied that need. We gave our first performance at the Canadian Women's Club on November twenty-eighth with a reception preceding it. I drew a word picture of Devil's Island, the Henneberrys and others, the finding of songs and something of their value. At the end, accompanied by Rosalind, Mr. Davis sang and the overflowing audience joined in the whistling chorus of "The Farmer's Curst Wife." The press was kind.

The following days were filled with appointments, preparing the other talks, and discussing possible uses of collected material. Should I take up lecturing professionally and if not, what other doors might be open? On December fifth I spoke to the English Folk Song and Dance Society where the reception was cordial but, as Rosalind said, not overwhelmingly so. Here I met Mr. Maurice Mattison, and when I found he was a collector of mountain songs I listened eagerly to all he had to say. I had met few collectors and was always on the lookout for ideas. For the Society itself I had a sentimental attachment because a few of their English members had given me useful advice when visiting Halifax and later, before the publication of *Songs and Ballads from Nova Scotia*, they had made an appraisal of the music.

During my talk I noticed that men seemed to enjoy it most, and indeed one sat on the edge of his seat with eyes and ears wide open, and I kept the tail of my eye on him for encouragement. Mainly to say I'd sung on a New York stage, I accepted Mr. Davis's invitation to join him in "The Quaker's Courtship," and when he sang, "Madame you are young and tender, and your waist is soft and slender," he looked me over approvingly and I blushed crimson, probably the most effective part of my singing performance. Afterwards I wired my family, "Enos amuses, Benny amazes, singer delights and lecturer rejoices."

At the final lecture at Columbia University on a Sunday afternoon I felt more relaxed. There were other programs on at Teachers' College but some sixty people turned out for mine. It was a pleasant informal setting but people were scattered and it took a little while to establish contact. Afterwards we met in groups and one of the staff said if I ever wanted anything from Columbia to let her know, from which I judged she was satisfied.

My hostesses had tremendous ideas for my future, many of which came true, but not for a long time. We talked of moving pictures, choral arrangements, a return lecture engagement, and I flitted from one appointment to another with the sky the limit. I even had an agent who sent a brochure to some three thousand people but she had only one nibble in return. Perhaps that was the Montreal club that found me too expensive. I have no idea what fee she was asking. I was in advance of my time and folk songs as a subject created little interest. The only immediate result of all this was an article in a Girl Scout magazine and it was twenty years before the moving picture envisioned here came into being. Nevertheless a beginning had been made.

My New York trip coincided with the abdication of King Edward VIII from the throne of England, and when we walked along Broadway we could see his name coupled with Mrs. Simpson's in lights with the latest news of their romance. The topic was on everybody's lips, and my hostesses studied my reactions as they tried to fathom why this marriage should not take place. At the same time I studied theirs, all done in the most friendly and open way as people do who want to understand each other. One day we met Mrs. F. H. Botsford who collected folk songs in the Appalachian Mountains. Unlike our Nova Scotia singers, these people were most unfriendly and she had to scheme before getting inside a door. She managed this in one house where the man and his wife conversed with her, but there were four people sitting on a bench with newspapers held in front of them which they deliberately held open so she couldn't see them. She tried every conceivable topic of conversation without result until she said, "What do you think of King Edward and Mrs. Simpson?" Immediately the papers dropped, revealing four of the most beautiful young women she had ever seen.

I hope I will never again have a trip at sea like the

stormy one that returned me to my family. With my occasional gift of foresight I knew that the luncheon in New York harbour would be my only meal in the dining saloon. In the worst of it I realized I might never see such a phenomenon of nature again and somehow crawled to the porthole and looked out. How were rescues effected in such mighty seas, and why would anyone as seasick as I care enough to get rescued? It was a daughter with scraggly hair and knees that would scarcely support her that my father met at the dock and it was a week before I recovered.

Chapter 5

Social events had an added zest now as I wore new clothes brought back from New York. Then one day while browsing around the local area I discovered Mrs. R. W. Duncan at Woodside on the outskirts of the town. She was a sister of Enos and Richard Hartlan and one of the dearest women ever to sing for me. Her husband had been in the navy and before their marriage King George V had come to Halifax. She loved to tell how the sailors were invited to bring their wives and respectable friends to a recepttion aboard his ship, one of the highlights of her life. Royalty was held in high esteem and every home then had its picture of some member of the royal family.

Like her brothers', Mrs. Duncan's songs were all old and she cherished them as another might her needlework or piece of precious china. She sang slowly and deliberately and often injected a little joke. One of her loveliest songs, and the first she sang to me, was a strange ballad of early marriage, "He's Young but He's Daily A-Growing." I could hardly wait for Doreen's return to get the music. I've had it since from four other singers, always with a beautiful tune.

Still enthused from the New York trip, I took a February jaunt by train to Lunenburg and stayed for a week and a day at the home of Captain and Mrs. Ammon Zink. There were no songs of any consequence here, but I wish

I had paid more attention to Captain Zink when he told me that he had been aboard the *Charles Haskell* when the sailors from the ship they had rammed at this spot on their previous trip had come aboard on their return and taken the ship over, thus inspiring the song, "The Ghostly Sailors." I had not yet started the diary I kept in later years.

Mr. and Mrs. Zink were kind, but oh dear, how cold bedrooms could be in houses where the kitchen stove provided the only heat! Fortunately I had taken a hot water bottle along, and this got to be a habit when I later started out in May and was often the first to warm up a mattress after a long cold winter. Then I moved to the "Sea Breeze," an inn in the nearby village of Blue Rocks. Because there were so many with the same surname, the proprietress was known as Mrs. Sea Breeze Lohnes. She was a kind woman, short, stout, jolly, an excellent cook, and her house was filled with knick knacks from voyages all over the world. She took me one day to the next village, Black Rocks, where as often happens along our shoreline, houses were built wherever the great rocks left room for a foundation. Here we sat in the home of Mrs. Ada Tanner and for the first time I heard that most popular of all ancient ballads here, "Bonny Barbara Allan." The singer had no sooner buried Barbara and her would-be lover and had the rose and briar entwined above their graves than she looked at me and in that frank manner you so often get in the country remarked, "You got fat legs, ain't it?" Doreen was to have the same remark made to her by a sea captain at Parrsboro who thought mosquitoes knew where to go for a good bite.

The next day I should have returned to Mrs. Tanner who probably knew many old songs but instead I visited a sea captain who didn't sing after all but talked for half an hour on the fluctuations of his weight. I met many delightful people on that trip and enjoyed Lunenburg's hospitality, but added little to my collection. I was to be much more rewarded later on. These activities however were a filling-in, waiting for Doreen's return. By now I was leaving all the music to her, realizing that only an expert should transcribe it. She arrived on July 9, 1937. I had much to tell her, particularly my discovery of Dennis Smith.

This had happened on the last day of May. Mother, my sister, Lil, and I had been picnicking at East Chezzetcook when I remembered that his name was on my list. I was tired and not in the mood and anyhow he was eighty-seven and wouldn't be much good at that age. Fortunately I have a terrific conscience, or was it mother's prodding? Anyhow I crawled wearily from the car and knocked at the door. What a pleasant sight met my eyes, a dear old man sitting in a rocking chair with his gentle wife in a straight-backed chair beside him. They lived in an ell attached to their son's house, which seemed a perfect arrangement. They greeted me cordially, and I told him I'd heard he was a great singer of old songs. He said he'd be proud and happy to sing and that although his eyes were failing, his memory was perfect. It nearly was and if he did forget a word or line, his wife was quick to remind him. I didn't stay for more than half an hour for fear of tiring him but in that time, among other things, he had sung a rare and ancient Child ballad, "The Grey Cock."

From 1882 to 1898 the late Professor Francis James Child published in five great volumes all the variants he could find of what he called the English and Scottish Popular Ballads. Highly dramatic, the songs give little description of the characters who are easily pictured from their actions. These rare and ancient songs became known to scholars as Child ballads and with a little experience are easily recognized. Many have gone out of oral tradition, so I considered it a great feather in my cap to be able to find any here. In time, of the 305 so designated, the Maritime Provinces have given me variants of 43.

On my next visit Mr. Smith was sitting in a chair

wheezing badly, the result of a long damp spell. He said, "You should have been here last night; we had a great sing." His friend, Tom Young, had come from East Petpeswick, and they often sang together. At Christmas they would sit at a table and hold hands, swinging them to the music's rhythm. This is the way they loved to spend their leisure, singing stories in song to one another. He wasted no time being coaxed but started a song which unfolded beautifully with some lines like those in the English "Waly Waly." Words and music of "Peggy Gordon" were so lovely I was to sing them over and over to myself for years afterwards as I drove alone over country roads. Now I thought what a calamity it would be if anything happened to the old man before Doreen arrived to capture the music.

Mr. Smith sang leaning forward, knees wide apart, whittling a piece of wood with a jackknife and, in the custom of old-timers, he spoke the last two or three words, sometimes with great emphasis, to show that the song was finished. His range was from middle C to high G, as in the song "Nancy" on page 189 of *Traditional Songs from Nova Scotia*, and he embellished his tunes with grace notes and embroideries which varied with his state of mind and mood. One day I took two prominent Newfoundland gentlemen to see him, Judge Higgins and Mr. Fred Emerson, barrister. He was so flattered that he excelled himself with twirls and flourishes and the emphasis on the spoken last words was triple any he had done before. When he forgot, he would say, "dooce take it," his utmost in profanity, and often when I left he would say, "Come soon again dear. Come as often as you like, I'll always give you a couple of songs," and he was as good as his word. When Doreen arrived that summer of 1937, we found that two songs were enough for one sitting, as he tended to mix his tunes if one followed another too quickly. To reach him was a distance of thirty-three miles. Suppose he sang fifty songs—you can see the time and mileage it would take to get the lot.

I also wanted to tell Doreen about my visit to Stanley Williams at Ostrea Lake further along this shore. He had sung readily enough but stopped suddenly and said, "No more songs, I'm going to have a shave," and off he went to the kitchen where I could hear him stropping his razor. He had sung himself out for the moment but didn't want to admit it. The stropping refreshed his memory and he called out, "Have you got this one?" So I joined him and as he scraped he sang—no mean feat with a sharp old-fashioned razor. Similarly Tom Conrod of Woodside had gone outside and refreshed his memory by looking to the southard, and later Walter Roast would say, "Now if only I was ploughin.'" Mr. Williams then startled me by suddenly stopping again lest I get all his songs and not come back, little realizing the effort it was to get there at all over what was little more than a rocky trail.

I'd found Walter Roast one day when mother and I were on a scouting trip. Walter was a bachelor about my own age so, to be sure he didn't get any ideas, I always addressed him as Mr. Roast—and his cousin John as well. People were not as free with first names as they are now. One day Walter protested, and I asked him why he didn't like it. He said, "It makes me too high feelin'." He never guessed the real purpose but it worked and we were excellent friends. The cousins had adjacent farms at Lower East Chezzetcook but in summer they were not free until dark, so we put up for the night at Mrs. Enos Roast's. With today's roads, it's only a half hour run, but not so then. Walter couldn't seem to remember many songs that night, perhaps from shyness but more likely because he wasn't in his own house. When he and John turned up next morning he brought a scribbler with him in which his songs were written out, and he said I could take it home and type out the words. Our little overnight trip netted twenty-five songs and three singing games and the total cost including room and breakfast was four dollars. On the way home we saw men boiling lobsters and bought six for seventy-five cents.

On Doreen's first free day we picnicked in Enos Roast's field where he, the only Roast supposed not to sing, surprised us with a song about pilfering gulls' eggs. At John's house when I asked him to sing he said he wouldn't, but we sat down and talked anyway and presently I remarked, "And when you sing this one," and before he realized it he fell into the song quite naturally. To get his two songs took an hour's conversation. We had been too early to go to the Dennis Smith's, and now I couldn't wait to show this dear couple off. Before asking for songs, I thought I would take their picture. Dennis was jubilant, but Mrs. Smith didn't want it. Finally at his urging she gave in, put his tie on, smoothed his hair with her gentle hands and then removed her apron. Later, when the picture was printed, I had it put in a blue frame for a present. Dennis took it in his hands and held it close to his eyes, examined it carefully, and with a contented smile remarked, "Ain't it purty?" Another day an artist friend, Peggy Covert, sat quietly sketching Mrs. Smith while her husband sang, and she became most agitated. I wonder if this could be connected with local belief in witchcraft; did she fear that someone might stick pins in her image to injure her?

Would "Peggy Gordon," the song I so loved, sound as well on a second hearing? It did, and Doreen shared my delight. Old as he was, Mr. Smith could stop and pick his tune up again without changing pitch or tempo, necessary in this case, for the tune wasn't easy to transcribe. After "Rochester City" we were all tired, and Doreen and I were glad to stretch out on the friendly grass and have our picnic. In the afternoon he sang "Lady Isabel and the Elf Knight", another Child ballad, and another song, a variant on the "Broken Ring" theme.

There were other visits that week, some good, some disappointing. Enos Hartlan had a cold and was polite but definite. Mrs. Duncan said shyly that she couldn't sing, but we pretended not to hear and presently she was singing without our asking. Thirty-three songs came during that period and it was all much easier for the preliminary work I had done during the winter and spring. With words in hand we knew what to ask for, and there was little waste of Doreen's time and energy. She taught with such vigour that there were times when we would drive to Chezzetcook and have our singers ready to perform only to find her too weary to transcribe.

A strange thing happened to a friend who, for some unaccountable reason, insists upon being nameless. She had taken a trip to Devil's Island without me and had returned with little to show for it. She put it down to sea-sickness on the ten-mile trip from Halifax and the fact that the island had been given a supply of "election rum," a local way then of paying for votes. Now with another friend we went together. I had phoned our intention, and Ken Faulkner met us in a boat he had made himself in which he had installed a Nash eight engine which transported us at a speed we found quite terrifying.

We went straight to Mr. Henneberry. I had words of nine songs for which I wanted his tunes, and we worked for two and a half hours. I could understand my friend having trouble with his voice because with his facial deformity he didn't always hit the notes head on. Then I saw her face turn a sickly green and I said, "Are you all right?"

"No," she replied, so I said cheerfully, "We'll stop then and come some other day," but she said, "If I don't finish now I'll never come back." Meanwhile Mrs. Faulkner had come to say she was expecting us at her house for supper which disappointed Mrs. Henneberry who had expected to do the honours. However Mrs. Faulkner was prepared, and my friend was in immediate need of something. As soon as the last tune was on paper two of us went to the lightkeeper's dwelling while she went alone to the great rocks that protect the island's shore. Here after I'd had a welcome cup of tea, I found her facing the sea with the broad Atlantic before her and no sound but the breaking surf. The whole world seems shut out here and one feels completely remote. She was sobbing but managed to apologize for upsetting our plans. I arranged then for the other friend to take her a cup of tea while I paid a short visit to Aunt Jane to explain that we had a sick girl on our hands and must leave. When I got back the sobbing had stopped, but one look showed that her raging headache was real. Half the island joined the procession to see us off and Ken slackened his speed on the return trip. Then the most remarkable thing happened. Once in Ken's boat and away from the island she was herself again. We had gone out the short way from South East Passage, and when we sat on the mainland hillside facing the island and opened our basket, she was jolly and carefree again and soon was even singing. She explained it this way.

On both trips, as soon as she put foot on land, she felt encompassed by something evil as though there actually were devils upon this island. She liked the people but, as on her first visit, the place revolted her almost as though an evil spirit had possessed her. She couldn't understand why I had never felt it, but concluded my consuming interest had precluded all else. In time I found that everybody I took to the island reacted in the same way although never with such violence.

The sunset was glorious that night and as though to reassure us, the sky produced a double rainbow. In the middle of the night my friend phoned to say she had concluded I'd got all the music there was to get from Mr. Ben's tunes, many of which were very good, and marvelled how I had done it. (Now many years later as I look back I marvel myself.) This was to make me sleep better. It didn't. Was I overtired, or had the devils beset me too?

By now I felt it unfair to expect father to walk back and forth to the ferry while I took the family car for collecting. Consequently, with Doreen Senior I called one day on the Premier, the Honourable Angus L. MacDonald, to see if the Province would be interested in helping out.

Knowing he was from Cape Breton, Doreen sang a few verses from songs we'd collected there and, when we got our car we joked whether it was because she had sung or in spite of it. Our first call was on Dennis Williams at his Musquodoboit Harbour store where Doreen sat on a chair that squeaked, our friend Jean Partridge on a packing case, and I on the counter. We got "Lord Loval" on that occasion and, since it was our first ballad collected with our loaned Hudson, we decided to christen it with that name. Perhaps Cecil Sharp objected; the new car proved greedy for gas and oil and thoroughly undependable, and no car since has been named anything but Cecil.

Everywhere people did their best to help us, but one day we approached a house and heard a woman singing a modal tune. We knocked on the door full of hope; she was hospitable but firm. She had led an unregenerate life (probably a very mild form of sin) and now no sound but hymns passed her lips. She may have been quite un-aware that she was singing when we arrived, but I learned to expect nothing where the repressive sects have come in and indeed, at a later date, met the meanest woman I've ever known.

We had been told that a man named John knew old songs but probably wouldn't sing because he had joined one of these groups. We decided to risk a rebuff and when his wife came to the door I said, "We hear your husband sings old songs. We're interested in writing them down before they're forgotten. Do you think he would sing for us?" "You can ask him," she said and pointed to the vegetable garden where he was working. We went over, said we'd been told he knew the ballad, "Sir James the Ross," and would he be good enough to sing it? He had reached the fourth verse when from across the road came one word, "John!" That wretched woman had purposely put temptation in his way.

On the eastern shore we met an eighty-seven year old matron whose name I've forgotten, but whose greatest dream was to visit Dennis Smith and hear him sing again.

Only with him beside her would she sing. We tried singing his songs to her but that didn't help. We climbed fences, clambered over rocks, and sat in a room where an idiot child rocked back and forth to the accompaniment of most unearthly screams while another almost as badly afflicted rocked in another chair in the yard. Pity that poor mother. That evening however rewarded us, for the Tom Youngs of East Petpeswick were old friends by now and had rounded up Mr. Grace Clergy and Freeman Young. The latter two sang little then, although later they gave me many excellent songs. This was probably in deference to Mr. Young, their senior, and the fact that many of their songs had been learned from him. As we were about to leave, tired but well content, Mrs. Young brought out for each of us a glass of pink syrup and a plate containing two date cookies, a piece of homemade cake, and a piece of orange, a crowning treat in the country then.

On our next visit to Mrs. Duncan we found her at the home of her brother, Enos Hartlan, at South East Passage. It was characteristic of her not to rise to greet us but to welcome us cordially and then sit like a duchess without moving all evening. Mr. Hartlan was outside and wearing a hat my mother had given his wife. Nothing daunted he said, "I've turned into a woman since you were here last." That evening Mrs. Duncan sang "The Famous Flower of Serving Men," obviously a ballad. Had Professor Child published it? He had, of course, but it was a rare and definite discovery. Sometimes the family got in an argument over the makeup of a song and it became so heated you'd think a battle royal would ensue. The men kept hinting that I should have brought something along to loosen their throats, but I had concluded early that if a young woman couldn't get a man to sing without bribing him with drink she wasn't worth her salt. Those who drink will take all the free liquor you supply, and then their singing gets muddled. The secret is to make your singer want to sing. A male collector might use liquor effectively, but he should have a limited amount; a woman, particularly a young one, would forfeit respect. Fishermen particularly have an old-fashioned veneration for a lady, and once they put her on a pedestal, they prefer to keep her there. With our high spirits, a genuine liking for the people, and our objective always in mind, any further stimulant would have been redundant and material came in a constant stream.

Shyness was not a common drawback, but one night at Chezzetcook the only way we could get the tune of the singing game, "Here Comes a Duke A-Riding," from the resident school teacher, was by going to the other side of the house where she couldn't see us. It took half an hour to get her started, and Mrs. Enos Roast, spinning on a huge wheel with its square frame for winding wool, marvelled at our patience as she watched us.

We often laughed with people, but laughing at them was another matter and sometimes difficult to avoid. On the western shore we stopped a man on the road to ask about songs, and he put his head in the car window and started a comical Irish song forthwith. It went on and on and he never stopped for breath. I thought I would get hysterics and we hoped he thought it was the song that amused us so.

On weekends we set off as soon as Doreen was free, saving Mr. Gallagher, lightkeeper at Chebucto Head at the western entrance to Halifax Harbour, for a special visit. He was over eighty and reputed to sing from "dawn to dark and never repeat." Discouraged by a few poor weekends, we now took another rutted, rocky road, this time along the western shore of Halifax Harbour. At the Chebucto Head turn we jogged over a side road where low scrub covered the land wherever it could get nourishment from the rocky ground. Every so often we would come to a bend and catch a glimpse of the ocean. Finally the lighthouse came in sight and at the top of another hill we saw three little boys playing. As we drew up beside the lighthouse a friendly face appeared, not the old man we were looking for, but one of middle age. I made what seemed an obvious remark, "You're not Mr. Gallagher."

"No," he retorted, "I'm Mr. Sheehan." Gallagher and

Sheehan were a popular couple in entertainment at that time. We laughed heartily until I realized that something was not quite right. Imagine our chagrin on learning that the Mr. Gallagher we sought had died several years before and the light was kept now by this man, his son. We were crestfallen and to cheer us he said, "My wife sings." We immediately concluded she would be too young to know the songs we wanted but fortunately we were polite and went inside. As soon as Mrs. Gallagher turned the pages of my book she was humming away as one familiar song after another appeared.

Dear Mrs. Gallagher! How we grew to love her. That Saturday afternoon her floor had to be scrubbed so her house would be in order for possible Sunday visitors. She wanted to sing, and then did the thing most natural to her which was to sing while she scrubbed. This was her songs' function in her life anyway, for they accompanied her housework. (Walter Roast sang as he ploughed and Ben Henneberry as he fished.) This is how we got "The Broken Ring", a song which became the basis of a folk opera. Her voice was true, and like Dennis Smith, she could stop anywhere and pick her tune up again in the same key. With other singers, Doreen made frequent erasures. This wasn't necessary here. When bedtime came Mrs. Gallagher's boys were well scrubbed and then wanted to say good-night to their baby cousin but the porridge she was eating covered most of her face. Their mother suggested her forehead, so each in turn placed a reverent kiss there and then scampered off. Our real work began then as Mrs. Gallagher recalled one gem after another.

This was a happy home and a musical one. Mr. Gallagher played the accordion and mouth organ and in time the boys played musical instruments. Mrs. Gallagher was of Scottish descent and had learned many songs from her mother. Before her marriage she had taught school. She and her husband never failed to see the comical side of any situation and they laughed easily, so it seemed we were always in a gale. Nevertheless they were responsible people, and the lighthouse would never suffer from neglect while they were in charge.

For this trip mother had rented for us a car that could be made up as a bed. It was anything but comfortable, and we had parked it beside the lighthouse, not realizing that fog would come in and the horn would boom all night. Probably because we were so happy in our work we slept like babes and were aware of the foghorn only when it stopped.

In the morning, to give Mrs. Gallagher a rest, we went to Duncan's Cove, a fishing village then, now an artists' colony. It is a narrow indentation with high cliffs on either side, no roads, and only faintly discernable paths. Here Mr. Holland told of his forty-eight years as captain of the lifeboat crew and the five thousand lives he had saved. It was interesting, but there were no songs and moments with Doreen were precious. We were more successful with Mr. A. E. Ettinger who lived close by, and we might have appreciated him more if we had not been under Mrs. Gallagher's spell. Even then we had little idea of her repertoire and considered going on to Sambro. Fortunately we stayed because whenever she had a free minute she gave us another song.

Doreen was now in charge of the commissariat. The cost was minimal as we took canned foods from home, and the Gallaghers said they would be much happier if we didn't pay for the few things we got from them. The weekend had given us eighteen new songs and variants of several already published in *Songs and Ballads from Nova Scotia*. Four were Child ballads, and Doreen considered at least ten of the eighteen publishable.

For a few songs Mrs. Gallagher needed help and suggested I visit her brother Andrew at Renfrew Mines to get missing words. The next week mother and I drove twenty miles to Enfield. Our route turned off to a side road which narrowed and worsened but even when there were no longer houses to be seen she poohpoohed the idea of turning back. When we reached the settlement we found Andrew was still at work, so we had our picnic while awaiting him. When he heard two women wanted to see him he approached with a long face, but at the mention of songs he brightened. We were disappointed that he didn't know the words of what we had dubbed "Mrs. Gallagher's Mystery Ballad," and for the others he said he would write them out if we would come back on Sunday, which we did. On the way back we called at another house but made a hasty retreat when a son staggered in followed by a friend also in on a drinking party.

The next day father was my companion and we drove to Kinsac to see Mr. William Nelson. We found a nice old couple but there had been a drowning accident in the village and they were grieving. I showed him my book of songs and decided to leave it with him for a little while hoping it would remind him of some he knew, and that by the time our picnic was over he might be inclined to sing. On our return we found he hadn't shaved for fear of missing us, and he'd been so engrossed in the book he had forgotten to smoke his pipe. He had been ill lately and the beginning wasn't encouraging, but he soon got used to us and slipped into real old time form with a variant of "Lady Isabel and the Elf Knight." The tune for this and also "The Three Ravens" sounded good, so we arranged a return trip on Saturday with Doreen. It proved a bad day because she had put on her display of folk dancing at the summer school that Friday and was too tired to be enthusiastic over anything. As so often happened, an hour's rest beneath a sheltering tree revived her.

We had planned a long trip to begin as soon as summer school closed, but Doreen collapsed and we had to postpone it. She was well enough for a few easy ones so we ambled down to the Hartlan's. Enos and Richard were out, and their brother Ferdinand hadn't sung since his wife died thirty-two years before. Dave was haying and we stopped for a friendly word. He who had never sung for us suddenly opened his mouth and a good song,

"Early Early in the Spring," issued forth. In a twinkling we had paper and pencil out and both were writing frantically. My fast longhand couldn't keep up with him; would he repeat when it had taken all these years to get him started? He pitched his song much too high and his breath came with increasing difficulty. We must have presented a comical sight as he raced through it. Doreen got the tune in the first singing and by the end of the second I had the words. He said when we came again he would try to put another one together and then said of the song he'd just sung, "Of course you've got that one," hoping we hadn't. Singers like to think they are the only ones who know a song and he was so pleased to have given us something new that he presented me with a huge bunch of carrots in parting.

Nearly every day while Doreen had been teaching I had gone exploring with father or mother or a few nieces and their friends as company, combining business with pleasure. And through the years I had often gone to the Thomas Osbornes' house at Eastern Passage. On such occasions Mrs. Osborne had sat quietly listening. Then we heard she knew the ballad "Katharine Jaffray," and one day Doreen and I went to collect it. She was always hospitable, but I suppose it was shyness that restrained her now. We were just giving up when our patience was rewarded. It seemed, erroneously, to be the only song she knew. This happens sometimes, as we discovered when Mrs. John Smith gave us one of the best tunes ever taken down for "The Cruel Mother," and she appeared not to know another song, at least of the kind we wanted. We visited Walter Roast who was not "in tune" but that day his cousin John sang two versions of "The City of Boston." Many times we climbed steep hills only to find possible singers absent.

One day along the eastern shore the road became impassable so we parked our car and walked to a picturesque little cove with two houses, a fishing shack, and several dogs that announced our approach. This was another "dawn to dark and never repeat" hopeful. He and I sat on a huge boulder and last week's porridge still trembled on his lips. Unthinkingly I sat to windward of him and whenever a breeze blew I moved over towards sweeter air. Then he moved too, so it became a little game, this moving every few minutes. The few songs he sang were of no consequence, and by the time I'd reached the edge of the rock I'd concluded he didn't know any good ones anyhow. Wishful thinking, maybe.

On the way back we got "The *Golden Vanity*" from a man with such a huge family that we invited him into the car and all the while the children surrounded us and peered in at the windows. At the Tom Youngs' at East Petpeswick we asked if we could park our car in their field and sleep in it that night. That evening Mr. Young sang, and this was home folk singing at its best, one story in song after another with no outside interruptions. In the morning he rowed us across the harbour to West Petpeswick where Mr. Garvie Young stopped his haymaking and sang for us as we sat beside the quiet water. Back on the east side, we asked the Youngs to share our picnic and Mrs. Young was so pleased that even with painfully arthritic legs she squatted, as we did, on our rug and loved every minute of it. In a farewell visit to the Dennis Smiths we lingered as long as we dared, working when Dennis felt inspired, or just enjoying their company. As we were leaving, one of us said, "I hope I'll be as frisky as you when I'm ninety," to which he replied,

"There's no use being dead when you're alive."

Somehow that day I got the car home and then it was my turn to collapse. I revived enough in the morning to take Doreen to her train and then to take my father shopping. I said, "I want a new mattress because I'm going to spend a lot of time on it in the next few months." Indeed too much of my life was of necessity spent resting and the pattern was either that or full steam ahead.

As I began to feel better, the ball that started rolling in New York picked up speed. A Montrealer had attended a lecture there which resulted in an invitation to speak

to the Montreal Women's Club in January, 1938. As I'd
learned in New York, good singers to illustrate the songs
were hard to come by, so I decided to take singing lessons,
though I knew I'd never be more than good, if even that.
I managed the comical ones easily, and even tackled such
demanding songs as "Peggy Gordon" and "The Broken
Ring." In Montreal I stayed in the beautiful mountain
home of the President, Mrs. Margaret Furness MacLeod,
and we have been close friends ever since. With successes
now in New York and Montreal, I considered further
lecturing, but the ball deviated along a path I hadn't expected.

Before returning home I took a short pleasure trip
to Ottawa, and it happened that the Canadian Authors
were meeting one night at the home of Mrs. Madge Mac-
Beth with Mr. Gladstone Murray, head of the CBC their
guest speaker. It seemed an unusual piece of luck for me
because I thought some day I might want to broadcast our
songs and I might get some good ideas from him. I had
done a series of folk tales, but these were from other
countries. Nothing had been broadcast from our own folk
material.

When Mr. Murray spoke I was profoundly impressed.
It seemed the CBC needed us, provided that our writing
could meet their standard. When he was through there
was a general discussion. Nobody presented a construc-
tive thought and it deteriorated into criticism of radio pro-
ductions. As time went on unexpected thoughts were set
in motion and a voice seemed to say, "This is your opportunity; you must speak." It was the last thing I wanted
to do but the voice was so insistent I knew I must. Not
meaning to be dramatic, but being very much so, I waited
until everybody else had finished and then got to my feet.

"Mr. Murray," I said, "I am here from Halifax for a
few days and will be going back at the end of the week. I
have an idea for a series. Should I write it out and send it
to you?" The room was breathless while he consulted his
note book.

"No," he said, "come to see me on Saturday at ten-thirty." I managed to say thank you and the meeting ended. The room was infused with new life, and friends gathered around to wish me luck.

That same Saturday the Women's Press Club had arranged a luncheon in my honour, and when I tried to plan my talk for them, it kept branching off to what I should say to Mr. Murray and I finally gave up. In his office I felt at ease and said, "This seems like a fairy tale. I've been collecting folk songs for ten years and am only now beginning to feel that I know enough to broadcast about them and lo, the opportunity is here!" He laughed and then questioned me. My plan was sketchy because it was all so new and I told him music would be a problem. He approved as far as I had worked it out and then called in the Program Director, Mr. Bushnell, to confirm it. They also asked if I would like to be an announcer, but I declined. It was agreed that I should return to Halifax and work out the details with Mr. Frank Willis, director of our local station. I left Mr. Murray's office walking on air and the luncheon talk must have reflected my happiness for I got good press.

This was a joyous homecoming. Although mother's arteriosclerosis turned her against me in so many ways, her interest and pride in my work never flagged. Frank Willis too was helpful in every possible way. The production was put in the hands of Robert (Bob) Anderson, a fortunate choice. He always seemed to know where changes would improve the script, and I respected his judgement. There were many problems, for nothing like this had been done before and professionals had not begun to sing folk music. Finally a pattern emerged; we would begin each program with a short string quartet of music to be heard during that half hour arranged by Doreen, and would end the same way. It was a rush assignment for her and many arrangements arrived just in time. Each program had at least one folk singer and I selected Walter Roast, Edmund Henneberry, and Mrs. Gallagher. We also had a professional male quartet.

When I told Walter Roast our plans he was very funny. Before we had found him, his friends used to tease him about his singing and he had an inferiority complex due largely to an arm withered from polio and the fact that he had not yet found a wife. He had suddenly become important in the community, for we were not only writing down his songs, but greedy for more. But this! He said, "You've done a big thing for me and a big thing for Chezzetcook." When I took him for his test he was so nervous he was nearly ill. Being talkative, he had told his friends who had said, "You don't think they'll let *you* sing on the CBC!" He could hardly believe it when he passed with flying colours, and he walked out of the studio more erect than I had ever seen him. Mrs. Duncan was not so fortunate. I thought she might sing a song or two but she was considered too old. Well on in her eighties, she was quite prepared to embark on a new career.

Edmund Henneberry, son of Mr. Ben, was shy and I didn't think I'd get him to the studio if I told him the reason in advance. He was in his fisherman's togs and the studio was in the Nova Scotian Hotel, but somehow I managed it. He sang well and Mr. Willis was so taken with his singing of "The *Mary L. MacKay*," a sea poem by Frederick William Wallace made into a song, that he asked to have it included in the series. With Mrs. Gallagher there was no problem for she loved to sing and would fall in with anything. Each singer received ten dollars a broadcast, which in 1938 wasn't bad, but the money wasn't half as important as their question, "Can I do it?"

Our first song was a long one and difficult to sing, "The Bold Pedlar and Robin Hood." I chose it because it gave an immediate impression of antiquity combined with a beautiful modal tune. Most of the audience hadn't heard unaccompanied singing before but in time got used to it and enjoyed it. Rehearsal time was much too short by today's standards for we met at four and went on the air at six. Nevertheless the other day I played one of these broadcasts over and found it better than I expected for those pioneer days. All the staff had been kind and help-ful and, most of all, interested. Fan mail was large and some letters told of tears streaming down the writers' faces, for what evokes memories more than familiar music?

By the end of the fourth week there had been no word from Ottawa so Frank Willis phoned and was told the head men loved the program and wouldn't miss it. There were backhanded compliments like, "To tell the truth it is much better than I thought it would be." For most listeners it was a revelation; people couldn't think what I would find to talk about for ten half-hour broad-casts. As for the Hartlans, they had no radio in those days but every Sunday trudged to the Osbornes' house to listen, and if they didn't like the professional handling of their songs, they would wait until the broadcast was over and then "sing them right." For me the big thrill came one summer evening when it was all over and I met Mr. Murray again. This was a social affair in Halifax at the home of Colonel Almon. Mr. Murray was sitting on a sofa.

"Come over here," he said, "I want to talk to you. Your program was magnificent; it gave distinction to the whole network." Then he went on to say I'd talked too much, but when I did it again. . . . So I said, "Oh?" and he said, "Oh yes, we'd like you to do it again," and he'd like to see me to-morrow. My brother Mac was there and I was delighted to have him hear these ecstatic words. The next day Mr. Murray greeted me with, "It was grand; it was grand." I felt this was an exaggeration, pleasant as it was to hear, but knew it must be partly true or he wouldn't have asked for another series. I came out of the office to find Frank Willis, Bob Anderson and Mr. Mor-rison of the production staff waiting and when they saw my beaming countenance, they all beamed too.

I wondered if Dennis Smith could be used for the next series. That would be a simple matter today, for he could be recorded in his own home. Then it meant a trip to town and, with the dirt roads as rough as they were, it was too difficult a journey. He too had been a regular listener, and one day he asked why when we'd had "Peggy Gordon" sung we'd left out a verse. As soon as we went off the air, like the Hartlan men he'd sung the whole song through and sung it right.

While the broadcasts were still on, Walter Roast had visited him and Mr. Smith had him come in to repeat the song he'd sung on radio the previous day. These were banner days for Walter who, incidentally, was timing his songs in advance to help me out. He delivered the local mail and every house knew about the broadcasts and many who had no radios of their own went to a neighbour's to listen. If Ben Henneberry felt snubbed when his son Edmund sang in his place he didn't show it. His facial distortion must have been a great affliction but he never mentioned it and I admired the way he rose above it.

That spring and fall of 1938 I accepted a number of speaking engagements and in August provided the CBC with three songs for a round-the-world broadcast, a great distinction in those days. In September mother and I set out on another collecting trip, making Antigonish our goal. Deciduous trees mingled with spruce and fir as we drove through heavily wooded country, and goldenrod growing beside the road reminded us that another summer was nearly over. It was suggested that we stay at John MacNeill's house at Loch Katrine. Directions were vague, which meant stopping often to ask the way, and this provided an opportunity to talk to people. We were impressed with their kind faces, and when they heard what we were looking for, all said we should see Angus the Ridge, so called to distinguish him from the many other MacDonalds. His father lived on a ridge and had been something of a bard, but not to the extent of the bard John MacLean who had emigrated to this province in 1819 after hearing glowing tales of it. What with bears and mosquitoes and perhaps a disinclination to work, MacLean wrote a song called "The Gloomy Forest" (which appears on page 296 of *Gaelic Songs in Nova Scotia*) depicting a depressing picture, and this went back to Scotland and stopped emigration for fifty years.

At the farm Mr. MacNeill and his daughter Jenny came out to meet us. Mrs. MacNeill was being hostess to a missionary meeting so we sat in the kitchen and talked until we were invited to join them. They had heard the broadcasts so we were already introduced. A Mrs. Sinclair said that when her husband on the opposite hillside gathered in his hay, Angus the Ridge always played the pipes on his side of the lake to lighten his neighbour's labour.

Mr. MacNeill sang that evening, but mostly in Gaelic. When a young man came for his mail, my host suggested he might sing and wasn't I surprised when he sang "William and Mary" to a very good tune.

In the morning Margaret, the older daughter, and I called on Angus who sat down at once to think up a few songs. We got a few local ones and a fragment of one his father knew, but I'd have done better if I'd had the Gaelic. He took his pipes outside and strode back and forth; he had to keep moving to play except in a car where there was movement enough. He showed us the Stradivarius stamp on the inside of his violin. When I suggested taking his picture he put his kilt on over his trousers and said I could photograph him from the knees up.

The next day Mr. and Mrs. MacNeill and their son Donald went with me to visit John Francis Sullivan and, with company, I enjoyed the wooded country. At the Sullivan home, which we reached by going up a very steep hill, there was a gorgeous sweep of a long fertile valley, but when we followed John Francis to his nephew's house where he was visiting, there was nothing to be seen for miles but treetops. John Francis looked frail and wasn't sure he could sing. As he got used to us he warmed up and his singing improved. He kept saying he and I would have to go away together because he couldn't think of songs all at once, and his wife teased him and said if he could sing like that he wasn't an invalid any more and could get up in the morning and chop wood. He thought I should hear a jig tune and sang Cape Breton's popular

"Judique on the Floor" all the while keeping time with his feet. It was so lively his nephew got up and danced. Not bad for a man short of breath.

We went then to see an Irishman who, like many others, said he'd spoiled his voice crying for bread and molasses, a staple food in those days.

That evening at the MacNeill's, Mr. John Kennedy sang the ballad "Geordie". Singing was almost continuous and when I drove Mr. Kennedy home, he and I took turns singing in the car. I had driven sixty miles that day over winding dirt roads and was not unduly tired. If the day had not been profitable and pleasant I'd have been exhausted.

A few evenings later we were coming home from John Francis Sullivan's—he had "humoured up" all the songs he knew—when Mr. MacNeill said we were in the Caledonia district known as "Mary Ellen Spooks." I pressed a little harder on the accelerator, remembering stories of unsolved hauntings in a house here attributed to a young girl, and perhaps sensing something of the atmosphere which to this day is said to be sinister. On a more cheerful note he explained how nicknames go here. His grandfather was Hugh, so his father was Donald Hugh. He, being John, was John Donald Hugh and his son Donald is Donald John Donald Hugh. Other nicknames have a physical association. Peggy the Grist Mill's father ran a grist mill. I decided then to nickname young Donald MacNeill who seemed to spend every spare minute piling wood for the winter. I dubbed him Donald the Woodpiler, but this wasn't right. They changed it to Donald the Woodpile and that he is to this day.

A day or two later we called on a widow, Mrs. Kenny, who was spinning on a primitive wheel. "I can't word a song," she said, "but my husband could word them good." A little conversation about her husband brought "The Ship's Carpenter" to mind and, once started, she was delighted to find she could remember it. This was followed by "The True Luvyers' Discoursion," a long dialogue between two very literate people which, surprisingly, is often sung by illiterate singers who can't possibly understand half the words. What attracts them to it? We made other calls, most of them unrewarding except for Mr. John Bray at Glencoe who kept me writing for two solid hours. Then mother and I left regretfully and drove to Country Harbour where there was supposed to be a singsong that evening. It rained and nobody turned up. Our host assured us there were songs but said we should go to the lumber woods to get them. There they sang every evening until nine and on Saturday they would sing all night. At that time they stayed in the woods for three or four months at a time. Similarly in head winds fishermen might sing for a week while waiting for the weather to clear.

We finished at Sherbrooke with three more Child ballads, ending a trip that was a mixture of ups and downs. We enjoyed the kind people who were pleased, as they said, to be of service, and the happy atmosphere of the MacNeill home, but the poverty and hopelessness of many farms where the soil seemed unyielding and the future unpromising was depressing. Mother was a perfect companion and fell in with everything I wanted to do. At the end of sixteen days I took her back and returned the car to father. Then after a good rest and an appraisal of what I'd found I went back to be driven around Guysborough County by the school inspector, Mr. Coldwell. Since he had to visit every part of the county at that season, I met people easily.

Of all Guysborough County, the village of Whitehead proved the most interesting. We visited a Mrs. Reynold who was sure she couldn't remember a song and anyhow before trying had to finish the favourite Nova Scotia card game, Forty-fives, before even thinking about it. The game seemed never-ending, but when it was over everybody thought she should sing. She tried, but nothing would come. Then suddenly at full volume she started in. This was from nervousness because later when she felt at home she sang softly and very nicely. As often happens, I was just putting on my coat to leave when she remembered another and when that was finished she said if I would come again she would take me to see her father. As we drove back that night, there was a magnificent spectacle of northern lights, like a marble stairway to heaven.

One day after a rather fruitless trip we returned by way of Giant's Lake where a wedding party was in full swing. Mr. Coldwell went in and first thing I knew I was invited to the feast. Earlier the bride and groom and immediate families had started the ball off with an eight-hand reel, the bride and groom leading. This was known as a Scotch wedding in the old manner. Tables were spread with cold meats, bread, cakes big and little, tea, and two wedding cakes. Angus the Ridge got a little circle about him which we joined with crossed hands. He sang a Gaelic song with the others joining in the chorus, pumping hands up and down to the music's rhythm. Then Mr. MacNeill led the singing after which Angus marched up and down the hall playing his pipes while some of the men got in a corner and step-danced. Liquid refreshment flowed and the mood was festive.

When we went back to Whitehead Mrs. Reynold, her son Herman and a niece took us to Yankee Harbour. It was a gorgeous day for the twenty-minute trip. There were no wharves for mooring our boat, but ready hands helped over the seaweed-covered rocks. Otto Munro sang first, a youngish man compared to the one we were hoping to hear later on. Sometimes Mrs. Reynold joined him as she used to do when living here as a girl. Or perhaps he would mention a song and Herman would sing it, or Mrs. Reynold would sing alone. If one undertook to "word" a song off, the others never interfered unless to help with a forgotten phrase, and I took down song after song in rapid succession. From there we walked along muddy paths over rocky hillocks and finally scrambled over more seaweed-covered rocks and tumbled into another boat.

The boatman stayed with us for the rest of the day sitting on the floor with his back against the wall and knees up in front of him.

Our next prospective singer was old and frail and said he couldn't sing any more. William, our boatman, expected this and said he would word off a couple for a start. I sat with my wet feet in the oven, writing rapidly. After the first words were down I asked him to *sing* and he did in the best voice I'd heard in the county. It isn't everybody who can remember words alone; most have to sing to call them to mind. By this time the old man was ready but William pretended not to notice and sang another song. Then he went out, and the old man started, sitting in a straight chair against the wall with eyes closed. He assured me he could do better if I'd brought along a little whisky and he was just getting started when we had to leave because Mr. Coldwell had an evening meeting. On the return trip Mrs. Reynold and Herman sang "Betsy the Waiting Maid" and, since I'd already written the words down on another trip, I could sit back and enjoy them with the rippling waves forming an accompaniment.

I had taken a dictaphone to Guysborough and found it a great help. Since there was electricity at John Francis Sullivan's, I took it there, but he had failed so in health I didn't urge him. Angus the Ridge didn't serve much better, being tired after spending the day making fifty pounds of butter. Years later I discovered I'd missed a great opportunity here for Angus knew some excellent folk tales. At that time I didn't know enough to ask for them.

There were many other calls, most of them disappointing. For one good singer there were probably ten who had either forgotten their songs or had never sung. I added to my supply of nicknames, each with a story to explain why the person was connected with the distinguishing noun. In my article in *Folklore in Action* (Volume XIV, 1962) published in honour of Dr. MacEdward

Leach who had worked here and discovered Angus the Ridge's tales, I wrote about these names, and he thanked me for bringing back memories. We have Hughie the Hide (he tried to steal one and was caught), Fourteen (he changed a cheque from $1.40 to $14), the Skunks (they painted their boat black with a white stripe which gave someone the idea), Angus the Bird (he flitted about from place to place), Signboard Alice, Angus Shoot the Cat, Rory the Lover, Billy Sunday (not the great evangelist, but one who bootlegged on Sunday), Kitty the Basket (nothing so innocent as eggs and butter in *her* basket, no, she carried a bottle), Sarah the Goat (her father was Dan the Goat), Rory Cold Day, Murdock the Mortgage, Boxcart Sadie, Galloping Sue, Kitty the Pullet, Hughie the Rooster, Duncan the Flea and the Seven Daughters. Two MacDonald sisters worked in the Antigonish library and were known as The Professors. You would never say, "Are you going to the MacDonalds' this afternoon?" but, "Are you going to the Professors'?"

Stories were everywhere, often on themselves. For instance, two Scots held this conversation,

"Poor Donald's dead."

"Is he now?"

"Yes," with a gloomy shaking of the head, "and he's gone to meet his Maker without a word of Gaelic in his head."

One story called up another. A stranger was reported in the district and somebody said, "It must have been the devil."

"No," in all seriousness, "it couldn't have been the devil because he talked to me in Gaelic."

Chapter 6

In 1938 the usual way to hear folk song programs was by short wave radio from England since we had few, if any, here. These were listed in our papers, and when I read that Canadian songs would be on I thought, "I wish they knew ours." My radio was upstairs where I heard it announced that there would be songs in English, French, "and finally from Nova Scotia where Helen Creighton has discovered—." I didn't wait for the rest but ran downstairs to tell the exciting news, for this had never happened before. We crowded around the radio. The voice would fade and static interfered but we heard enough to realize this was a lovely voice and the choice of songs was to my liking. The singer was Eve Maxwell-Lyte and the next day I wrote her the first fan letter she ever received. She had wondered if she should have asked permission to sing our songs but thought, "It's the middle of the night; nobody will be listening in Canada." She had a concert tour planned which would begin in January in Montreal. The Halifax Ladies Musical Club invited her here and on March 16, 1939 under the distinguished patronage of the Lieutenant Governor, the Premier, and the Superintendent of Education, our songs were introduced.

Eve was the great granddaughter of Rev. Henry Francis Lyte author of that most comforting hymn,

"Abide with Me." There were set ideas then about how folk songs should be sung and I was told that in England purists objected to the beautiful costume she wore. We loved it and were fascinated by the way she used her voluminous skirts for a shawl at one time when she impersonated an old woman, and to cradle a baby when she sang a lullaby. Until then I'd heard only two solo recitals, one entirely in foreign tongues and so deadly dull that nobody came to hear the delightful Danish singer, Engel Lund, who followed a few weeks later, and who conveyed the meaning whether you understood the words or not. Eve was different again, and reviewers all over Canada agreed that the little acting she did added to the enjoyment of the evening. She was our house guest while here and I entertained at a tea for her. Later she sang our songs in England and said she considered Enos Hartlan's "When I Was in My Prime" one of the most beautiful in the English language.

In April, 1939, Professor Henry Alexander came from Queen's University to work on a Nova Scotia speech map. He used literate and illiterate informants, and interviews could run for several days. My father was interviewed and when I realized how long the questions lasted I said, "Are you enjoying it?"

"Yes," he replied, "it doesn't do to get in a rut." No wonder at eighty-two he was still young. Not so Enos Hartlan. He would answer politely and then suddenly get up and disappear. I introduced the professor to many people in the district and one day he went with me to see Mr. Willie Hartlan. He was sound asleep on a kitchen couch but in two minutes was up and singing. The professor's eyes popped wide. "How do you do it?" he asked later. "You go into a house and wake a man up and he sings for you. A man couldn't do it." I smiled modestly, knowing it wasn't all that easy. Nevertheless it did happen more often than not.

The second series of broadcasts started in May. This time I turned the professional singing over to Nina Bartley Finn, known later as Emma Caslor. Hers was the only trained voice that satisfied the folk singers. When she was through there was no singing them over again "right", for they could tell she loved them as much as they did. Those who had been on the first series were relaxed, and Walter Roast walked into the studio as though he owned it. He told me people were getting special batteries in their sets to hear him. This was long before transistor days or even electricity in every house, and the radios we take for granted now were luxury items then.

When driving Walter home after a broadcast, I noticed a new roof on his house. He said I'd helped to put it there and added, "You made it possible for me to keep my horse for a whole year and, if it hadn't been for the broadcasts, I couldn't have kept my horse." Another day, driving Mrs. Gallagher home, I looked at the low scrub growing there and thought of the persistent fog that spring which had prevented her husband ever coming to the studio to watch her perform. I remarked, "Mrs. Gallagher, do you like living down here?" to which she promptly replied, "I might as well like it; it's my home."

Planning, typing scripts, and timing of broadcasts all fell on me. Nina's health had been bad before we began so there was a great risk in using her, but this was therapy for her, and she strengthened while I, on the other hand, wondered if I could last it out. When the series ended and the last note played I sighed with relief. All twenty broadcasts had gone without any real hitch and we had worked together happily. But these were hard days at home. Mercifully when mother's condition had almost brought me to the breaking point, I was appointed Dean of Women at the University of King's College in Halifax, to begin in September. Meanwhile the Canadian Authors Association was to meet in Halifax and I'd been asked for a program. I felt such a gathering would be interested in source material and when I asked Walter Roast if he would sing he said, "Does that mean I'll have to face an audience?" I said "Yes," so he thought a moment and said breathlessly, "When I tell them down home that I'm going to sing at the Lord Nelson Hotel, oh my!" Mrs. Gallagher assented readily, but Edmund had to consider. Nina was also to sing, and Ken Faulkner to play the fiddle for Edmund's "False Knight upon the Road." We would also have our male quartet. On the night of the performance I met Edmund, Ken, and Walter at the ferry and as we drove to the hotel listened to their exchange of compliments.

Edmund to Walter: "You have a fine voice. I like to listen to you on the radio broadcasts."

Walter to Edmund: "I like to listen to you too. It's a funny thing, people down home downfaced me that I had sung 'The *Mary L. MacKay.*' They wouldn't believe it was you."

Edmund to Walter: "My little feller, he's only three years old, and the other day when you sang he said, 'There's daddy.' " It was a good evening and a memorable one for the Authors.

Two delightful visitors that summer were Joan and Betty Rayner, originally from New Zealand. They were New York entertainers known as "The Troubadours," and liked to visit a country before interpreting its songs. When I took them to Chezzetcook, Dennis Smith was in excellent form and sang lustily and, since I already had all his words, I was free to notice things I'd missed before like the way he pursed his lower lip for the e sound. Eyes wide open, body motionless, knees wide apart, often whittling a stick or opening and closing his jackknife, he gave his full attention to his performance. Joan Rayner said, "We like your songs, they're so cheerful. In so many others we've heard the heroine dies in the end." Dennis Smith called them "the little girls" and where "Peggy Gordon" had the line, the "girls adore me," he made flirtatious eyes at Joan. They took pictures of the old couple, Mrs. Smith in long cotton dress and boots, dust cap, and a shawl over her shoulders, he wearing his waistcoat with brown buttons which he liked because it was part of his uniform when he sailed coastal vessels along this shore. Later, when the Rayners performed our songs, this is the way they dressed. As we passed the house again returning from our picnic, Dennis came running out to give us a verse he'd forgotten before. He must have stood for an hour awaiting us.

We found Walter picking strawberries, and with the Nova Scotia faculty for turning the moment into a joke he said, "I see I got lots of help coming." He told them I was his boss now (the broadcasts were still on), and "whatever she says goes. When she first come I was going to run away, but all she has to do now is to crook her little finger."

Before the Rayners left in their beautiful caravan, a great novelty in Halifax at that time, they gave me a set of china for the suite I would occupy at King's. When war came they sang for troops and eventually established a travelling theatre for children in Australia. Every year or two a mimeographed letter keeps their friends up to date.

By August of 1939 Doreen was back, but Dennis declared he couldn't sing any more. He did, but his choice was uninteresting, and when he repeated a song he'd given us the previous year he changed the tune. We weren't used to being disappointed in this house and were filling in time with polite conversation when he began to sing the lovely riddle song, "I'll Give My Love an Apple." Pencils went into quick action, and Mr. Smith was amazed that it excited us.

"It's only a little one," he protested, "only as long as my thumb." We didn't get it all at that sitting though, and it was only because he got absent-minded that the final verses popped out. The last riddle went, "How can there be a baby and no crying?" and the answer is, "When a baby is a-getting there is no crying." A-getting is probably begetting which he must have thought not fit for our ears.

We explored the Noel shore and discovered how a

grandpa could be so discouraged by grandchildren who laughed at his songs that they were all but forgotten. Teen-agers were eager to entertain us and incredulous when they had to take a back seat. Here we met Leander Macumber, a farmer who had returned from the United States where he had sung in the evangelist Billy Sunday's choir. His tune for "Do You See That There Bird?" is one of the loveliest I've recorded and one of the most difficult to sing. When Kenneth Peacock arranged it for a CBC prestige broadcast, I wrote Mr. Macumber, and he invited friends in to listen, but when he learned it was to be sung by a woman he was so angry he turned the set off. In 1969 a new arrangement was made by Dr. Dennis Farrell and sung at the closing exercises of the Halifax School for the Blind. They carried it off beautifully.

Not getting a great deal on the Noel shore, Doreen and I went to Parrsboro and met a man who boasted he could sing two hundred songs but when he tried to recall them, came up with two. We were not so light-hearted that year for the clouds of war hung overhead and if conditions worsened, we knew Doreen would have to return to England at once. A fruitless twenty-six mile trip wasn't laughed off as a wild goose chase. However there were bright spots such as our meeting at Musquodoboit Harbour with an elderly retired banker who was living alone and on a milk diet. He said we should go to Ostrea Lake and he would go with us and introduce us to his friends. I recalled what a lonely rough road this was and was happy to have a protector, even one so old and frail. He said he'd take along some bootlegger's rum. I assured him it wasn't necessary but he was so insistent and had been so kind that I gave in, never dreaming he would drink with his friends.

When we arrived the men were getting towards the end of a celebration and because they'd had just so much their songs were not what we wanted. I thought, "What a waste of opportunity," and then had an idea.

"Does anyone know the one about the milk white

steed?" I asked. Many songs have this phrase and they are usually Child ballads. They nodded negatively, but the seed had been sown. A face brightened and a voice said, "I know one about a little page boy," and away he went. Doreen got the modal tune easily but it went quickly and was twenty-seven verses long, so the most I could get was the opening line of each verse so nothing would be lost when repeated.

That was a good night, for we had "Little Musgrave and Lady Barnard," a rare ballad indeed, and I had again successfully used my device for getting singers in the frame of mind for old songs. Later when I mentioned this at Indiana University, Alan Lomax found it very funny. He had a mental picture of me approaching a burly fisherman and saying, "Excuse me, but do you know the song about the milk white steed?" If that failed, I learned to ask if they knew one with broadswords in it, or one that began, "As I walked out one May morning," or "Early early in the month of May."

Our protector on the way home was full of argument, but as soon as we reached our hotel all argument ceased. A message had come for Doreen to return to England. That meant war was coming. The next day with heavy hearts we saw her sail away, and it was many years before we met again.

September followed quickly and with it a new way of life as I assumed the duties of Dean of Women at King's, a college founded in 1789 and with a proud history. Buildings were in the English style, and the women's residence, Alexandra Hall, stood between the main building and President's Lodge and chapel. The President, Dr. Stanley Walker, and his wife were close personal friends, so there was much visiting back and forth. My suite was tiny but I bought a luxurious sofa with down cushions and had it covered with an English cretonne with curtains to match. Students would come in any say, "My room's the same size but it doesn't look like this." It was the first time I'd had things around me entirely my own, a new and startling experience. I got along well with those of the fifteen co-eds who were serious students, but those whose main interest was in courting were a problem I wasn't prepared for. I made a few mistakes, but on the other hand, with the help of the president, new rules were drawn up which made residence life better all round. Meals were served in a common dining hall where the girls had their own table and at the evening formal dinner we wore our academic gowns and all stood for the Latin grace. There was a short chapel service every evening before dinner and the girls often went, though not obliged to. On Sunday morning we paraded there in cap and gown. I would have enjoyed these services more if I had not once fainted in church in 1938 which has made me nervous ever since. Even yet I seldom get through without at least once feeling I'm slipping away and I wriggle my toes and stand on the soles of my feet to prevent it happening.

The year was pleasant but a strain, due largely to late hours. In the summer when I felt the need of a holiday, the Fred Emersons came from Newfoundland and said they were taking me back with them. This seemed exactly right, but from the moment I started to get ready, I felt I wouldn't go and mentioned this several times. When we finally left in their car for North Sydney I couldn't believe we were really on our way, and when we arrived in North Sydney and were going to a restaurant for dinner, I told the purser not to have my things put aboard just yet. On our return from dinner a long distance call from my brother Paul awaited me. Mother had suffered a cerebral stroke. I was not to see Newfoundland until 1964 when I set up a branch of the Canadian Authors Association and spoke on folklore at Memorial University.

Duties were heavier the second year at King's, and I dreaded the summer because our nurse was leaving. How could I look after mother who was heavy to move and resentful? To prepare for this, as soon as college closed

I went with my cousin, Belle Albro, to Bear River for a short holiday. The good Lord took a hand then and I was helped as I have always been, for while I was there mother slipped quietly away. I determined then to forget the bad years, and in time the lovely memories came back. Now I had father to care for and that was pure joy. Lil had been spending her summers in West Gore and this was extended to full time for she was happier in the quiet village with friends of her own.

I have said little about wartime Halifax as it was now where every moment was fraught with danger, for ships with explosive cargoes came and went, making a repetition of the 1917 catastrophe almost a probability. On the night of April tenth, 1942, while we slept, the *S.S. Trongate* with a deadly mixed cargo was afire less than a mile away. About 3 a.m. we were awakened by the sound of gunfire, and although we knew we shouldn't, we rushed to the nearest window and saw a spectacle unlike anything we had seen before. What was it? It couldn't be a naval engagement because one ship was doing all the firing. Left alone, I would have run for cover, but not father. He would enjoy his moments to the last, so he placed his chair in front of the window and we watched breathlessly. It must have lasted for half an hour and the whole activity was centred on our side of George's Island. Suddenly it stopped but we had to wait until morning to find out what had happened. The burning *Trongate* had been towed to this point where they planned to scuttle her. That wasn't possible, so the *Chedabucto*, with Captain Creery in command, opened fire as the only way of sinking her. A shot in the wrong direction and we wouldn't be here today. A vivid account of that hazardous night is in the January 1963 issue of *The Atlantic Advocate*.

As I looked forward to being housed with father more and more, and realized the shortage of accommodation for service personnel, I said, "Why don't we make an apartment upstairs and have a nice young couple here to live?" Everybody with a house of any size was doing this and it could be quite a financial boon. To my surprise he welcomed the idea, even though it meant turning his commodious bedroom into a bed-sitting room for others, and his dressing room into a kitchen. I had a couple in mind, and soon Jerry and Dick Garrett moved in. I stipulated they must be self-contained for I would do no menial chores. I had to eat my words, of course, and found myself one day down on hands and knees cleaning out their grate and lighting their fire. Jerry was sick, Dick was in his plane escorting the *Queen Elizabeth* or some other great ship to port, and I didn't feel I should ask Ruth, our maid. This didn't keep me from suggesting a while later that we make a second apartment upstairs. I did this largely to get father on the ground floor where he would be nearer the coal furnace. He enjoyed taking out the clinkers. It was dangerous, but the last physical task he could do. We therefore made our drawing room into two bedrooms, moved Ruth into the library, and took in Major Peter King with his wife Margaret and baby David. On fine days father would sit in his chair at the front of the house with David in his playpen beside him, and it was touching to see the two, one at the beginning of life, the other so near the end.

On one of these happy days, President Stanley of Dalhousie University phoned to say Mr. John Marshall of the Rockefeller Foundation was in his office and would like to see me, but he did not say why. Mr. Marshall turned out to be a man of great charm. He asked about the work I'd done in folklore. Then he asked if I had heard about the Institute of Folklore to be held that summer at Indiana University and what I thought of it. I replied that the literature I'd had on it looked more scholarly than anything else I'd ever had on folklore.

"Are you going?" he asked.

How we throw away our opportunities. "Going? I wouldn't think of going. There's a war on." This was 1942. I had a feeling he expected something more than

that, and I suggested that if his foundation planned anything in folklore in Nova Scotia I would like to be kept in
mind. All the way home I had a sense of unfinished business. Why had I gone so obligingly all the way over to
Dalhousie, and what had I neglected to do? In the morning Dr. Stanley phoned again.

"How did you get on with Mr. Marshall?"

"Very nicely," I replied. "I enjoyed meeting him."

"Did he say anything to you about the Institute of
Folklore?" Then it dawned on me, I was being made an
offer. I changed my tune in a hurry.

For the first time I was enjoying domesticity. Also
Mac was home, for he had joined the Canadian army and
was stationed in Halifax. This swung the balance in
favour of leaving because, being a doctor, Mac could check
father's heart and see that he didn't overdo things. Ruth
was well used to our ways, the Garretts had become close
to us and Jerry would take over from me as chauffeur.
Although we all felt an opportunity like this must not be
turned down, two months seemed a long time to be away.

I was late for my class on the first morning I went
to the Institute and slipped quietly into a back seat. The
moment it was over the other students came crowding
around saying, "I've always wondered if I'd be able to
meet you," and that sort of thing. They all knew my *Songs
and Ballads from Nova Scotia*, and told me it was in their
libraries and often used in their courses. Three of the professors took me to lunch; one of them was Alan Lomax
whose father had made a name for himself as a collector
of cowboy songs. Alan had grown up in the tradition, and
said that for a while he hated it. He had become a collector himself, however, and at that time was assistant in
charge of the Archives of American Folk Song in Washington, D.C., and has been active in folk music ever since.
The next day, four of us went swimming in a quarry pool,
and on the way back Alan asked if I would consider using
a recording machine in Nova Scotia.

Little did Alan know what that meant to me because,

shortly before, someone had come to my province and had attempted to take for herself on disc all the songs I had collected so laboriously, at the same time insinuating that only someone with her massive brain could operate a machine so intricate. If I've guarded my material jealously ever since, it has been because of this unfortunate encounter. I was overjoyed, particularly as our songs would have a place in the Library of Congress, and also I would have a recording set of my own.

John Jacob Niles was one of our lecturers, and he had for his collecting field the Appalachian Mountains. He illustrated his talks by singing in a countertenor, and I would be transported with the beauty of his music. In the middle of a lecture he would stop and shout, "Ma'am, have you anything like that in Nova Scotia?" or he'd finish a beautiful ballad, and while I was still breathless with the joy of it I would hear, "Sister Creighton, what do you think of that?"

The course was meant for graduate students. I knew practically nothing about folklore from the academic side, but we had excellent teachers, chief of whom was the internationally-renowed scholar Dr. Stith Thompson, author of the great *Motif Index of Folk Literature*. He and his wife soon became my close friends. Our class had picnics to country parks where we would listen to one another's folk songs. In lectures it seemed the letter Z was always coming up and when Dr. Thompson used it with the American pronunciation he always looked apologetic. One day I penned the following and passed it around the class:

> I find it very strange to see
> A people using letter zee
> Because when everything's been said
> The older form is letter zed.

In the morning a reply was on my desk:

> If in the ancient British way

For zee you must have zed,
Why then, Miss C. there's heck to pay
For dee, poor thing, is dead!

One stipulation of my fellowship was that there must
be no interviews and this I explained when visited by
Irene Harris of the *Indiana Daily Student*. Nevertheless
a comprehensive write-up appeared, saved by the heading
which read, "Miss Creighton, Folklorist, Knows Plenty
of Songs and Folkways but She Can't Give Out Interviews." I could lecture though, a challenge in this company of experts, and when I'd mention a song Mr. Niles
would demand, "Sing it!" I hadn't expected this. One
verse wouldn't do; I must sing another.

One day at lunch in the cafeteria we were having our
usual lively exchange of songs and stories when Mr. Niles
announced, "I have a lot of friends who are deans of
women." This seemed so out of character that we looked
at him in astonishment so he added, "but some of them
are awful cows." I put on my most hurt expression and
said, "Mr. Niles, you called me a cow."

"I did not."

"Yes you did," I said and turned to Dr. Boggs sitting
next to me to confirm it. We made the most of it. Then
at Mr. Niles' farewell corn-roast a few evenings later I
presented him with a gift for his farm. It was a cow bell,
a nice dainty one. Four years later when I was back at the
university the Thompsons invited me to join them on
their trip to North Carolina where Stith was to receive his
first honorary degree. On the way we stopped at the Niles'
Kentucky farm where, in our host's absence, we were received cordially by his charming Russian wife. When we
were leaving I said, "Mrs. Niles, have you any idea what
became of the cow bell I gave your husband?"

"Did *you* give him that bell? It's our front door bell."
There it was, so we all gave it a tinkle in passing.

I came home in 1942 by way of Washington where
I spent several days in the Library of Congress learning

how to use a recording machine. At that time Dr. Charles Seeger, father of Pete of later folk song fame, was head of the Music Division of the Pan American Union, and his second wife, also a musician, worked with him. Pete's mother had died a few years previously. One evening they invited me to their home for dinner. We drove to their Tudor-style dwelling where their three children eagerly awaited them, and after dinner their father played the piano while they expressed themselves in rhythm. I believe they did this for about twenty minutes every night and loved it. Years later when Michael sang in Halifax I said, "We've already met." In New York the Rockefeller Foundation confirmed a second fellowship, this time to pay expenses while I used Library of Congress equipment.

Every moment at home now was precious as father's health failed, and I devoted myself largely to his care. These moments would have been most happy if it had not been for the impending separation, and one remark made then comforts me to this day: from a clear sky he announced, "You've earned every cent I've ever spent on you."

At Indiana University I'd studied Negro music. We have a large black community in Nova Scotia. I called first on a Mrs. Bundy. She was friendly and told how in the old days when few people could read and anyhow there were not enough books to go around, the minister would line the hymns out. That is, he would read a line and the congregation would sing it. One day he found himself without his glasses. He stood up saying, "My eyes are dim. I cannot see to read this hymn," and they sang it. Then he said, "Yonder comes my brother Jim, I guess he's got my specs with him," and when they sang that too he protested, "I did not mean this for a hymn, I only said my eyes were dim," and they sang that too. She said that the best church music came at collection time and that at a recent baptism when they were dressed in white "and all took to the water so nice," that they had a special hymn. It seemed promising.

133

A letter from the Rockefeller Foundation advised that Mr. Charles Dunn would be in Halifax on his way to Cape Breton to study Gaelic. I suppose I selected nearby Preston as a place to take him because I was getting interested in the music of the Blacks. We separated at North Preston and I found myself at the home of Mrs. Cassie Downey. In deference to the day, she would sing nothing but religious songs. On Monday she would sing anything. I was just leaving, pleased with the words I'd taken down, when I saw a big man weaving his way across the field. Mrs. Downey told me there was a lot of drinking on Sunday, so I beat a hasty retreat, and wondered if I should come back to this district alone. On the way home I told Mr. Dunn the "eyes are dim" story and he said he'd heard exactly the same thing from his grandmother in Scotland who, like Mrs. Bundy, could tell you the place where it had happened. Later I took it down in Lunenburg, and they too could point out the spot. So we have it from a Negro, Scottish, and German background. Did it really happen in all three?

Mrs. Downey had told me of her father, Mr. William Riley of Cherry Brook, so my father went with me to see him. Another Mrs. Downey, also a daughter, was keeping house for him, but he was ill in bed and probably wouldn't be able to sing for a week. Meanwhile she was learning his songs and seemed genuinely anxious for our return. He then sang readily but the words, "Lord, I wonder shall I ever get to heaven," with its picture of the blessings to come were too much for him and he broke down and cried.

Someone had told him I was going to make a lot of money from his songs so I explained the true situation, and then he sang the haunting slavery song, "Auction Block," a song which has been reprinted in many text books since. He also sang "The Twelve Joys of Mary" and, after I'd said good-bye and was about to leave, he remembered one of the most beautiful songs I've found anywhere, "The Cherry Tree Carol." This was sung to a tune different from those usually found, presumably one he had made up himself as this family often did. In parting he said, "Come any time you like. I like to occupy your time; I'm a lady's man." A few days later he sang for two and a half hours. At one point I thought he was falling asleep but Mrs. Downey said no, he was studying (trying to recall the words).

It was in July 1943 that the recording equipment came. There were seven boxes, including a heavy machine and a heavy box of blank acetate discs. The microphone fitted on a steel stand; there were sapphire needles for cutting the groove, and a converter to be used with batteries for making electricity. When assembled it was formidable. However the less sophisticated the singer, the less it worried them. Mrs. Duncan, for instance, was delighted and at the first recording sang until I, not she, was tired out.

To justify the Library of Congress in sending out recording equipment in wartime, I had to do some work among the Service personnel. I had heard that they often made up their own songs, but when I mentioned them they looked horrified, for few were of the parlour variety. One or two whose words I didn't understand I sent on to Alan Lomax and later, when I learned their meaning, my blushes could be felt from here to Washington.

At the naval base, H.M.C.S. *Cornwallis*, I discovered young Henry Sherman who was writing most of the material for the navy paper, *The Crow's Nest*, and had dreamed up a serial about a mermaid named Miranda who wanted to become a Wren (the women's branch of the service). I became interested in his career and we've been friends ever since. Gordon Kushner, now with the Royal Conservatory of Music in Toronto, was, like Henry, in the Special Services Branch. He was a concert pianist. They were experimenting with programs of classical music on Sunday afternoons. Some officers protested the sailors wouldn't go, but they always filled the hall and were so proud of their gifted musicians that the applause was deafening. I made a number of recordings here and elsewhere and, of the navy's original songs, those made up about a trip to the Aleutians are probably the best.

At home, Richard Hartlan sang for one whole evening, and when at the end I gave him two cigars, he felt he should take only one. Walter Roast came to our house too to record and told me he always knew when I was going to call him. This time he'd dreamed I was being married and he was singing at my wedding. To sing his best he had actually gone first to a doctor to have his ears blown out at a cost of two precious dollars. Another singer now recording for the first time was Edmund Henneberry who could go through *Songs and Ballads* and sing every one of his father's songs. He would hum them over soundlessly first. His tenor voice was clear and musical but nervousness makes him sound much older than his years.

Edmund's house had electricity, but at Dennis Smith's I had to take along my converter and newly charged batteries. At ninety-two Dennis was still in good form, and when he sang "Lady Isabel and the Elf Knight" and came to the part where she pushed the villain into the river he slapped his legs. In his younger days he probably dramatized his songs a lot. You will remember that like most old timers he spoke the last word, but this time he shouted it so vehemently I feared he would smash the microphone. One Saturday afternoon, the time most people did their shopping, I went to Dennis Williams' store. What was business compared to this wonderful new machine? He closed the store, and customers and all went into his house. Between songs he would run out and wait on them.

My last visit to the Black community in this area came to an abrupt ending. The old man I sought was sitting in his doorway so I set my machine up in the quiet roadway. I had words of a number of his songs and, fearing an interruption, asked for the most important first. They went well enough; then in the middle of a song we heard approaching wagon wheels. His daughter got excited and spoiled the record by talking, and then her brother arrived and said it wasn't good for his father to sing and he must stop. I was saying it was very good when one of my companions whispered that there was twenty-five dollars worth of liquor in the carriage. I realized then that a party had been planned and had indeed already begun for I'd noticed someone going into the room (the parlour), shutting the door, coming out in a few minutes to be followed by someone else doing the same thing. I packed up in a hurry, and was too discouraged to go back. However at the Nova Scotia Home For Colored Children nearby I was more fortunate and got some excellent singing games.

There are pockets of Blacks in many parts of the province and I have always regretted not following up a young lad in Guysborough who passed my hotel singing a beautiful modal tune. Many years later in Bridgetown I met Mr. Charles Owens who at the age of ninety-nine was still singing with the Salvation Army. He lived with many descendants at Inglewood on the outskirts of the town and those that didn't sing played musical instruments. I've always felt that families should be courted, but babies are a mixed blessing. If their gurglings come through on the playback the family will say proudly, "The baby!" while I growl to myself. But here when all the family joined the old man, harmonizing and playing musical instruments, the voice of the baby coming in the middle of the song seemed just right.

My mother had once said, "You need never worry about your father until he refuses his food." Prophetic words, and it happened on October third, 1943. I was to record the Navy Show on the seventh and decided to go ahead because I knew that after father died I would not be fit to work for some time. There were last minute panics because permission hadn't gone through, but at two minutes before curtain time Captain Connolly arrived and said I might do it if I would send a complete set to the Navy Minister. At that point I would have agreed to anything. My friend Marjorie Sircom was with me and we had our equipment set up in the aisle of the Capitol Theatre, a very different process from holding it on your lap as people do today. She kept me supplied with blank records and held a flashlight so I could see that the threads didn't tangle around the sapphire needle. The show was tremendous and the audience soon forgot us. I was glad I had gone because the challenge and excitement helped me over the next sad week. On the morning of October fourteenth, soon after my niece Kay had gone off night duty and I was alone with him, father suddenly sat up in bed and gazed high up on the opposite wall as though seeing something that was drawing him there while at the same time he clung to the earthly life he had so enjoyed. In a moment he fell back and I knew there was nothing I could ever do for him again. Like my mother he died highly respected and with his lifelong ambition fulfilled, that the world would be a little better because he had lived in it. I seriously considered then adopting two children but concluded that folklore seemed to be my calling and that this was where I should stay.

Soon after this, when I was feeling very sad and lonely, a strange thing happened and I wondered if perhaps I was not to remain single after all. You will remember that during the first war when the *Old Colony* was here, a young American had come courting. I had liked him but felt no romantic response. Now married to a much more suitable wife, and once more in the navy, he turned up again and I reacted exactly as I'd done so many years before. But there had been another at that time for whom I did feel a romantic attachment although there hadn't been time for it to go very far. He had left on his ship with the understanding that he would come back, and for a while corresponded and sent beautiful gifts such as embroidered tablecloths and fine linen. These stopped, and I supposed his ship had been torpedoed. One afternoon my telephone rang and I learned that the Second World War had brought him back too. What would he be like and how would I feel now? Lorna and Joan Gregson were coming for dinner, and I felt that was good because I could get over any embarrassment of meeting again, and by nine when Joan would have to be taken home to bed, I would know how I wanted things to proceed from there. This was a good idea, and I discovered that he had always intended coming back but had fallen on one misfortune after another. Whether he had married I have no idea, but there was no difficulty in picking up where we had left off. He was charming. We all liked him and he seemed to like us, and I wondered what further revelations there would be when we were left alone.

Alas, that never happened because his ship was in convoy, and when the others left his time was up too. Again he assured me he would be back and I laughed and said not to wait another twenty-five years or I would be all bent over and full of rheumatics, and I acted the part. Rising to the occasion he hobbled out like the old man he expected to be at that age, also laughing at the prospect, and it was all very light-hearted and jolly.

The twenty-five years have long since passed and I am not yet bent over and rheumaticky, thank goodness, but what happened? The old attraction seemed to be there on both sides, but did I perhaps look too prosperous? Too well set up in life, and was he still struggling? It was tantalizing not to know if he had a family of his own, which he probably had, but whatever the reason, I have never heard from that day to this. The Dominion graphologist who had said I was the investigative researcher type had also said that love demand was small, but that there was enough love tucked away to melt a Labrador iceberg. I have always felt that the one who might have melted that iceberg had probably been someone I had never met who had died in the first war. Now in this latter war was there another casualty? I will never know.

Chapter 7

With apartments to rent, I could live on at "Evergreen" which had been left to Lil and me jointly, her part in trust. Our monthly cheque was small, and it took all of my income combined with hers to keep her in West Gore. At Christmas she came home to be one of the family again. This legacy of money was soon exhausted, but it seemed that when one source failed another opened up. This time occasional cheques came from my Uncle McCully Terry in Denver, Colorado, so I concluded the means would be provided. I made the house over gradually and did less socially, partly for financial reasons, but often because I was too tired, and nobody will take fatigue as an excuse—nobody sympathizes with plain tiredness.

My parents had always been public-spirited, so it was natural that I should join clubs and preside. I had done so for many years. Now I filled my need for outside contacts largely through these associations. Also they interfered less with a writer's time than did social engagements. Wartime tenants were grateful for such accommodation as I could provide, and after being so much with old people I selected young couples, usually with a small child or two, and found the patter of little feet above me comforting. Forty children have lived here through the years and fifteen were born while their parents lived under my roof.

One of these tenants, Lieutenant Commander E. O.
Stockman, told me one day that Staff Sergeant Larsen,
who had sailed the R.C.M.P. *St. Roch* from Vancouver to
Halifax by way of the Arctic, was at the Dartmouth Ship-
yards, and he thought I should record him. When I
phoned, the poor man was so surprised he couldn't think
how to refuse but called back a few minutes later to say
he didn't think he could find the way. I laughed and said,
"If you could find your way from Vancouver to Halifax
by way of the Arctic, you can easily find my house because
you can see it from where you are."

The first session went on for two and a half hours.
Once he got over his initial shyness he was ready to talk
of the north indefinitely. To record, however, meant getting special permission, and once the purpose was understood the Force was anxious to have it done because they
were proud of their famous navigator. Have you ever seen
a frightened mountie? With the machine in front of him
he froze, so I tried my favourite trick of recording a little
bit and then playing it back. Most people are delighted.
Instead an incredulous look came over his face, and he
said, "Do you know who I sound like? Mortimer Snerd,"
(Edgar Bergen's dummy, popular then on radio.) Finally
he wrote out his story of the *St. Roch* and read it; then he
forgot all about the machine and talked about the Eski-
mos for six records—a feat of loquaciousness that later
made him blush whenever it was called to mind.

Stocky (Lieutenant Commander Stockman) was also on hand when Tyneside sailors were brought to the
house, and he listened with delight as songs and stories
from his old home came as fast as I could record them. I
was amazed that they knew so much about their history
and folklore. Then Stocky himself recorded a Tyneside
song, and when he was later lost at sea I had a copy made
for his widow Margaret for whatever comfort it might
give her.

I had mentioned our Micmac Indians to Staff Sergeant Larsen, and he said he would like to talk to them and

compare them with the Indians of the north, so we went one day to the reserve at Shubenacadie. John Knockwood had already recorded at my house and was now joined by three friends of whom William Paul, chief for thirty-five years, was spokesman. Indians nowadays sing mostly parts of the Roman Catholic mass translated into their native tongue, but I managed to get a war dance from Mr. Paul, a story of how their dead were buried in the old days, a talk on their demi-god Glooscap, and a legend of their arrival in Shubenacadie. The former are now on my Folkways record, *Folk Music from Nova Scotia** and the story is in *Bluenose Magic*. In this period I also got recordings of Hebridean, Afrikaans and Maori songs.

On one of my trips to Lunenburg, Mr. Joe Langille, aged ninety-five, talked into my machine, and when I played it back and asked him whose voice it was he said, "I was the only one who was talking." To tease, he pretended to totter down the steep front steps, then he ran down the last lot, cut capers in the road and said he could still lead an eight hand reel. That spring evening frogs were singing so lustily that I set my machine up at the side of the road, and a hawk in the background contributed a few notes too. Two girls came along and I imagined the report they might make of strangers with broadcasting equipment at the side of a lonely road. I let them listen through the ear phones lest I be taken for a wartime spy.

The Lunenburg accent is most pronounced at Rose Bay, and here Mrs. Anna Mossman recorded early history and stories of ghosts and witches. Then the grandmother said grace in German as her grandmother used to do and once more I was in a folklorist's paradise. When I visited Captain Maynard Colp, I couldn't use his house because it had no electricity, and a neighbor to whom he explained

**Folk Music from Nova Scotia*. (New York: Folkways Records & Service Corporation, Ethnic Folkways Library Album #FM 4006, 1956).

142

what was wanted said he wouldn't "subscribe to anything like that," neither of them understanding what it was all about. I decided then to work in the car, resting the tripod with its feet against the back seat and the microphone in line with the captain's face. He must have wondered what I was doing back there. He told many sea stories in a thick German accent, and I felt these would be useful as personal reminiscences of the time, and also as a study of the dialect. Five times the cumbersome machine was set up that day mainly for lively conversations, and all the material recorded was good.

Cape Breton beckoned again, and this time I took as companion Miss Isabel Dimock of Windsor, a friend who had often taken me scouting around the Hants County area. For her, as for most people who went with me, this was a great adventure, and when we were in Port Hood, good Father MacPherson locked the door until Isabel could say a greeting in Gaelic. She felt she had stepped into another world.

A highlight of this trip was our meeting with Mrs. Sandy Hamish Gillis of Gillisdale. Her son Neil, a soldier home on leave, was considered the best Gaelic singer in the county. A guide, Alex Collins, showed us the way over a six-mile back road, and at times we climbed such steep hills that I dared not look into the valleys far below. I remarked that I wouldn't want to drive over that dirt road after a rain, but felt such a trial would not occur because this was a glorious day.

We told Mrs. Gillis our errand, and while Alex went to fetch Neil, Mrs. Gillis gave us homemade bread and cake. When Neil arrived we sat on the verandah and he began to sing. He was soon joined by his mother, a neighbor, and a brother. For recording they all felt we should go to the home of Jack Malcolm Gillis who could play an organ accompaniment, so I transported them in relays over a road so steep it was like driving up the side of a house.

This was Neil's embarkation leave. He didn't want to

go back to war and had been drinking to forget. Whether or not this was the reason, his mother stood beside him and when he finished one verse, she whispered the start of the next. It was touching to see this rapport between them. Then three of them sang a milling song, a special type used when shrinking newly woven cloth, and then the ten year old twins sang and in between the old grandmother talked to them all in Gaelic. We were so engrossed we hadn't noticed the weather and had just finished when the rain came down in torrents, lightning flashed and thunder roared. I recalled what I'd said about driving these roads when wet but they assured me they didn't get slippery. Nevertheless as I made my way gingerly down the steep incline, the mirror showed Mrs. Gillis crossing herself.

The next day we saw Neil walking along a country road with a haversack over his shoulder. He had two hours to wait for his taxi. The Doyles who owned the general store had electricity and offered us their house to record in. Now cold sober, and looking towards the ceiling all the time, he sang much better even though his heart was heavy. Later we called on his mother and found her weaving on an old-fashioned loom to ease her sorrow. She told us if women didn't weave here they would never have warm bedding, but first they had to raise and shear the sheep, wash and pick the wool, send it to the mill to be carded, then spin, dye, and weave it. Many of her complicated patterns had been learned from her grandmother.

Of all Gaelic songs, those used for milling are still the most popular because they call for group participation. As late as the depression of the thirties, many Cape Breton Scots wove the wool that made their clothing, and for the milling, or shrinking, they would gather at one another's homes and sit around a table. Songs were familiar, but the leader who sang the verses would often make them up as he went along; then all would join in the chorus much as sailors did in chanty singing. As they sang to a strongly marked rhythm they would thump the wet cloth on the table and pass it from one to another until it was dry. It demanded great energy, but work done joyously is never too strenuous, and they knew that supper and a dance would follow. These occasions are known as Milling Frolics and today are a tourist attraction. Expatriates often plan their holidays so they can take one in. Our "Land of the Old Songs", a CBC television show which will be mentioned later, demonstrates one done in Gaelic. The Acadian French do it too but call theirs *une foulerie*, and it may be seen on the National Film Board's presentation, "Nova Scotia Folksongs."

Mrs. Gillis thought I should record a frolic, and arranged one in the school. When we called for her she greeted us with her customary, "How is time since?" There were ten around the table. Mrs. Gillis got the giggles and I had to stop and start over again. Then they got too solemn so I asked if they didn't act up a bit in a real frolic, so one of the men interjected, "Hooray for Margaree!" Alas, the light had been dim, threads had knotted, and the records were useless. Twenty years later when Major Calum MacLeod and I were preparing our book *Gaelic Songs in Nova Scotia*, I let him hear them and he said, "Those songs are guid," so back I went and found Mrs. Gillis still singing. She got another group to join her, and now with tape in place of disc we recorded all we had done before and a few more to boot.

There were miners at Inverness, and I felt they too would have songs. When we saw one walking home with his lunch box we offered him a ride. I said, "Have you miners' songs down here?" and was delighted when he said, "Yes, we have a lot of them." I said, "What are they like?" He looked so surprised that I said, "How do they go?" To this he answered, "Mine are here." That seemed a strange remark so I said, "Who sings them?" Then he began to laugh. "Did you say songs? I thought you said sons." In Montreal many years later my songs and sons got mixed up again when a newspaper stated that I had four thousand sons!

In Cape Breton, Gaelic-speaking Scots and French-speaking French live side by side and occasionally marry. The story is told of a Gaelic-speaking woman who married a French husband who knew no Gaelic. A man named McCrimmon used to visit her when her husband was away, and one night the husband was heard coming home unexpectedly. Houses had huge fireplaces then, so she told him to climb inside which he did, but he left his feet dangling. As her husband came in the door she picked the baby out of its cradle and walked up and down singing in Gaelic:

> Pick up your feet McCrimmon, McCrimmon,
> Pick up your feet, McCrimmon my boy.

We recorded Acadian songs at the Petit Étang school, and the children not only heard their own voices for the first time, but heard the teacher tell them not to sing too loud, and this caused much merriment. At the next village, Grand Étang, we called on Moses Chaisson who advised us to fetch Tom Doucette from the other end of the village. Like all singers, Tom Doucette was intrigued with the machine, now set up at Moses Chaisson's, and when he sang, his host sang with him. I felt he could fill all my records, but after a while the others said we should get a younger man, Peter Chaisson. It is usually best to go along with people in their own territory, so, with Mr. Doucette as guide, we went in search of Peter, but he said he would not be free until evening. On the way to his home, I photographed Mr. Doucette and he looked more pleased than when he had heard his voice on the machine. He and Peter spoke English fluently and said they had to in order to make a living. Tom said exactly what he thought and ended with "Poor fella," no matter what the subject, and sometimes he surprised us by singing in Gaelic.

When we called back we found him all dressed up and triumphant because his family had said we wouldn't return. We then called for Peter. When we arrived people were staring from their windows and Peter announced he had brought along a couple of bottles of beer to get them started.

In no time there were twenty-five in the little kitchen and ten or fifteen outside. Peter sang well, prefaced by a speech of introduction by Moses, his own idea. There were comings and goings all evening, and when a new singer was presented Peter would fetch another bottle of beer from his car. One man was so nervous that he perspired freely, rubbed his hand over the top of the coal-burning kitchen range and then on his forehead with such a grotesque effect that it brought forth peals of laughter. When that was nicely washed off he absent-mindedly repeated the performance, this time with new paint. I recorded from seven until ten, filling the ends of the discs with short songs and lullabies. Everybody had a grand time, and when I took Peter home and offered to pay for his beer he wouldn't hear of it. You will hear more of Peter when we return at a later date to film him. Isabel was excited, for this had been such a gay, happy evening, and Tom Doucette would have plenty to tell his family. Poor fella.

We recorded some excellent fiddle music on that trip, but there were flaws in the recordings. We saw sheep shearing, old-fashioned country dancing, and gaspereau at the peak of the season dipped up in nets so heavy with the catch that one man could scarcely lift one alone. In Whycocomagh I asked an Indian about their music, knowing that the Eskasoni Reserve on the opposite side of the Bras d'Or Lake was the place to go, but not feeling quite up to it. He said there would be a funeral at nearby Nyanza the next day and that all the important Indians would be there. He assured me it would be all right to go there as the mourners would be around all day with nothing to do. It seemed a strange place to make records.

We arrived at 9 a.m. in time to see the remains taken to the graveyard on a hand-drawn wagon. I decided to consult Father Rankin, the priest, and what a lucky thing

I did. He thought recording a fine idea and took us to the home of the deceased where a woman said she knew lots of stories but didn't feel like telling them then, though she had no objection to others doing so. Chief Silliboy offered to record in Micmac, not the masterly oration he had given at the funeral which he considered too personal, but the story of the Scots arrival and how they made peace with the Indians. We assembled our equipment in the yard and everybody crowded around. Then Father Rankin selected a young man to sing, and then another. After a while I noticed a restiveness among the other young men which grew into open resentment. Then one, looking angry, said, "This is the last one, see. We want to get on with our business."

When we got away with what dignity we could, Isabel said, "You know what all the trouble was?" Apparently it was their custom to spend all morning and early afternoon getting money from the mourners to pay for the funeral. While recording was going on the people wouldn't give, and they were afraid they wouldn't get their money. We drove back and gave a small donation, but I'd had enough of menacing looks and didn't set up again.

Our funniest encounter was at the top of Mount Young overlooking the lovely valley of Lake Ainslie. James D. Gillis lived there. He was author of *The Cape Breton Giant*, and now full of years. From a distance his house looked spic and span because the sides were newly painted and ladders were up for finishing the job. From a closer view we were not too sure and we had to park outside his fence because the two driveways were blocked with spruce boughs. There was no sign of life but, when I tooted my horn, he came out and seemed delighted to see us. I explained our presence and felt he didn't quite understand but was willing to do anything. He had forgotten most of his Gaelic compositions but suggested playing the fiddle. He had vaulted the fence to talk to us and now vaulted back again, and every time we suggested a change, he would vault again. We were set up at the side of the road but the machine might have been part of the car for all the interest he showed in it. His best fiddling days were long past but he sawed away, eyes closed, and on his face was a look of sweet content. I was working from the back seat of the car and could crouch low and have my chuckle, he was so deadly serious. Isabel had more control and signalled to him when to start and watched that he didn't stroll away from the microphone. He read from *The Cape Breton Giant* in the preface of which he writes, "I have twice been to Boston. I do not say so for the sake of boast." He read also from *The Great Election* and his poem, *Miss MacKay*, accompanying it by picking on his violin strings as he recited,

> Miss MacKay, dear Miss MacKay,
> Why did you go away Miss MacKay?

James D. Gillis is part of Nova Scotia's history, and perhaps these records will have little value except in the province where he had many friends. He is written about in *The Four Jameses* by William Arthur Deacon. I once watched Halifax artist Ruth Wainwright do a pencil sketch of the back of his head, all she could see from where she was sitting. It was a noble head. Had he possessed a sense of humour, he might have been a genius.

When the recording equipment went back to Washington, I had to work again by hand. In October, 1944, I was in Chester visiting two former tenants when Bev Gaby said, "Helen have you been to Tancook Island? No? Well, you should," and she told me why. I got a list of possible places to stay and, with suitcase in hand, set forth. The sea was rough on this seven-mile trip, and it was bitterly cold. When we arrived a truck was going in my direction and I clambered aboard.

The first house couldn't take me, the woman was too old, and the second was too busy cabbaging. Fortunately Mrs. Ralph Cross, plump, motherly, and next on my list, saw me shivering and said I could stay with them. Reverend and Mrs. Bezanson lived on the other side of their house. He was doing an article on the island's folklore and wanted help, so we spent the next three days visiting and helping one another. It was a rich field, and my notebook filled quickly. The Crosses were full of fun and loved a joke. One evening in the midst of lively conversation Mr. Cross rose and said, "Time for bed; teeth go first," and out came his false set to spend the night on a kitchen shelf. A delectable tidbit to them was a stick of cod eaten like candy. Fish, fresh as fish ought to be, was our main diet, and one day a pool at the back of the house froze over enabling Mrs. Cross to make ice cream in the good old-fashioned way, by hand. Houses here, as in all Lunenburg County, were clean as wax. The men were skilled boatbuilders and were then making small craft for use in the war. I loved my three days, and when I asked Mrs. Cross for my bill she said I didn't owe her anything, and when I gave her four dollars she wouldn't take more than three. And then she kissed me good-bye.

I had stopped at Chester on my way to Queen's County. I had thought of studying Queen's County folklore to see how much it had changed from that of New England, the place of origin of these settlers. Now, with such a start made on Tancook Island, I thought I would concentrate on Lunenburg County instead. On a short trip back to Halifax I mentioned this to Dr. Munro who suggested I ask the school inspector, Mr. Maxner, to take me with him to the outside communities which he visited at this season. By staying with Mr. and Mrs. Eleazer Nauss in Mahone Bay, and then with the Norman Veinottes in Lunenburg, I did double collecting every day because at night we would go over the notes taken during the day, and these would remind them of similar items. Six weeks gave me enough material for a good sized volume and occupied me for four years classifying and writing it up.

One day at East La Have I spent an hour or more in

Recording at Seabright with Mr. Edward Deal (1954).

On the skidway at Bon Portage, with Maida Parlow French.

Mr. Grace Clergy, Mr. Freeman Young, Mr. Bernard Young, at East Petpeswick

The Gallagher family at
Chebucto Head, with
Doreen Senior, their three
boys and a little friend.

On Devil's Island with
children. The melodeon is
being pushed in the
wheelbarrow.

Doreen Senior with Mrs.
McInnes, in Northern
Cape Breton.

On the way to Devil's
Island to film for the CBC.

the general store and asked a lot of questions before making other calls. When I returned they had made me a present called a Spanish row galley. It was a puzzle made like a miniature boat with four thwarts and had a double length of cord passed through its own bight on the top thwart, double half hitch knots on the other three, and a long line of slack. The cord had to be removed by working from the slack end, and a recalcitrant sailor might be imprisoned until he could "unlash the longboat." Another day at a spinning party three wheels whirred merrily together, for Mrs. Hyson's friends had come to spin for her as she in turn would spin for them. I soon discovered they knew no songs, but women can be excellent informants about home remedies and early customs. These Oakland women also knew riddles, some of which sounded questionable but had the most innocent answers, and were told to embarrass the listener. They invited me to stay for their chicken dinner with fresh peas, carrots and potatoes, barley bread, preserved raspberries, fruit cake and coffee. In season these same women would meet to hook mats for one another.

At Petite Rivière, Reuben Sperry, eighty-eight, did a step dance that would put a younger man to shame. He told of a cancer cure, made of old oak bark, taught to his grandmother by Indians. His father had used it successfully on surface cancers for years. At Canaan in the heart of thickly-wooded country, I got my first Paul Bunyan story, and then from Mr. Edward Collicutt the story of Big Claus and Little Claus which took half an hour to tell. It had been learned orally, and when compared with the Hans Christian Andersen tale, proved almost identical. What a memory! As we were leaving, the man who had told the Paul Bunyan yarn called down from the rooftop where he was working to tell me a fish story he swore was true. These, and other results of that memorable trip are written up in my *Folklore of Lunenburg County.**

*Shortly to be reissued.

For the next two years I typed and classified my material. One day I noticed on my desk a letter from the Rockefeller Foundation asking if my present activity had any relation to the training they had provided. I began idly to fill out the questions and found myself writing about what I had on hand, that I required a folklore library to work in, and was there any chance of another fellowship? Almost by return mail a letter came from Mr. Marshall saying they would like to look into this further, which meant that I had it. At the end of December 1945 I joined Dr. Stith Thompson and Dr. Inger Boberg in Chicago at the American Folklore Society meetings and we travelled to Indiana together. On New Year's Eve at the Thompson's house I met two professors of the Mormon faith who were to become outstanding folklorists, Dr. Austin Fyfe and Dr. Wayland Hand. Dr. Thompson helped me work out a plan for my book and after that I was on my own. It gradually took shape, and when I finished he went over it with meticulous care. Again I returned by way of Washington to visit its Library of Congress and in that city had the great pleasure of seeing again two of my former Mexican pupils, Fanny and Ena Howard. They had matured beautifully and carried themselves like foreign princesses. In New York I reported to Mr. Marshall who was pleased with my manuscript. Twenty-five years later requests are still coming in for it. Of all the books I've done, this gave me the most enjoyment.

In late September one of my tenants was taking his family to Ottawa and wanted a spare driver. Would I go? That spring with the Thompsons I had seen dogwood blossoms in the Appalachian Mountains, and now I saw the brilliant autumn colours of four Canadian provinces. On that visit I saw Dr. Marius Barbeau at the National Museum. He had already proved my good friend, and he set wheels in motion so that the following summer I was on the Museum's staff to collect folklore, mainly music, in the Nova Scotia I was getting to know so well. Of all my writing years, the ten that followed were the happiest and most satisfying, and, as they used to say enviously at meetings of the American Folklore Society, I was paid for doing what I wanted most to do. At first I had four months' field work and one month to write up my notes, but I needed more time, and it gradually went to eleven months' employment. Dr. Alcock, Museum Curator, left me to work entirely on my own initiative and promptly attended to any request. This was exactly right for my temperament, and I gladly worked my head off.

That first summer, 1947, at Victoria Beach, I met Martha Banning Thomas, a poet from Massachusetts who had a cottage beside an inn run by Mr. and Mrs. John Casey. Mr. Casey and his son Joe were great raconteurs and they were at their best in the evening as they relaxed over coffee in the kitchen. This whole district was exciting, and I found more ghost stories from Annapolis Royal to Victoria Beach than in any other part of the province. Their name for ghost sounded like appegashen, perhaps a combination of apparition and ghost. If you hesitated about sitting down when visiting, your hostess might say, "Why don't you throw over the second anchor and stay?" Speech was coloured by the sea which provided their living. About songs, one Everett daughter said, "When pa was through with work he would lie on the couch in the kitchen and ma would sit on a chair with a child on each knee and another on the arm of her chair. They would say, 'Sing, Pa!' and he would, and his feet would go too. Didn't we love to hear him."

A Casey clam bake was fit for a king. The picnic ground was at the top of a cliff. Blue iris grew in swampy ground and at night fog hung over the horizon. A fire was made on a flat rock and everybody gathered wood to feed it. When hot enough, Mr. Casey brushed the coals off with a spruce bough, laid the clams on the hot rocks and covered them with seaweed. They soon began to steam, and were left until the shells separated. Meanwhile other clams were put in hot water to steam and the clam water served as broth. There were crackers, devilled eggs, cucumbers, homemade bread, cheese sandwiches, lobsters with chopsticks made of twigs for eating them, tarts and tea. This is one of the few places where you see the sun setting over the water. Now it was so brilliant it hurt our eyes. At times great billowy clouds of fog would lie on top of the Bay with changing light effects, always different, always fascinating.

Two old friends, Horace Johnston and Norman McGrath, camped in a hut on the shore for a few weeks every summer and fished for fun. Both were good story tellers, but the local people had heard their yarns. Mine were new eager ears. Here I got an all too rare "fable story" from Mr. McGrath, "Seven Years Before the Wind." Mr. Johnston's were ghost or tall stories and you had to choose which ones were true. A young man passing by called out, "Did you have a good catch today?" Everybody knew he hadn't caught a thing but, after nodding in the affirmative, he drawled, "Might as well say yes as no; it don't cost no more." One day they surprised us by making biscuits and tea—delicious. Jim Apt told of a whale that took a fishing boat on its back and kept it there playfully for an hour or two, and of another whale that frolicked so close to his boat that he could have jumped in its blow hole. Another man caught a hundred pounds of pollock on his shirt tail; he had run out of bait and, remembering that he was wearing a red shirt, a colour pollock like, had cut off a piece and put it on his hook. A coat on the mast or a blanket would sail them home if their engine failed. When Mr. Casey's engine failed to start one day he simply left the key in it knowing that Buzz Ring who couldn't resist engines would soon be along. When Jim Apt heard his voice on the tape he remarked, "If a feller knew what it was going to sound like he could get it a bit more broguey." And after extolling the virtues of his father-in-law he wound up, "He was a nice man—for an Englishman."

It was generally considered bad policy to pay for

material. Yet when I called on Louis and Evangeline Pictou, an Indian couple, my inner voice told me to break the rule. This was easy money for Louis because he could relate stories learned from his grandmother and continue basket-making at the same time. Sitting beneath spruce and pine, he and his wife talked easily, and among other things Evangeline told me that her father was a witch and had the evil eye. I mentioned this to a newspaper reporter who wrote it up as I learned on a return trip to Dartmouth. Immediately I went back, fearing they would think I had abused their hospitality and perhaps Evangeline would suffer, for she had said, "If my father says you'll die, you will die." As I turned in to their camping ground they raised their hands in greeting and I said, "I see we're still friends."

"Why wouldn't we be?" so I told them and Evangeline said her father would be proud to be called a witch in the paper, and she would be too, to know she had that power. Louis was soon off on another tale but I could see they were thinking this over. Finally she said, "I know what we'll say if they mention it. We'll say, 'Of course we told her that stuff; she gave us money.' "

For a few weeks the long drives through wooded stretches were no longer lonely. Joseph Raben, a New York student, had asked if he could come and see me work. He was particularly interested in square dances, and at a hall at Kempt in Queen's County we saw dancing as I'd never see it before. Joe said that what they called an Eight was a mixture of an Eight and a Running Set which Cecil Sharp had found in the Appalachian Mountains of Kentucky. It was dignified and stately, and when the couples promenaded with a polka step I felt I had stepped back to another age. On Sable Island the fishermen were intrigued with my Austin car's little engine and wondered how it would serve in a boat. At Pubnico we met Mrs. Laura McNeil, née Pothier, a mine of information. We visited many of the little places in between and finally came to Yarmouth where we visited a man who was supposed to sing. He was alone and talked instead of his wife's death and his own incarceration in a mental hospital. When I tried to get him back on songs he said fiercely, "Don't ask for those things," and then gazed fixedly into space. He seemed to be getting completely unbalanced, and Joe was wondering if he could hold him while I escaped, when mercifully the man snapped out of it.

I missed my young companion when he left and was glad to have made friends in Pubnico. There is neither great wealth nor great poverty here and the church dominates the scene. The people were happy, kind, loving one another, and the atmosphere was idyllic. I said to two of the older women one day, "Now don't quarrel over these songs," to which they replied truthfully, "We wouldn't know how."

Mrs. McNeil had taught school for many years and, like all the Acadians here, was bilingual, intelligent, and willing to share her folklore. Women are often better informants than men, but this is the only place where everything I got was from women. A few years before, through Mrs. McNeil, folk tales brought over by settlers in 1751 had been published in the weekly newspaper, and the editor had been so fascinated that he padded them to make them last longer. This ruined them for scholars, but I managed to have them all republished exactly as the old people remembered them. Their Cinderella story goes much further than those from English sources and includes two little songs. All Pubniconians are descended from Baron d'Entremont, and on their tercentenary they put on a pageant composed of scenes from their own history. Neighbouring villagers envied their familiarity with their past.

When I was working along one shore it was suggested that I visit a man thought to be a witch. (The word witch is used for man or woman.) I said, "What will happen if he doesn't like me?"

"You may have a flat tire on your way home." That

didn't seem too bad so I paid my call. We got along famously and when I seemed to have exhausted his information he said, "Why don't you go down and talk to Stewart? He might have something for you," and he pointed to the shore where two men were standing dressing (cleaning) fish. There was plenty of nourishment for seagulls to feed on, so I took their picture with the gulls in the background and said that I'd bring them a copy when I came back. I returned before the film was finished and found Stewart at their stand alone. His immediate question was, "Where are the pictures?" I explained about the film which he couldn't seem to understand, and after that any attempt at conversation proved fruitless so I went to the witch's house. He had seen me and said, "How did you get along with Stewart?" I said I couldn't seem to get along at all, to which he replied, "No I don't suppose you would. You see, Stewart's tetched." He was just a week out of what we always used to call the Insane Asylum. He was angry with me, and in his hand he had been holding a very very sharp knife.

I was turning in some two hundred songs a year at this point and many items of folklore as well. I suppose I drifted, but for me that was right as it left me free to linger as I did at Seabright, a summer resort about twenty miles from Halifax, where I expected to polish everything off in a week. Instead I arrived before school closed in the spring and was there when it opened in the fall, feeling my way along and taking whatever material offered. John Obe Smith lived with his grandson whose children stayed home in the evenings for the pleasure of hearing the old man sing. When I went to the home of Edward (Eddy) Deal, it was to hear stories they were saving for when "the ghost lady" called. I soon discovered they were more interested in singing even though Mr. Deal was so shy it took him an hour to clear his throat and start. At the season's close he put on a special performance, for he had composed a song and as he gardened had practised it on the squirrels. When he came to the part about my visit there was a certain triumph in his voice and it took on a richer timbre. Set to a well-known traditional tune of his choosing it is in my *Maritime Folk Songs*. In 1949 recognition came from my own home town when the Dartmouth University Women's Club made me an honorary member. I can't tell them how much their encouragement helped me.

Chapter 8

A new era began in 1949. No more great Presto machine to carry, no more converter and batteries, no great box of blank discs and no more sapphire needles to break, for tape recording had come in, and the Museum had its own machines. I must have looked pleased with life on the first day I used mine, for I got two proposals of marriage from singing farmers I had never met before.

In July I was working at Clark's Harbour when the Toronto author Maida Parlow French joined me for a visit to the island home of another author, Evelyn Richardson, author of *We Keep a Light*. I went to see Eddy Whiskers about taking us over. When he wouldn't shave for a dance one evening his wife had given him this appellation not realizing it would stick and that she would henceforth be known as Glady Whiskers. He was fishing, but Dewey Nickerson was at the wharf so we asked what he would charge to take us over. "Would ten dollars be too much?" I looked doubtful so he made it eight. I told him we were writers, and he asked if we knew the author Tom Raddall. Indeed we did. Well, if we knew Tom, he'd make it right about the price, but he ended by charging eight dollars, probably a fair amount.

Cape Island is noted for the boats built there. This one had a fine cuddy with a little stove and a windshield against the weather, and we stood behind it all the way going and coming. The fog was thick, and when Mr. Nickerson stopped the engine and seemed to be listening I asked what he was doing. "I'm listening for the rote," he explained. "The surf breaks with a different sound all along the shore." Presently he heard it and in no time Bon Portage Island came in view. When the boat was anchored we clambered aboard a small skiff. Mr. Richardson had made a skidway where boats were drawn up by motor power, an ingenious rig, as fishermen would say. Then we walked half a mile over a wide road with spruce trees on either side, surf on the sea side, and blue flags in bloom on both sides. Everywhere were signs of loving care. Mrs. Richardson was painting the interior of the house, and the morning passed in animated conversation. We picnicked in the lee of the lighthouse with a gentle summer mist caressing our brows. She gave us macaroni and cheese, lobster salad, wonderful homemade bread, the best peas I've ever tasted fresh from the garden, and for dessert bake apple, a small fruit that grows in a few places along the coast. She told us that when her elder daughter was married she threw her bouquet not from the steps of the house, but from the lighthouse.

When we were ready to leave, the hired man hitched the oxen to a wagon with rubber tires. It was filled with hay and, with a blanket over the hay, we three women rode in style. Soon we were enveloped in fog again but we knew now about the rote and that it would guide us safely back.

Cape Sable Island, better known as Cape Island, lies on the southwestern shore slightly over a mile from Barrington, and for years could be reached only by ferry. This made for isolation and, as in many places along our coast, inbreeding. It was one of the few places where I was nervous driving alone, though perhaps I needn't have been. People were more than kind. Mrs. Caroline Murphy, an enormous woman with a soft-spoken pleasing voice gave me the cumulative folk tale, "The Old Cat Spinning in the Oven" which I have found nowhere else. Cape Islanders take special pride in stoves that shine, and Miss Evelyn Swim's spotless kitchen often became my workshop. Earl Smith contributed history and folklore, and with Miss Swim recalled games played in their childhood. Eddy Whiskers at eighty-six could name from memory eighty sea captains from this one island.

The new causeway linking the island with the mainland was about to have its opening, and I heard that the women would shuck lobsters for the banquet. This gave me an idea. There is no better way of getting to know people than working with them, so I offered my services. What nonsense, for I don't open a lobster more than two or three times a year. These women were factory-trained. My ineptitude was the best thing that could have happened, and when I left it was with a whole bag of lobster bodies as a present and the feeling that any gap had been bridged.

At Baccaro on the mainland, Otis Purdy got his bills paid by "songing" his debtors. If they had heard what he sang about them once, he need only begin with:

Come all you jolly jokers, listen to my song.

He would sit squarely down, knees apart, heavy rubber boots on his feet, dressed in fishing togs, cap tilted over one eye, corncob pipe in mouth, and he would preface his song by stating, "My voice ain't melodious tonight." At the Everett house at Hillsburn on the opposite shore, a young man entered and his mother said, "That's my son. His name is Biggy. He's a twin." So I said, "The other must be Littlely," and he was.

At Sambro near the mouth of Halifax Harbour, everybody knew William Gilkie as Bill. He sang slowly and deliberately with eyes on the floor or looking straight ahead, making the most of every precious note. When I first knew him he sang with a child on each knee and a wad of chewing tobacco in his mouth. When he was working in his boat, his old mother would climb down a steep ladder to sing familiar parts with him, and on many of his tapes her high quavering voice may be heard at the end of line or verse. One day at the Gallagher's I asked him for the tune of "The Baffled Knight," in which a girl tempts a man and taunts him when he lets her go free. He had sung it before when I was without recording equipment. He felt he shouldn't record it and said, "It has something of the blue in it" (improper).

"Yes," I said, "but it has a beautiful tune."

"But it don't end right," he objected. Then he compromised, and said, "I'll tell you what I'll do. I'll sing a verse or two and then we'll see how it sounds," so with stops for him to censor it we finally got it down. Most fishermen have definite ideas about what to sing to a lady. At Little Harbour on the eastern shore I was once recording Ned MacKay in a fishing shack with some half dozen of his friends sitting around listening. A young Lunenburgher came in and contributed a number that not only had no merit as a song, but was definitely vulgar. I let the machine run and when it was over the young man went out laughing while the local fishermen fidgeted in embarrassment. I put the machine in reverse and remarked that I had erased it from the tape. You wouldn't believe how those few words eased the situation.

In another fishing village I had left my machine at the top of a long steep hill while I went exploring. My singer was in the mood, but while the tape recorder was much lighter than my earlier equipment, it was still too heavy for me to carry any distance. The fisherman's wife took me to her son's house. He was willing enough to help, but he had been drinking all day, and the girl who had been drinking with him objected. We had just started our descent when she refused to go any further, and while they argued it out he stood teetering on his toes with my precious machine on his shoulder. On flat land I used a grocery

push cart if it had to be carried any distance, a slight re-
finement on the wheel-barrow of Devil's Island days.

For enjoyment all round, there was no comparison
between disc and tape recording. A disc had to be handled
with great care lest the original get scratched, but a tape
could be played any number of times and was a novelty.
When Oliver Hubley of Seabright heard himself for the
first time he blushed to the roots of his hair and confessed, "You know, I'm kind of a little proud of meself."
"Sidey Pete" Boutilier of the same village had suffered a
paralytic stroke and was sure his singing days were over.
I coaxed him along by playing what his friends had recorded. Finally he sang one verse himself and then finished the song and sang two more, the best therapy he
could have had. Laughing for the first time in months he
said, "You've got a way with you, you'd bewitch the devil."

Two big moments in 1950 were the arrival of proofs
of my second book of music, *Traditional Songs from Nova
Scotia*, and *Folklore of Lunenburg County* in its final book
form. I went shortly afterwards to a tea at my brother
Syd's house and a guest got hold of a copy and refused
to take his nose out of it all afternoon, taking the food
offered him automatically and scarcely lifting his eyes
from the book, a grand sight for an author. Included in
this book are a number of stories of witchcraft which I
got in a surprising manner. I knew it had been practised
in that county and said one day that I could believe in
ghosts but not in witches. This proved a challenge and
they explained that there are witches in the Bible and that
it is written "Thou shalt not suffer a witch to live." Then
stories came easily.

For years I had wondered why Halifax County had
so many more songs in English than the rest of the province and mentioned the fact at the home of Mr. John
Dorey in Seabright.

"Halifax County people are restless," he explained.
"We can turn our hands to almost anything although we

may not be able to do any one thing very well. We go to sea in ships and to the lumber woods. We keep meeting different people all the time and we sing for each other, and that's how we remember our own songs and learn others. Also Halifax County has a very long shoreline."

It was in this year, 1950, that I saw my work used in an original and dramatic way. At Hubbards the Adult Education Department put on a concert in which they included the ballad of "The Farmer's Curst Wife." On one side of the stage a group sang the story. On stage acting the words were the farmer, the devil, the shrewish wife and, in a corner, four other devils. When the wife "up with her foot and kicked out their brains," down the four went, and when "three little devils peeped over the wall," up came three more heads. You will recall that the story is about a woman who was taken to hell where she proved such a nuisance she was taken home again. With a good tune and a whistling chorus, there was scope for all kinds of original treatment. Another time the same group dramatized the folk song "Gallows." They had a gallows on stage and the hangman dressed in black stood beside a waiting noose. The clergyman, also in black, was there. The young man approached his doom and hesitated as singers offstage sang,

> As he went up the first step of the gallows
> His own dear father he chanced to see.

At the next step it was his mother and so on. As he went higher the tension grew and I was glad I knew that on the final step his sweetheart would appear with his pardon. One child who didn't know the ending screamed. Since ballads are action stories they lend themselves to this type of treatment and all that is needed is the skill to portray them visually.

Various people have followed me into this field, notably Richard and Lyn Harrington of Toronto, who got stories and pictures for many publications out of one short afternoon at Seabright. Frank and Edith Fowke called on me at the Lazy Tide Inn at Musquodoboit Harbour, and that evening I took my tape recorder to the open verandah overlooking the water and played what I had on hand. This included a cumulative song called "The Twelve Apostles," which went so far and then stopped. I said, "Isn't it too bad she's forgotten the rest of it?" An "old residenter" had been standing on the road listening and called out, "I know that song," and forthwith contributed the missing verses. When I went for the words the next day I found that it and one other were the only old songs he knew.

The Fowkes had found me in one of our most fertile grounds. I took them to see Mr. Grace Clergy, the fisherman whose photograph is on the jacket of the first edition of *Maritime Folk Songs* and whose singing eased the arthritis that crippled him. Then to Mr. Bernard Young, a huge man with large blue eyes whose songs were so dear to him that, like Walter Roast, he had neatly written the words in a book. Until he heard his voice played back he was so nervous that perspiration streamed down his face as he sang. In his house nestled between low hills, John Roast said he wouldn't sing, but of course he did. The Fowkes also met Mrs. Duncan, but other people were away. This showed them it isn't always easy to get singers when you want them. This was their introduction to field collecting and the beginning of a career that Mrs. Fowke has pursued diligently ever since. They were the last people I took to see Ben Henneberry, now confined to his bed.

In October of 1951 Mr. Henneberry died. Just before hearing of it I had a curious dream in which a white fluffy mouse appeared before me and I was startled by its purity and beauty. Was there a connection? Mr. Ben was not perfect, and certainly not beautiful, but his soul may well have been because nobody without sterling qualities could have been as beloved as Grandfather Ben. My flowers were placed at the head of his casket, and as I looked upon him lying there I thought of all his songs had done for my life, and the fresh interest I had brought to his. Sometimes I have visions after death as in father's case when I saw a white cloud float across the room. This happened again in 1967 after Michael Wood, who had lived in my house as a little boy, was killed in a motor accident.

The year before Mr. Henneberry died, the National Film Board had entered "The Rising Tide" in an American competition, and Mr. Eugene Kash asked permission to use five songs from my collection in this film. At last, I thought, I might get a little money for the singers, and asked that they be paid. I received fifty dollars, forty of which were Mr. Henneberry's share. I drove to the house with the money in five dollar bills, told him about the film and asked him to put out his hand. When twenty-five dollars lay there I asked if he'd had enough and the poor man didn't know what to say. When I reached forty I slipped away while he was still inarticulate with surprise.

I had never envisioned a folk opera based upon our songs, but in 1953 this happened when *The Broken Ring* was presented in Halifax by the Nova Scotia Opera Association with music by Trevor Jones and libretto by Donald Wetmore. Words and music were woven into the story practically unchanged. There are over twelve hundred songs extant on the theme of a ring broken between lovers when parting. The man returns, usually after seven years, and in disguise tries to woo the girl. When he finds her faithful he reveals his identity through his half of the ring and she swoons in his loving "arrums." The Halifax Symphony played the Overture in its 1954-55 series and CBC radio produced the full opera in 1956 beginning with Mrs. Gallagher's clear unaccompanied voice singing the first verse. It then lay dormant until Dartmouth High School students took it for their centennial project and were invited to perform it at Expo '67 in Montreal. A student said, "We love the music," and that was after they had spent two years working on it. I hope some day it will be televised. It has a beautiful nautical flavour.

While I was working in Lunenburg, Ian Sclanders of *Maclean's* telephoned to ask for an interview. We met in Halifax first and then he followed me to Kennetcook, an inland village where he could observe me approaching a singer and new district for the first time. We heard about Mr. Jack Turple who lived alone and when we called I said, "Are you the famous Mr. Turple who sings old songs?" He acknowledged that he was and said, "Come on in. It isn't very clean, but come in anyway." We followed him into his bed-sitting-kitchen-all-purpose room where his laundry was suspended from the ceiling over various clothes lines. He sang a long murder song "Benjamin Dean," and told us he made up songs. Woe betide any who ran afoul of him for, like Otis Purdy, he would "song" them to their sorrow.

Ian asked what use these songs were and that evening his question was in part answered. He, an Acadia University professor, and I sat in the hotel's parlour and listened to a CBC radio presentation of "Sam Slick" whose background music had been composed from my collection. Ian asked many questions, some while drinking in the beauty of June foliage as we searched out our singers. His article gave readers a better understanding of my work than I had been able to do. However when I tried to laugh off one or two items, my friends would have none of it. They had seen it in print so it was right, and I realized that an innuendo or snide suggestion could turn the public against you, a frightening thought.

Ian was to return in a few weeks with Mr. and Mrs. Yousuf Karsh. She had read my *Songs and Ballads* and wanted to meet me, so we had a day together. They were doing a series of photographs for *Maclean's* and Ian was in charge of their tour. We drove via Terence Bay to Peggy's Cove and as we approached, Karsh spotted the church with morning light on it which reminded him of the Biblical phrase, "Upon this rock I will build my church." He declared, "The light on the church is just right," and although we showed him the great boulders and lighthouse, nothing else would do. For a congregation he recruited from a tourist home a New York singer, a Toronto professor named Tait, an artist named Paton, a Texan and so forth. Women, recognizing him, came out hatted and gloved, and some carried prayer books. As cars stopped with sightseers they too joined the procession of worshippers, and I looked on fascinated as he got in all sorts of contortions, taking one picture from a space underneath one of Peggy's Cove's huge rocks. Passing tourists either recognized him or realized this was no ordinary photographer and stopped to photograph him and he would flash a smile towards them for their picture. From there we went to Donald Wetmore's house at Indian Harbour to photograph a fisherman, and Mrs. Wetmore invited all four of us to stay and share the delectable meatballs bubbling on the stove. It was a temptation, but in Lunenburg the author Thomas Raddall would be waiting for us.

For the Raddall pictures, Karsh wanted a waterfront scene, so I solicited the help of Dr. Hewat, husband of one of my many cousins. He promptly got in his car and led us to Zwicker's wharf, and when Tom arrived a few minutes later a fisherman confided in me, "There's a famous man here to take some pictures."

"Yes," I replied, "there's a famous man here to take a picture of another famous man and," pointing to Tom, "he's it." When this was done we all went to the Hewat's for refreshments.

We were due at Murder Point, home of Mr. and Mrs. Ralph Bell, at four but didn't arrive until six-thirty. The Bell property overlooks a magnificent sweep of bays and islands, seen from picture windows on all sides of the house. We roamed over the spacious grounds, had light refreshments, and plans were made for photographs to be taken the next day in Halifax. A drizzle had turned to pouring rain which would have meant miserable driving if Yousuf hadn't sat next to me and told about his experience at the Vatican where he had been so overcome by the presence of Pope Pius XII that he had lost his voice completely. He said it was impossible not to feel the eminence of this man, and he told how he had to change all his plans when the Pope appeared robed in red instead of the white Karsh had requested.

When we parted in Halifax they invited me to look them up on my next visit to Ottawa for they would love me to see "Little Wings" where they lived. I went soon afterwards and was immediately invited to lunch. To my disappointment, Yousuf was at a luncheon for Lord Mountbatten. Solange and I chatted in a leisurely way, and she would often slip into the kitchen to supervise the commissariat. For one guest she served roast duck, a course with celery prepared in a specially delectable way, and a frozen sweet which had been set in a mold and which looked thoroughly professional. I had learned after their visit that they were gourmets and thought of the places I had taken them here. One was a tourist home clean as wax but designed for hungry labouring men and the other a roadside restaurant at the end of a busy weekend with nothing left but bacon and eggs and nothing to sit on but stools at a counter.

My final visit to their house was sad because Solange was dying of cancer. I wrote her occasionally, and when she died I was one of her many friends to receive a telegram announcing the event. Since then I have seen Yousuf once in his studio and we exchange cards at Christmas. I found him a warm, kind, thoughtful, sensitive person, easy to talk to, friendly and grateful. Knowing them is a cherished memory.

One last word about Ian and his article. After reading it I concluded I'd got myself in a rut, but it was such a pleasant rut I decided to stay there.

In 1951 Mrs. Abbie Lane, prominent in civic affairs, social activities and many forms of welfare work, told me that Zonta, an international club for executive and professional women, was interested in having a branch in Halifax and I had been selected as a possible member. My sixth sense told me to consider this, and when Zontian Helen Robertson from Toronto invited eighteen of us to dinner at the Lord Nelson Hotel, I was there. A bond was immediately established, and we all felt we would like to know each other better. We, and subsequent members, were so carefully screened that when Queen Elizabeth was crowned, the mother of the membership chairman was heard to remark, "Now Elizabeth can join Zonta in her own right."

When I heard myself proposed as Zonta's first president I thought there must be some mistake and still don't quite understand it, for these were all outstanding women at the top of their professions. At a formal dinner at which the Mayor of Halifax and heads of all service clubs were guests, Zontian Helen Cleveland from Toronto presented our charter and gavel. At that time I hadn't the assurance that people probably thought I had and this has helped me more than any of the many offices I have held. Also I needed this new impetus in life with women of varied professional and business interests, particularly as so much of my own work was done alone.

In 1952 Dr. B. C. Woodroofe of Chester sent word that he had a patient who was always singing, even when waiting for an appointment, and he thought the man's songs were old. This was Nathan Hatt who lived at Middle River, six miles from Chester. His daughter, Mrs. Nellie McInnes, looked after the old couple and was a great help to me. Mr. Hatt had run a mill and had learned his songs from men who brought him lumber. Being illiterate, songs took the place of books, and love stories of young men and maidens were sung with tenderness. He sat in a rocking chair, and in something less than a minute after our introduction he was singing "The Gay Spanish Maid," head averted shyly. At the end he made a comical remark, turning suddenly toward me, and his whole expression changed when he laughed. Then he said, "Now I'll sing you an old-fashioned song," and he was off, this time looking towards me but with hands covering his face. Now and again he would peek through his fingers to make sure I was enjoying it. He used to sit on his back steps on summer evenings and sing for hours, and neighbours on the other side of the valley would come out and listen. On the slow trip to Beech Hill with his oxen he would sing all the way going and coming and he said people missed him when he stopped.

The first visits were devoted to taking down words and titles, but how could I record him when his house had no electricity nor I a battery-run machine? Old people are best in their home surroundings. Perhaps the Light and Power Company in Chester could run a line in from the next house.

"How long will you want it?"

"A few days, I expect."

"How old is he?"

"Somewhere in his eighties."

"Then one afternoon should be enough," Mr. Hennigar said. "If you find you need it another day come in before we close at five. We have a man living out that road; he can set it in the morning and disconnect it at night."

The wonder on Mr. Hatt's face when he first heard himself set us all laughing and he would make remarks about the voice from the box. "That man in there says it all right," or, in disgust, "That man forgets," or, "He's bound to say whatever I say." He knew it was himself, and this was a little game. He thought up a new lot of songs for recording and when my car whizzed up the road at two minutes to five to ask for more electricity the men were amazed. At the end of two weeks when he was still singing they began to feel proud. To spare him, I recorded only in the afternoon and when I was exhausted and had to rest, he, nicknamed Chippy because he made the chips fly, was just getting started. His recompense was root beer, and he was so unworldly that when I drove him to the doctor's one afternoon he offered to pay me.

It bothered him that he couldn't sing as he used to do and when I complimented him he would say dolefully, "Yes, but how are they sung?" When his throat got husky he would say to his daughter, "Nellie, bring me the salt." Then with the roguish look that was so endearing he would explain. "I've got a toad in me troat. Do you know how to get rid of a toad? Put salt on him. That'll make his toes turn up," and he would chuckle happily. Indeed he was happy as the day was long.

At the end of a song hundreds of years old he would describe the characters as though they were his personal friends: "She was a good girl. She didn't go out on the roads on Saturday nights but stayed home with her parents, and he was a fine young man." I've often wondered why most of the ancient ballads come from illiterate singers who sometimes have to learn the long verses a line at a time over a period of months. What mental images do they make of noble lords and ladies and the castles in which they lived?

In concerts and on professional records, our songs have been most widely sung by Alan Mills and Ed McCurdy. One afternoon I was being interviewed at home by Professor Lambertson and we stopped for a break. I remembered that Ed was performing at that time and switched on the radio just in time to hear, "I will now sing a song from Helen Creighton's fine collection." It couldn't have been more pat if I'd planned it. Later Ed came to Halifax and I went to the airport to meet him. As the passengers disembarked there was no doubt which was Ed. He was quite detached, feet widespread and toes turned out, lanky, tweed jacket open in spite of the cool breeze, no hat, and he was carrying a guitar and phonograph records. His face and figure were long and thin and his eyes expressive, and now they registered delight for he hadn't expected to be met. I drove him to see Devil's Island and Eastern Passage which had provided so many of our songs that he sang, and then brought him back to the house for tea and Lunenburg's good barley bread which he enjoyed so much I had two more loaves sent up as a present. He would sing no matter where we were or how many people were around, including in a coffee shop where he ate broiled lobsters, smoked oysters, and clams all at the same meal. He told anyone who would listen that Halifax should give me a medal; in fact cover me all over with medals and, if Halifax didn't, he would have one cast in bronze and pin it on me himself. In his concert he praised me to the skies which brought a hum of approval from the audience which he hadn't noticed the first night, but listened for and appreciated on the second.

He particularly wanted to meet Mrs. Gallagher. She was nervous and sang breathlessly at first but this was one woman he didn't try to embarrass and they got on famously. Among other songs, she sang "The Gallant Brigantine" which I have since heard him perform, and when we finally tore ourselves away he kissed her tenderly on the forehead which touched her so that she couldn't sing the farewell verses in "Come All My Old Comrades" as she had intended.

Pete Seeger was another visitor and, like Ed, he would think of a song he wanted me to hear and he would give voice to it as we walked along a busy street or rode in a crowded elevator. Pete gave a concert at Dalhousie and I went with Finvola Redden whom you will meet later. At the end of the third encore he remarked, "I'm told I've made an omission; I haven't sung anything from this neck of the woods." Apparently he thought "neck of the woods" not too tactful and explained that he came from a neck of the woods himself, and then remarked casually, "I don't know any anyhow," as though our songs were of no account. The following morning my telephone rang and I heard, "This is Peter Seeger. I'm here to give a concert to students." "Yes," I said, "I was there." You could feel his intake of breath. He said, "I'm afraid I owe you an apology." I said, "Yes you do, for you belittled our heritage to students, and that's unforgivable. I had to get that off my chest, Pete, but now I've said it, what can I do for you?" It was arranged that he would come to my house the following afternoon.

I learned later that he spent that afternoon at the CBC viewing our "Land of the Old Songs" film, and when he came the next day he wasn't long in finding my books, thumbing through them, which he'd never thought to do before, and making notes. I think he enjoyed his visit; I know I did. A few months later his agent wrote to say Pete wanted to use one of my songs on a record and would I sign the enclosed contract which would give me a share of the royalties? I replied that I could think of nothing better than to share Pete Seeger's royalties. I wish other singers had used equal courtesy. I often find my songs in books or on commercial records without even an acknowledgement of their source.

I have digressed, and we left Mr. Hatt with his tunderin' bad cold and his distress at his failing memory. I went back and got what seemed to be his complete treasure trove, a song for each of his eighty-six years, many of which are now in *Maritime Folk Songs*. We caught him just in time. One more year would have been too late.

How I hopped around in 1956! There was a film made by our international award-winning Margaret Perry for the Nova Scotia government called "Marine Highway," and, since it covered the eastern shore, she thought it should include folk singers who had provided so many of our songs. Ned McKay looked picturesque with shaggy beard and kind eyes beneath bushy eyebrows, and Isaac Doyle was at ease sitting on the edge of a wharf playing with a rope, the wind blowing in gusts while men in the background stowed away their lobster traps. Margaret wondered if Mr. Doyle weren't too gentle for a fisherman, but I assured her gentleness was one of their characteristics. Another week I would be in Pubnico recording Acadian folk tales, and the next in Karsdale, Annapolis County, to check a few facts in A. B. Thorne's forerunner story* (that racket, he called it) which turned out to be the most frightening in *Bluenose Ghosts*. Then I was back in town to address the University Women's Club Regional Conference and after that a national convention of Canadian Authors.

Folklore came in for a practical testing then, for I developed neuralgia in my left cheek. In Stewiacke I often dropped in to the home of Reverend Kennedy Wainwright. When the pain was severe, Mrs. Wainwright said, "Would you like Kennedy to put his hands on your face? He often does it for us; we think he has healing hands." He did this and, I suppose, said a short prayer. The pain didn't stop immediately but began shortly afterwards to decrease, and in a week or two it was gone. A few years later it returned so I asked him to do it again. This time he took it more seriously. The family gathered around and we all said our little prayer. The pain failed to develop further, and I've never had it since.

When people nowadays say they couldn't sleep after reading *Bluenose Ghosts* I say, "That's fine; I couldn't sleep after writing it." All that summer I tried to write for one hour at least, but I would get so absorbed it often ran to more. The chapter on devils I found particularly disturbing and was careful not to make it bedtime writing, but a good deal was written at night and it was probably the exhilaration of getting on with the job more than fright that kept me awake. There was new material everywhere, and many of the stories were collected while writing the book. Although Nova Scotia is particularly fertile ground, it seems that no matter where you are in the world, if five people are together and the supernatural is mentioned, at least one will have had an experience for which there seems no explanation. People keep these things to themselves for fear of being laughed at. Some-

*Forerunners are supernatural warnings of approaching events and are usually connected with impending death. (*Bluenose Ghosts*, p. 1).

times they have seen a loved one after death and they have been comforted and don't want anybody telling them it is just their imagination activated by grief.

At least four times through the years I have visited old people with cerebral strokes who were sure their singing days were over. Clarence Thompson at Springhill must have had a most musical voice when younger. The trick was to get him started. The machine could magnify the sound and once he heard himself he went on, just to see if he could do it. Mrs. Ruth Morse at Middleton suffered greatly from arthritis but, once started, recorded everything she knew including a beautiful love song, "Down by the Seaside." They weren't gloomy songs either, and some were comical. In Cape Breton, Captain Allan Morrison managed two verses of a paraphrase in Gaelic. Their pleasure was one of the things I loved best about collecting.

The Alex Morrisons of Marion Bridge took me to the home of a Gaelic singer, Lauchie Gillis. He was working on his car but said his wife would be delighted to see us and he would join us in half an hour when he would be glad to sing. There were eight children running around and there would soon be a ninth, but we didn't realize how soon.

It must have been nearly an hour before Mr. Gillis and the children joined us, and the room was soon spellbound as one song followed another. All the while Mrs. Gillis, a gracious hostess, sat on the piano stool in apparent enjoyment. But even though he was an excellent singer and I wanted to make the most of the opportunity, by ten o'clock I felt I could work no longer. They wanted to make us tea then, but the Morrisons refused as our hosts had so many children to be put to bed. I was surprised they were dissuaded so easily because it is almost a point of honour for a Cape Bretoner to serve tea to guests. Then because the day's work was well done, the evening fine and warm, the company congenial and the road unfamiliar, I relaxed my usual speed and dawdled home. Two days later Mr. Gillis appeared at the Morrison's door.

"You nearly had a picnic on your hands the other night," he announced. "Just before you came my wife said she was ready for the hospital. When you left we followed you to Marion Bridge but didn't like to pass in case you'd think you'd kept us from something. Then we raced to Sydney and an hour later the baby was born." This was hospitality carried to the nth degree and that's the nearest I ever came to being a midwife.

That year brought Captain Charles Cates, then Mayor of North Vancouver, to Halifax where he and his wife visited her relatives. He cherished songs his father had learned on this coast and wished to record them during one of his few leisure periods. We presented a comical sight because, unlike any other singer, he performed standing up, and it was all I could do to reach high enough to hold the microphone in position, a necessary precaution because singers forget about it and wave it about. He said he often enlivened Vancouver meetings by breaking forth in song, and in all recorded forty-three here. He found it relaxing, and I was a nice, a very nice person, thank you. He was happy perpetuating his father's memory through his songs, just as Fred Redden and Angelo Dornan had felt towards the fathers they loved. His version of "The Carrion Crow" has been set for male voices by the University of Toronto's Hart House Glee Club.

Shortly before they became television stars, I visited Don Messer and his Islanders in Charlottetown. Their instrumental music was very old, but they were recording it themselves. Few of their songs were folk in the old sense although Charlie Chamberlain sang a beautiful variant of "Lost Jimmy Whalen" learned in the lumber woods of New Brunswick. At a home for the aged there, when John Archie Campbell heard his Gaelic songs played back he remarked, "That man sings well. Yes, he does sing well." He did too, and must have had a beautiful voice when young.

At Charlottetown's Confederation Chamber I visited Mr. Fraser, a big man and former farmer and fisherman who would have put everything aside if it hadn't been for the telephone. For an hour he alternated between discussing the road situation with some unseen caller and telling me ghost and witch stories. It was much the same when I called on Mr. Neil Matheson who ran a column in *The Guardian* and often told ghost stories there. A singer in English, Mr. Edward Sellick, sang among other things a lament for a sick cow, "Drimindown." I had recorded it a few weeks before from Captain Cates. It is curious how often you pick up a song for the first time, and almost immediately hear it again.

At Mount Allison in New Brunswick I saw the other side of the coin, which is what makes this life so interesting. Here the librarian, Laurie Allison, and the head of the music department, Howard Brown, discussed folk songs from the intellectual angle and played recordings from other places. I wrote in my diary that except for two singers' unwelcome embraces from which I was lucky to escape, this was the happiest season yet, little realizing that much bigger things were waiting.

At the end of the season's field work, homecoming was pleasant these days for a new interest on the personal side. Much as I loved children and have always had them in the apartments, I had never envied my friends their babies. I felt differently about their grandchildren. A navy couple, Susan and Roy Portchmouth, had come to live at "Evergreen" in the 1950s, and when their first child was born far from its English grandparents, Susan said, "Helen, you're to be Keith's foster grandmother." This was a novel idea, and I was delighted. Later I became Eric's godmother and Richard followed to be a third foster grandchild. Their mother always referred to me as granny and I envisioned the day when the boys would see me in the supermarket and rush over calling, "Hi, Granny!" What would fellow townspeople make of that? They left me for a Newfoundland posting, and after three years years returned to "Evergreen." Jean Bruce who lived here then said, "Are you sure you want three little boys in the house?" I realized then how much I'd missed them, for I said from the bottom of my heart, "I'd love it." Many tenants have become fast friends, and one of the joys of a later coast-to-coast trip for the Canadian Authors was in visiting these friends in their own homes. In Ottawa, Bus Morrow loves to tell that when he was a young navy lieutenant living here with his wife, the only time he wore his gas mask during the war was when taking clinkers from my furnace. I would never have chosen to be a landlady although I do like setting people up in a happy home. I've made a few mistakes through the years, but not many, and my career as a homemaker may be my greatest accomplishment.

For some time I had worried about my papers which had accumulated through the years and needed weeding out, and I pitied my executors if anything happened to me before I could do it. One night I felt myself going up like an astronaut, only at a much slower speed. I was startled and thought, "I'm dead. I've just died." At that point all the cares and worries, some of which I didn't even know I had, seemed to drop away, and I had the most wonderful feeling which must be like the Biblical peace which passeth all understanding. Then I thought, "The poor people who will have to look after my papers," and back I came. It was probably a dream, but I will never really know. However if that is what dying is like we can take heart.

Chapter 9

The banner year was 1957, so many important things happened then. It all began with the arrival from Toronto of producers and film makers Klenman and Davidson to do a television show for the prestige program, "Graphic." For this, Mr. Joe McCarthy sat in his office in Hart House, Toronto, and appeared to hold a conversation, although few of us who were interviewed ever saw him. Passers-by wondered at the huge CBC van parked outside my house, and would have marvelled more if they had seen my sitting-room which had become a forest of lamps and microphone stands. Plans were made in advance so no time would be wasted when they arrived with two technicians on the morning of January twenty-eighth.

Photography at home means being up, and dressed, breakfasted, house and self immaculate and everything ready for filming. Shortly before, at his farm at Middle Musquodoboit, I had met Fred Redden who sang folk songs mainly from Scotland and Ireland. His daughter Finvola, named for the heroine of his favourite song, often sang with him and also composed, although she was only fourteen years of age. Having sung so much with her father, her songs were in the folk idiom. I had asked the family to share this event with me. The program dealt with my work as a collector of folklore, and the Reddens illustrated it with songs.

At that time a cable had to be laid by the Light and Power Company to service the powerful lamps, and it seemed the CBC's call for service was no sooner put in than we saw eight men wearing yellow helmets climbing a nearby pole, and in jig time the lights were burning. Similarly, after a call to have the line disconnected at the end, they got immediate service. Realizing our visitors found this phenomenal, I called the next day to thank the power company for the service, and Mr. Canty's explanation was, "I didn't like that Gordon report." This referred to Mr. Walter Gordon's suggestion that we should all be moved to prosperous Ontario. Here was Mr. Canty's proof that we *could* do well here. I date Nova Scotia's upgrading by the degree of general indignation at the thought of being uprooted.

When I finished writing *Bluenose Ghosts* I began to have misgivings. How would the public receive such a book? I can't remember ever hearing a ghost story told at home, but I do remember my mother on several occasions saying that she had once been told she would make a good medium. Although she seemed impressed by this information, it never went further than that, and I have no idea where this opinion of her originated. I had read little on the subject, partly because ghost stories frightened me, but mainly because I wanted to present the Nova Scotia viewpoint with an unbiased mind. Before submitting it for publication, I asked my good friends Phyllis Blakeley, archivist, Marion Moore, historian and newspaper correspondent, and Doane Hatfield, teacher of high school English, and all members of the Canadian Authors Association, to read the manuscript. They all voiced approval and suggested minor changes, each reflecting their own activity. With these revisions I sent it off, never dreaming I had written a best-seller. It has had ten printings. To write it and still keep up with my work had been a long hard grind, and when my cousin Ralph invited me to Nassau for a holiday with his family, I jumped at the idea, but, alas, I went to the operating table instead. A day or two after a fibrous tumour had been removed, my surgeon, Dr. Atlee dropped in to see me and I said grumpily, "If it weren't for your old carving knife I'd be lying out on a beach today in Nassau." He retorted, "If it weren't for my old carving knife, a year from now you'd be lying out indefinitely." It wasn't malignant then, but would have become so.

A few days later I realized mail had been brought in which I hadn't opened. Listlessly I broke a seal and suddenly came to life. Dr. Ross Flemington, President of Mount Allison University, had written to know if I would accept an honorary degree at their spring convocation. I thought it safe to accept since I had no duties but to receive it, but what to write to him on? I hadn't expected an operation and had no stationery except a post card of Evelyn Richardson's lighthouse which she, also a patient, had sent through a friend; on this I wrote my acceptance. A few days later a nurse came to my room and seemed to be looking for something.

"You haven't a telephone have you?"

"No, I don't want one." Then I realized someone was calling and the message confused her. Somehow I felt this was important and made my slow painful way down a long corridor to find Dr. Flemington on the other end of the line asking if I would give the convocation address. I thought if he could see me at the moment he wouldn't be asking, but said I would if the doctors felt I could. They agreed and gave me a pattern for living which would give the quickest recovery. For the next six weeks I followed it to the letter. I lived so carefully that when the time came I had no idea what my reserve strength was. Friends and family rallied around, and my niece Lois drove me to Sackville. I wanted to get the fullest enjoyment from what should be one of the happiest moments in my life, so we went up the night before convocation so I could take in the banquet and also get the feeling of the next day's audience. At Marshlands Inn I had breakfast in bed and lay perfectly still until noon.

*Indians on the
Shubenacadie Reserve.*

*Mr. William Riley, Cherry
Brook.*

*Mrs. R.W. Duncan,
Dartmouth.*

*Enos Hartlan,
South
East Passage.*

*Walter Roast,
Chezzetcook.*

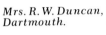

"Evergreen".

Helen, in 1967, below a portrait of Great-uncle Edmund Albro and a photograph of her father.

Testimonial dinner given by the Nova Scotia Government in 1974: The Honourable A. Garnet Brown, Minister of Recreation, Helen Creighton, Mrs. Brown, Mr. Ronald Napier, President of the Canadian Music Council.

Helen at home. Photo: David Street.

We lined up for the procession at one-thirty, and it was five before I got up to speak. Providentially, Hugh John Flemming, then Premier of New Brunswick, sat next to me, and as the graduates came forward for their diplomas he whispered, "I'll tell you what we'll do. You clap for the Nova Scotians and I'll clap for the New Brunswickers." Then a Newfoundlander would be announced and he said, "Let's both clap," or a particularly pretty girl from Nova Scotia would appear, and he would say, "I'll *have* to clap for her." With this cheerful nonsense I had no time to think of myself, bless him.

When the honorary degrees were conferred and I was led to the front of the platform, Mrs. Laurie Black, who I learned later had suggested my name, read the citation. She looked as nervous as I, and when our eyes met I found myself smiling encouragement to her. If my heart missed a beat when the President placed the beautiful scarlet hood with its royal blue lining over my shoulders, it is little wonder. My address had been carefully prepared, but my borrowed mortarboard with its beautiful gold tassel was a hazard because the reading stand was so high that when I turned a page and had to tilt my head far enough back for my bifocals to pick up the script, the cap nearly fell off. Lois's bright and interested face gave encouragement. I talked of their library and about my work, including ghosts and stories of rumrunners, unusual subjects for a convocation address. When I went back to my seat, Mr. Flemming shook my hand and congratulated me. One of the nicest things came in Dr. Flemington's following remarks when he said I was a lover of beautiful things. At the reception afterwards I stood next to the President and heard myself introduced six hundred times as Doctor.

What should I do about this new title? Should I use it? I had been given it for my work in folklore—and from a university particularly interested in the subject, for Mount Allison has one of the most complete private folklore libraries on the continent. As I understand the story, years before, Mrs. Mary Mellish Archibald was principal of the Ladies College, and her son Raymond taught violin. When certain Christmas holidays came she wanted to go to one place and he to New York. They went to New York and she came down with pneumonia and died. He was so conscience-stricken that he never touched his violin again but turned to his other great talent, mathematics. In her memory he established a library at Mount Allison devoted to drama, music, and literature which included everything he could lay his hands on in folk music and lore, as well as phonograph records and a magnificent Ampex player with earphones so music could be listened to without disturbing anybody. He himself taught at Brown University where he built up a fine library in mathematics.

Dr. Archibald was a prodigious correspondent. He wrote me first in 1934 to congratulate me on the publication of *Songs and Ballads*, and that was the beginning of a friendship that lasted until his death in 1955. We didn't meet until 1946 when I accepted his invitation to visit Mount Allison. I had expected to find a fuddy-duddy old man with an exaggerated idea of his library but instead found him charming, full of fun, and with every reason for being proud. After hearing Dr. J. C. Webster introduce him one day to the lieutenant-governor of Manitoba, the Honourable R. F. McWilliams, I thought I'd better consult the American *Who's Who* to see whether this was just one home town product praising another— or were the plaudits justified? Actually Dr. Archibald was one of the foremost mathematicians in the United States. In honouring me, the university was also calling attention to their folklore library of which most people were unaware, so I decided to use the title, a wise decision for one whose professional life was paramount.

When I got back to the business of collecting, I was saddened by the illness of Mrs. Gallagher, and when I called there she said she had written a book about their life in the lighthouse and she wanted me to read it. I read some of it aloud, with her husband an anxious listener. Other pages were read silently while she watched every expression for approval or otherwise. Her sweetness and love for family and friends were in every line but, while it had a personal interest to me who was so fond of her, I felt it was just too sweet for the average reader. Yet I must not convey this by word or gesture because she had not much longer to live. The manuscript was finally put in my care and I am still at a loss to know what to do with it.

The "Graphic" show shot in January was televised in June and resulted in telegrams and long distance and local calls. Once you have appeared on television in peoples' homes, they feel they know you, and the preliminaries of making new contacts are much easier. At a Government House garden party that month, it was gratifying to have many guests congratulate me on my new degree and the "Graphic" interview. It was my first social function since Mount Allison, and when I gave the aide my name as "Doctor," he looked astonished and gulped, viewed me as though to say, "Are you sure that's right?" and finally stammered the word while I manager to suppress a giggle.

In early July the National Film Board sent Mr. Ian McNeil to my home to discuss making a film, so I took him visiting. Despite Mr. Clergy's arthritis, he sang willingly. As we approached Bernard Young's, I told of a former visit when a line from "Lost Jimmy Whalen" had resulted in the greeting, "and cold was the bosom he pressed to her heart," hardly a cheerful welcome except for the smile accompanying it. At Freeman Young's they were having a fish supper which recalled my last visit when he had called out, "Come on in. We're having a mess of eels. Sit down and have some." At the Gilkie's we also arrived at meal time and were invited to share their herring and potatoes. This was a preliminary tour to see what I had to suggest.

Filming was done towards the end of July with Ottawa's Grant Crabtree the producer. He had filmed here before, but Peter Chaisson was new to him. As we drew up to Peter's house, there were children's eager faces at every window, and they presented such a charming sight that he had them repeat it for the film. Mr. Chaisson was the most vivacious singer I had ever seen and the most fun to watch. Most Anglo-Saxon singers sit motionless except for keeping time with their feet, but every bit of Mr. Chaisson was alive, and his feet did triple duty.

A milling frolic was arranged for that evening, and we found the Acadian custom slightly different from the Scots'. Here the cloth they were shrinking was composed of blankets sewn together and tied at the ends, and it was made wet with soap and water. Milling was done by sixteen men who stood. They didn't pass it to one another like their Gaelic neighbors but did an up and down movement raising their arms above their heads, the cloth held in their hands, and they pounded it down on the table to the rhythm of the music. Singing was done by a group off side and there were no solo verses. Here work and play were combined and each ecstatic face was a study. Peter was our leading man, and even his moustache was bristling with delight. The film was called *Songs of Nova Scotia*, and it has had many showings, particularly on the tourist boat between Yarmouth and Bar Harbor. It had required calls on many people and took twenty-one days to make. I found it most pleasant to be a movie star for a brief period!

For several years I had been getting letters from Mrs. Agnes Metcalfe, a widow with a nursing home in Ontario. She had heard of me through radio and thought I might be interested in songs and stories from the Louisbourg–Gabarus area of Cape Breton where she had grown up. When she planned a trip to Cape Breton, I offered to drive her around, knowing that as she visited her relatives I would have an opportunity to learn of the district.

In Louisbourg we were sent to two Newfoundland families named Fudge. The men, who worked in the fish plant, were Benjamin and Esau, and it took twenty minutes to strike the right note to get Benjamin started. Finally I asked if he'd ever heard himself. He jumped up then saying, "Let's get the machine." His first song was uninteresting and I was disappointed. Not so Mrs. Fudge who was so overcome that, woman fashion, she wept, and when it was played back again for a neighbour, she said with breathless pride, "That's my dearest 'usband's voice." Then Mr. Esau came in and sang a little treasure that began, "I merrily sing from morn to night," and of course Mr. Ben's next song was better. On his accordion, Mr. Esau played reels that had Mrs. Metcalfe and Mrs. Fudge doing a step, and not only his feet but his knees kept time with the music. Mrs. Ben said to Mrs. Metcalfe, "Maid, I loves 'un," meaning, "Girl, I love the music."

Mrs. Metcalfe took me to meet Mrs. Lillian Crewe Walsh at Glace Bay, but had built me up so it took Mrs. Walsh a while to feel at ease. A Newfoundlander, she had grown up in Cape Breton's Neil Harbour and wrote folksy poetry which was dear to the hearts of people there and which touched many facets of Cape Breton life. The first day she "worded off" a few songs insisting that she couldn't sing, but at the end of the second visit suddenly burst into song and gave me tunes for all of them. Among her treasures was a shelf scarf from Scotland said to have been beaded by Mary Carmichael and Mary Seeton, two of the Marys in the ballad, "Mary Hamilton."

Another friend of Mrs. Metcalfe's younger days was Mr. Charlie Weeks who lived with his son. He seemed to take a fancy to this attractive widow from Ontario, but he was crippled with arthritis so that he moved with difficulty. Perhaps with matrimony in mind he said to her, "If my legs were only equal to my ambition." Mrs. Metcalfe's father had been a sea-faring man and had often brought friends home. She had relished their salty conversation and had a retentive mind so that stories, often with a supernatural flavour, were as big a part of her contribution as her songs. An account of how her father at sea knew of his wife's death ashore is one of my favourites in *Bluenose Ghosts*. Listening, you would think there was no music in her singing, but some tunes she recorded are quite lovely.

I'd had this same experience with Mrs. H. H. Power of Little Harbour when she and her husband lived at Canaan, King's County. Their house had no electricity so I took her to a church hall. Then I saw that a rat had been there very shortly before. However she'd had such a rugged existence I felt she would cope if it returned, and I connected the machine. Closing your eyes you would think a man was singing, and I wondered why I'd gone to so much trouble to record this unmusical woman. Yet by some miracle the music was there and several excellent tunes have been transcribed from her singing. In collecting it seems that nothing can be taken for granted, and it is best to take down everything available and weed out later.

The President of Mount Allison wrote again—this time to ask for a program on folk music for their Summer Institute in August. I thought of Finvola Redden and suggested she help to illustrate the songs. We performed in Tweedie Hall to a distinguished gathering who had just heard a program of music from the West Indies. It isn't easy to jump from field work to the lecture hall, but after a little while I felt relaxed and then introduced Finvola. There is something about her that touches the hearts of an audience, and I found it exciting to watch them, especially Mr. James B. McGeachy, prominent in journalism, who later came up to congratulate her. Another was Dr. Albert Trueman, Director of the newly formed Canada Council. Two days later we gave the same program at the Festival of the Arts in Tatamagouche, and for this Mr. Redden also sang. How he loved to sing! Two school teachers had once been found listening outside his barn as he milked the cows to the accompaniment of his own songs. Like most folk singers, he sang as he worked.

Through the summer I had corrected proofs of *Bluenose Ghosts*, and at the Summer Institute when talking to editor-in-chief at Ryerson Press, Dr. Lorne Pierce, and his associate Mr. Flemington, the subject of reviews came up. I said fearfully, "I wonder what mine will be like," and was astonished when they said emphatically, "You've got nothing to worry about." Later in a letter, Dr. Pierce referred to my incomparable ghosts. When the book finally appeared, the CBC had a Sunday afternoon radio program called "Critically Speaking," and book reviews always came at the end. I knew when mine was being done and paced the floor alone. The first two were favourable which augured badly, for there were never three good ones in a row. Dear Mr. Miller Stewart, a stranger then and now, he said all the things I wanted most to hear, and I breathed at last. Before long I found myself recommending the book to all kinds of people including the men who serviced my car. Hearing the conversation, two heads popped up from the pit where they were working to tell of ghosts at Sable Island. Nevertheless it was several years before the book came into its own. The frightened fisherman on the original jacket, painted by Adrian Dingle, with a huge pirate ghost behind him gives just the right note of fear and yet has a touch of humour to attract the reader. *

It is strange that stories of the supernatural, something I looked upon as purely incidental to my main work, should perhaps be my best effort. It is difficult to compare the two fields since songs and stories are so different, but my book has certainly reached many people, and it has helped them to discuss their own unexplainable experiences. To this day I receive telephone calls or letters sharing some strange event. From the book have come radio and television interviews, radio dramas based on its stories, two long profile-type television shows in colour, and so many invitations to speak that I have to turn most of them down, for they take too much time from writing. Children tell me their teachers read from

*Current editions of this book have a new jacket.

the book in school. At social gatherings or even when out shopping, people I scarcely know come up and discuss the subject. Having had a number of strange things happen in my own life, I suppose I am in tune with the subject, A few who had kept things to themselves for as long as thirty years now feel free to talk, and at times I have been able to help them. I never dreamed I would be a consultant on the supernatural.

The Canada Council, financed by death duties of two former Maritimers, had recently been set up to foster the Arts in this country. The more I read about it, the more I felt it fitted my needs to the letter. For years I had worried about my original tapes in the National Museum at Ottawa. There was the danger of fire and also of irreplacable material being erased, which could happen even in the hands of a competent person. Unless I went to Ottawa, I had no access to them once I had transcribed the words and shipped them off. I wanted a complete set to keep in Halifax, and a musicologist to note the words on paper. With backing from Dr. Marius Barbeau on the Museum staff, and Canada Council Board members Sir Ernest MacMillan, Mrs. Agnes MacDonald and Mr. Fred Emerson, I applied for ten thousand dollars and got it. A new life opened then, and by the greatest good luck musicologist Kenneth Peacock heard about it and wrote to ask if he could transcribe the music.

That summer Mac had accompanied Lord Beaverbrook to his home in Fredericton, mainly to treat his asthma, and he invited me to spend a few days with him. We met in Saint John, and as we drove along the Saint John River he revelled in autumn colouring such as he hadn't seen for years. *Bluenose Ghosts* was hot off the press, so I was able to present him with a copy and also tell about the Canada Council grant. On our several stops he would reach for the book, and I thought, "This is more than brotherly interest." I asked if he'd had an experience himself. "Yes," he said, "three."

One story was about a dog in a garden whose

hackles rose at certain times when there was supposed to be something supernatural there. The second I've forgotten, but the third was about a night he spent at a friend's home in the English countryside. He awoke to hear what sounded like a chain being pulled along the floor of the hall, but when he opened his bedroom door to see what was going on, there was nothing there. The noise continued and presently another door opened and another guest looked out to see the cause of the disturbance. Finally they decided there would be no more sleep that night and went downstairs and sat beside an open fire. In the morning he said to his host, "What were you doing dragging a chain up and down the floor outside my room last night?"

"Oh," he said, "did you hear it?" This had been going on for years so that the family thought nothing of it. He explained what ancestor had been doing it and why. It wasn't a nightly occurrence, but happened occasionally.

Next morning when we met, Lord Beaverbrook said, "You've got a fine thing here." Which did he mean? My folk song collection with which he was familiar, the new book which Mac would have told him about during his morning treatment, or the grant? Not wanting to embarrass him, and knowing it was the last thing he meant I said, "You mean my brother?" which broke the ice nicely. Then we set out for Newcastle and Lord Beaverbrook had a picnic hamper prepared which we were to enjoy sitting on a horizontal gravestone in The Enclosure, a park Louise Manny had fixed up for him. Louise met us there, but it was so cold she suggested we take our goodies to her house.

Mac was, of course, the doctor of the family, and I the little sister, so it was something of a shock to him— and brought the most comical expression to his face— when Louise quite properly introduced us as Dr. Creighton and her brother. Lord Beaverbrook liked to give an impression of a poverty-stricken boyhood and Mac wanted to see the house where he had grown up. It is a large comfortable dwelling, now Newcastle's library, and the family had lived well. When Mac said to him later that he didn't think he'd done too badly as a boy, Lord Beaverbrook replied, "I've done a lot better since."

In October with field work done and many new songs recorded, I went to Ottawa to see about spending my grant, one of the first the Canada Council had given. Ken Peacock was well started on his music. Should the dubbing be made on disc or tape? It was finally arranged that Crawley Films would duplicate a set on tape to be kept in the Public Archives in Halifax, and at the same time Radio Station CBO offered to make another set for the Museum if I would provide the tapes. What a blessing this was because I discovered a few years later that the sound had faded on some of the originals.

For part of the several months I spent in Ottawa overseeing this work, I stayed at the Chelsea Club where there were rooms for eight women residents and a guest. Ottawa members often came in for meals and receptions and the friendly and gracious atmosphere was a pleasant change from living alone.

Hope's Book Store in Ottawa roused my curiosity, and I looked around timidly for my new book. Would they be interested enough to sell it? I saw no sign of it and was perhaps looking glum when a saleswoman with a bright eye and pleasing manner said, "Are you looking for something?" I asked where the new books were. "The new fiction is over here," she said, so I replied that I wasn't looking for fiction.

"Is there a special book?" she enquired, so I gave her the name.

"Oh," she said, "shipments are so slow." I knew then they meant to sell it and my spirits soared. I admitted writing it and found I was talking to Helen Dacey Wilson, later to become author of *Barrett's Landing*. She had been brought up on just the things I'd written about. The upshot was that as each shipment arrived I autographed the books. With a prominent place in their shop window and in the Saturday newspapers, this was the most advertised book of the season, and it was so much on Helen's mind that when an order came for the Creighton book, meaning Donald Creighton's study of Sir John A. Macdonald, she sent *Bluenose Ghosts* instead. No, it wasn't returned, but the recipient must have been surprised. Every day while the dubbings were being made I went to the Crawley studios and made notes as the reels were run off. I could also note what songs would be suitable for radio from the point of view of quality in production and singing voice. What surprised us was the preponderance of murder songs, and I've wondered what psychologists would make of this. Lullabies in English were few and far between, a fact that had puzzled me until one day after a Miramichi Folk Song Festival at Newcastle, New Brunswick, a young father came to Louise Manny's house with five children all under the age of six. We sat on the wide verandah watching the Miramichi River flowing by, the children cross-legged on the floor, and the sweet smell of pine trees in our nostrils. When we asked them to sing they did so with all the aplomb in the world, but their choice was a horrible murder song that affected them not a bit, and it was most cheerfully that their little voices rang out with the words, "He took her by the yellow locks and drug her o'er the ground." I realized then that this is what the children had for lullabies. Their father would sing whatever came into his head, be it a murder or love song, and the tune and rhythm would carry it—words had little meaning.

In the collection there were, of course, many love songs, (most of them with a sea motif), humorous, topical, and local songs; many subjects were covered. Altogether, two hundred and fifteen tapes were processed. Now I no longer lie awake at night worrying about the originals and, with copies in Halifax, I have been able to prepare *Maritime Folk Songs, Gaelic Songs in Nova*

Scotia, and *Folksongs from Southern New Brunswick** for publication. Through the following years as Kenneth Peacock transcribed the music, he shipped it in lots of fifty tunes at a time, each melody, at my request, graded for musical quality.

Frank Willis of CBC Toronto must have been so wrapped up in his plans that he forgot the time difference between Toronto and Dartmouth, because it was at twelve-thirty one night in April of 1958 that he phoned to tell about two hour-long broadcasts to be produced on the life of that great Nova Scotia statesman, Joseph Howe. He wanted two twenty-minute programs of folk songs to precede the broadcasts. Now with Ken's transcriptions at hand, the songs were easily provided, and I went to Toronto to give a verbal introduction to them; they were sung by a choir under Dr. Richard Johnston.

On the way I went to the CBC in Montreal to watch Alan Mills give his weekly program for children. After that he took part in what the actors called The Bible Show on which Rupert Caplan dramatized stories from the great Book. I had often listened to this and also to Neil Chotem's original music that accompanied it, and I wanted to meet the composer because he had written an orchestral suite on Newfoundland and Nova Scotia folk music. While we were talking, a tall young man, Michel Perrault, came up and said he had written a ballet based on tunes I had collected. He said that it would be performed later in the season by Les Grands Ballets Canadiens and I must come up for the première. I did, but we'll come to that later.

In Toronto the CBC put me up at the Frontenac Arms, a respectable hotel in an unrespectable district where women didn't walk alone at night. It was only a

Folksongs from Southern New Brunswick. (Ottawa: National Museum of Man, Canadian Centre for Folk Culture Studies, 1971).

block away from the studio, but after the dramatic rehearsals, which I liked to watch, they had me escorted the short distance by a commissionaire. My own part was, in a sense, small, but it was nonetheless important, and while the other experienced performers were so relaxed that one singer, Joyce Sullivan, did a little dance between verses, I was pretty tense, and at one point felt that I might collapse. Then in some extraordinary way that I can't explain, I got a message from my old singer, Ben Henneberry who had died some years before. He was saying, "You're doing very well; just keep it up." Had the singers known I was having a supernatural experience in the middle of a broadcast, they would have been the ones to collapse. Mr. Henneberry had never appeared to me before, nor has he come since, but somehow I knew the message was from him and I was immediately strengthened. We had good mail response after these broadcasts, including letters from members of parliament and several senators.

On the way back I stopped off in Ottawa and went to the home of Dr. Barbeau for a meeting of the Canadian Folk Music Society's prospective members. These included Sir Ernest MacMillan of Toronto and Mr. Fred Emerson of St. John's, both then on the Canada Council board; Dr. Graham George of Queen's University music department; Mr. Arthur Price, son-in-law of our host, and illustrator of many of his books; and Mr. Harold Pfeiffer of the National Museum. Later Mr. Leonard Brockington, also on the Canada Council board, arrived and while there had been animated conversation before, it now sparkled. He was tall and crippled with arthritis and sat without turning his head but knowing the position of everybody there. I told my story of Bernard Shaw's address to the Canadian Authors in London. When the last of our stories had been exchanged and refreshments served, Mr. Brockington offered to drive me home. As we drove off in Graham George's car I realized I hadn't said good-bye to my friend Fred Emerson. Mr. Brockington, for years Canada's most eloquent speaker, said he would do it for me. He said, "Yes, I shall say Helen asked me to say good-night, and he will think you have been over-tender and I am impertinent."

Soon after my return I came down with a thump. Dartmouth put on its first evening of folk music. All the songs were from other places, and there had been no attempt to include any of our great heritage. Isn't that typical? This was remedied a few years later, but any real encouragement and use of our songs has come, until very recently, from outside. It was only because I believed in them so thoroughly myself that I set my jaw and kept stubbornly on.

Perhaps that is why in 1958, for the first time, I faced my new field season with a heavy heart and felt I couldn't take the discomforts that were bound to lie ahead. This wasn't helped by my first trip which was to the Gallagher home where I found a sorrowing widower. However things soon picked up with the aid of my Toronto friend, Richard Johnston. Collectors are loathe to share their singers with others in the same way that a person with a treasure map keeps the information, hoping that he will some day be able to find the place for himself. From somewhere, Mr. Augustine MacDonald of North Sydney had got hold of Richard's name and had written that he knew fifteen hundred songs. This information was passed on to me, for Richard realized his chances of finding time to collect them were slim.

Mr. MacDonald was a little pixie-like man with one tooth up and one down and grey hair that stood on end. He had cherished his songs against his later years when he would sing them to a delighted public and reap rich rewards. He may have pictured himself as a great artist or travelling troubadour, not realizing that with age his memory and singing ability would diminish. Like many singers, he thought nobody else knew his songs, so I was careful not to tell him when a prized possession had been sung elsewhere. He knew no songs about milk-white steeds or little page boys, but after a few days he recalled the ballad of Lord Bateman, also a good song of whale fishing, and a few interesting songs in Gaelic and English. As well, he talked intelligently about life and customs at Meat Cove, further north, where he had grown up. He had to be taken out to record, and the Carl Masons, who ran a home for visiting seamen, made us welcome there. It was the season of year when the town was alive with Portuguese fishermen, and we had to dodge the times when they would be coming in. These fishermen were always asking for "figurines," catalogues to take home to wives and sweethearts who would give them orders to submit on their return. Poor Mr. MacDonald, he enjoyed the recording, but his fifteen hundred songs dwindled to thirty, all he could remember. All MacDonalds in Cape Breton have a nickname and his was Juice. I suspect his life had been far from easy, but it was a pleasure to record him, especially when laughter rippled from his happy heart to the willing tape.

He had a number of stories about the devil whom he assured me he had seen and one of his beliefs proved surprisingly useful the following year. I had been speaking to a high school group and had told a devil story. When I finished a girl stood up and said, "My father saw the devil beside his bed five days before he died and he was terrified." My immediate thought was, "I wonder what your old man's been up to." I managed to look interested but casual. Her face haunted me, and I felt that she and her mother must have worried over such an apparition. Then I recalled a remark of Mr. MacDonald's to the effect that if you see the devil in this world you won't see him in the next, and it was a relief to telephone her teacher and ask her to pass this belief along. The strange thing about this encounter was that I had repeatedly refused the invitation to speak to this class until this occasion when I seemed to feel the time was right. Was I being used to allay the fears of a troubled mother and daughter?

In June of that year I was to give the luncheon address at the Home Economics Convention in St. Andrews, New Brunswick. As I approached Sussex, my mind absorbed with thoughts of buttercups lining a Cape Breton roadside, I recalled that the Deichmann family of pottery fame lived here. I'd heard they were a delightful Danish family and skilled craftsmen, so I thought I'd look at their work and see if they lived up to reports of them. That was Saturday afternoon at four. When I left on Monday morning I wore their gift of a medallion they had fashioned and Erica's voice whispered softly, "We love you." I had driven up their long driveway to an imposing house set well back in its own grounds. Sitting on the front steps were Mrs. Deichmann (Erica) and her daughter Anneka. Erica was painting designs on boxes for packing gifts and Anneka, then a university student, was helping her. We must have been on the same wave length for we made friends immediately, and I found they were as interested in me as I in them. I was invited to stay for the weekend, and that evening Erica sang a twenty-two verse Danish song called "Dronning Dagmars Dod." People kept coming in to view the pottery and to buy, and many were invited to the inner sanctum for coffee or mulled wine served in handmade mugs that were a delight to hold.

After my St. Andrews speech I stayed on to do field work there and one day was invited by Senator Wilson to a luncheon at her summer home. As we strolled through the grounds, I noticed a fountain with figures of young children in different poses on its rim. One had a fish in his hand; another was about to release a bird. She told me an Italian sculptor had come especially to make these replicas of her grandchildren. She had a similar set on the grounds of her Ottawa home. I often think of them with pleasure.

As long as I could remember, I had heard snatches of "The Chezzetcook Song" about various articles of merchandise brought from that village to the Halifax market. I supposed it was locally composed. An article in the

1957 December issue of *The Atlantic Advocate*, "The Bellefontaine Club," by Mr. J. J. F. Winslow, Q.C. told how one of Fredericton's young intellectuals had once visited the Halifax market and talked to a Mr. Bellefontaine there. The young man was so fascinated with the variety of Chezzetcook wares that he wrote a poem about it. The organist of his church in Fredericton set it to music, and a literary club became The Bellefontaine Club. The song, very similar to the way I knew it, had been sung for years in the Winslow home as part of their Christmas celebration, and Mr. Winslow was good enough to record it for me on tape. It had come into being in the true style of the old-fashioned folk song, and among those who contributed to its making was the poet Bliss Carman.

Back in Sussex it was evident that the Deichmanns were deluged with tourists, and we agreed it would be better for me to stay with the town's historian, Miss Grace Aiton, but they were always calling us to go up, and they had a way of making every occasion festive. They were genuinely interested in what I was recording, and many a time I was asked to play a tape for their visitors. The greatest enjoyment came when the three Deichmanns sang together, Anneka on the left with her youthful enthusiasm, singing with head held high; Kjeld, her father, in the centre, tall and strong and grey, with his rich voice giving depth to the music; and Erica with her sweetness contributing her part—a happy united family. After one of these sessions we were showing guests the displays when Erica picked up a vase and, loving it herself, pressed it against every cheek. When she came to me I ejaculated, "My dream is out," for I had just recalled dreaming that morning of Erica waking me by pressing her cheek against mine.

The Canadian Folk Music Society had been formed in affiliation with the International Folk Music Council. Our president, Dr. Barbeau, could not be present for the second annual meeting and suggested that I, as vice president, arrange and chair it in Nova Scotia. I thought of Tatamagouche on the north shore where the United Church had a comfortable house which they used as their Training Centre, and this was available in August. Rooms were found in the village for our little group, and, among other business, we drew up a constitution. Attending were Sir Ernest and Lady MacMillan, Mr. and Mrs. Fred Emerson, Miss Louise Manny, Mlle Simonne Voyer, Professor Luc Lacourcière, and Rev. Germain Lemieux, S.J., a small number but with sufficient courage to offer ourselves as hosts to the International Folk Music Council three years hence. Our evening meeting was open to the public, and local folk dancers performed for us. Then Sir Ernest demonstrated orchestrations he had made of folk tunes, and we showed my recently released NFB picture.

I was scarcely rested when it was time to leave for Bishop's College, Lennoxville, to give four hours of lectures on folk music to the National Assembly of the Y.W.C.A. I suggested Finvola Redden go with me, a happy thought. Again everybody loved her, and she got into people's hearts so that some had tears in their eyes and others confessed to goose pimples. Then an odd thing happened. The audience came forward not to me, but to Finvola. I knew now how a mother must feel when she is no longer Mrs. Smith, but Barbara's mother. Alan Mills had driven us down from Montreal, and on that trip it was decided Finvola should study under Mr. Bernard Diamant who unfortunately was out of town. However Alan took us to the home of Maureen Forrester whose star as a singer was just beginning to rise, and who studied under Mr. Diamant. Her husband, Eugene Kash, violinist, and John Newmark, the pianist, were there. Finvola without a qualm sang for this distinguished trio.

I had a singer in Tatamagouche who had given me "The Strawberry Roan," and when I returned I thought he might have remembered something else. He had, and asked if I would set my machine up in a restaurant where his friends could see him recording. The tourist season was over and it was past meal time so I did. When everything was ready he pulled out his dentures and called out to anyone who would listen, "Hold my teeth." Ill-fitting teeth sometimes fall out when people sing, so they frequently remove them. When nobody obliged he went on with his song, pounding them on the counter to keep time. I call that my denture accompaniment.

At our Tatamagouche meetings Louise Manny had told of a folk song festival she was planning for September in Newcastle, New Brunswick, and asked if I would be a judge. Singers who had never performed before on a platform were recruited from the lumber woods and fishing villages, and nobody had any idea how it would work out. The opening speech was made by the lieutenant-governor, the Honourable Leonard O'Brien. It is interesting to compare his somewhat hesitant remarks with those made in later years after the festivals had proved themselves. There was some excessive tipping of the elbow as contestants sought to calm their nerves, but Ken Homer, a Nova Scotian now living in New Brunswick, acted as Master of Ceremonies and smoothed over many a crisis. Our work as judges began before the festival started when people phoned Louise Manny to know if they could enter such and such a song. She would give the title to Edward (Sandy) Ives of the University of Maine and me, and then say, "No, the judges say that isn't a folk song." We were strict about this which was fortunate as we were setting a pattern. Some of the songs were long and gloomy and perhaps had little value. Others were rare, beautiful, and exciting to us who were collectors. Many threw light on life in the lumber woods and on the fishing vessels, and many a song had been recovered by a singer who had consulted friends to help him piece it together. The festivals have also resulted in the composition of original songs in the old style of commemorating current events. The most outstanding was written by thirteen-year-old Bernadette Keating after the Escuminac Disaster when a sudden storm took an appalling toll of lives.

I loved to watch the different techniques of the singers. Nick Underhill used to look down at me out of the corner of his eye. It looked flirtatious but was actually for encouragement. He would hold a top note for an unconscionable time at top volume which would have the audience doubled up with mirth as he intended. Wilmot MacDonald always ended with a loud whoop, while John Holland, in his late eighties, finished off with a little step dance, and shuffled his way off the stage, eyes dancing with mischief. Sam Jagoe could stand with hands clasped and no movement of his body or raising or dropping of his voice and keep an audience on the edge of its seats through seventeen double verses of a long tragic ballad. It was his sympathy for the characters that did it, and some in the audience would have tears running down their cheeks. As I watched these unaccompanied singers I thought of modern youths who must have an instrument to support them and wished they would come and take lessons, for this is a great art that is dying. Sometimes the festival's spirit would be so contagious that in the intermission a visitor might take out his fiddle and an old woman might get up and do a step dance in the aisle. Pete Seeger once asked if he could come. Louise said she'd be delighted to have him but he couldn't sing. This was right, because in no time the local people would be copying his style or feeling inferior in contrast to his professional ability. Alan Mills was allowed to give concerts for children, but, as far as possible, this was a production solely from the district of the Miramichi. One year's festival was scarcely over before singers were planning for the next year.

I usually stayed on for a few days after a festival, and on one of these occasions Wilmot MacDonald and his wife arrived to visit Miss Manny. Logs were burning on the hearth, he had been acclaimed the best woods singer, and he was in the mood for story telling. I set my tape recorder in motion and got a ghost yarn so well told that I've used it over and over again to finish off a lecture, it was told with such obvious zest and enjoyment, and always with his receptive adult audience in mind. Another time he told the same tale to Sandy Ives not with the purpose of spinning a good yarn to make him laugh, but as he had told it to two young boys to frighten them. It was an abbreviated version without the high spots achieved on my recording when every sentence was his own dramatic experience. Because storytellers and singers are so sensitive to their surroundings, it is often a good idea to go back and then, if the mood is right, to record them over again. For both of us he recorded several folk tales which we published jointly in a little volume called *Eight Folktales from Miramichi,** and you can see from these how his stories varied with his mood. I have been fortunate working in a limited area where I would make return calls, and I've seldom come away without getting something new or another slant on something that needed that extra touch.

In November, CBC's John Hobday invited me to a luncheon with four writers he thought might dramatize stories from *Bluenose Ghosts* for radio. These were Barbara Grantmyre, Kay Hill, Doug Fraser, and Ian Fraser. In time each produced two plays which ran in a series. This, I believe, was Ian Fraser's first experience in drama, and we like to think we started his career, for it was he who in 1967 produced the great *Military Tattoo* for Canada's centennial celebrations. In December of that year, the name of the film *Songs of Nova Scotia* appeared in lights at the Capitol Theatre in Halifax, but it was so close to Christmas that few, if any, of my friends saw it. Soon after that, in January 1959, I went

Eight Folktales from Miramichi. With Edward D. Ives. *Northeast Folklore*, IV. (Orono, Maine: University of Maine, 1962).

to Ottawa for a meeting of the Canadian Folk Music Society and to have more tapes transposed. While I was there the film was shown at the National Museum, and invitations were sent. The thermometer registered twenty below, but we had two senators; two Museum directors; the former curator, Dr. Alcock, with whom I had worked so happily; Inspector Kelly of the RCMP; Admiral Houghton's wife; Dr. Carmen Roy, head of the folklore department; and others—a distinguished gathering.

In spite of 1958's distractions, many songs had been recorded and words from these tapes had to be transcribed. Also I applied for and received from the Canada Council a further grant of $3000 for more dubbings. The CBC asked for a radio series profile and sent Ken Homer to record it. There was a panel discussion at Mount Allison University and talks given here and there, but the most exciting event of that spring was the première performance of *Sea Gallows* by the Montreal ballet company, Les Grands Ballets Canadiens. If I hadn't gone up, my province would have received no publicity, for the ballet was advertised simply as based on Canadian folklore, which I felt was a mistake. It would have been much more interesting if a specific location, in this case Nova Scotia, had been designated, and actually, the set with its fishnet drapes and waterfront scene might well have been our Devil's Island. The dancers wore grey sleeveless blouses and short grey skirts with red and white checked aprons. The heroine wore a simple sleeveless dress and the villain was in black and wore sea boots. As I watched the melodrama unfold, I was caught up in the gaiety of the dancing and the beauty of the love scene, while at the same time I was trying to identify the tunes upon which the music was based. There were six of them: "Auction Block," "The Bailiff's Daughter of Islington," "I'm Going To Be Married on Monday," "Gallows," "The Kangaroo," and "I'm Scarce Sixteen Come Sunday," all from my *Traditional Songs from Nova Scotia*. Milenka Niderlova and Brydon Paige played the leading roles, and Eric Hyrst choreographed the dances. At the end there was loud applause and cries of "Bravo." I saw it twice and heard later that it had been performed one hundred and fifty times and was considered one of the company's most successful numbers. Afterwards there was a reception at the Windsor Hotel. I gave a number of press interviews, and it was then that *The Montreal Star* had its comical misprint stating that I had 4000 sons, most of them from Nova Scotia.

For twelve years I had served the National Museum far beyond the call of duty and for a very small stipend. Any plums had gone quite rightly to Dr. Barbeau, Canada's dean of folklore. He couldn't go to the 1959 meetings of the International Folk Music Council, so I decided to ask for that privilege and so establish myself in the position I felt I'd earned. I didn't pay much attention to where it was to be, since any place in Europe would be new to me, but I was lucky that it was Rumania. I had practically forgotten the application when Dr. Russell, the Director, wrote to say it had been approved. The Canada Council granted $700 for the trip, and the Museum would pay my living expenses.

Chapter 10

Before starting the three months of field work that would precede the Rumanian trip, I went again to Ottawa for meetings of the Canadian Folk Music Society. There Professor Luc Lacourcière of Laval University told of a Folk Tale Congress to be held in Kiel, Germany, immediately following the one in Rumania—so why not take in both? It seemed like the opportunity of a lifetime, and so it proved to be.

I had joined the International Folk Music Council soon after I began collecting and had received its annual publication ever since, and also, at times, wise and sympathetic advice from its members. Chief among these was Miss Maud Karpeles, general secretary. When I first corresponded with her she was in Newfoundland taking down songs Cecil Sharp would have collected if death had not intervened. In all these years we had never met, so this was one of the first things I arranged in London. We couldn't travel together, but she gave me a list of the English delegates who would be on my plane. Mac drove me to the London airport, but there was no one to point out the delegates, and bifocals are a nuisance when trying to read names on luggage tags. He solved the problem by having the loudspeaker ask the English delegates en route for Rumania to come to the information booth. Immediately two appeared, Dr. Laurence Picken, professor of zoology at Cambridge University, musicologist and linguist who was said to speak seventeen languages; and Miss Bartlett from Dartington, fair of hair and blue of eye whose first name appropriately is Winsome, and who does all kinds of interesting things for sick musical instruments. We were five in all, and the others were obviously world travellers. I had worried about arriving alone in a communist country, but now I settled down to enjoy every minute.

The Sabena plane to Brussels was luxurious and had a glamorous stewardess, but the Tarom plane to Rumania was small and old and the stewardess was glum. On this, my first trip to Europe, I would have had little idea where I was, but Dr. Penton of our group kept us informed. Our only stop was Vienna, and as I entered the airport I heard, "Look, there's Helen Creighton!" This was Ruth Rubin whom I'd met in Washington and Ottawa and who was now on her way to give a paper at our conference.

We had noted the absence of boats on the River Danube, and I had supposed that landing in Bucharest at night would be exciting as in other cities where cars on the roads make moving ribbons of light and prominent buildings stand out in brilliant illumination. Here, even at the airport, there were only dim lights, and we were soon aware that there were few private cars in the country and few private boats on the Danube. We were met by a welcoming committee which included Mr. Mihai Pop whom we promptly dubbed our glamour boy. He was tall, grey, and handsome, but spoke no English and depended upon a young woman to interpret. Passports were taken from us and our money declared, such as it was, for we could get no Rumanian currency outside the country. Other delegates had trouble with the Customs, but we were more fortunate and soon found ourselves being driven along wide streets with many trees and parks on either side and lights down the centre. Our hotel rooms were large but on different floors, and although mine looked comfortable, I felt a long way from friends. I would have liked to call it a day then, but we had been invited to a four course dinner, and I felt it would be unwise to refuse. As it turned out, we might as well have stayed up all night for there was loud music from the square outside until two a.m., and then a cement mixer rolled until six, proving to visitors that progress in Bucharest is continuous, twenty-four hours, non-stop.

The next morning at breakfast we watched life passing in the square outside, but we were given no opportunity to wander. Most people were dressed like us with the occasional peasant in costume, and there was practically no traffic. It was Sunday and we were put in buses for the sixty-mile trip to Sinaia, a wooded resort in the Carpathian Mountains. We observed many people walking; they have to, of course, for so few own cars. Some owned horses, most of which looked ill-fed. We passed an oil refinery and were reminded that oil gave Rumania most of its wealth. Houses were small but prettily designed and were made of wooden laths covered with plaster. They all had pitched metal or thatched roofs and many had gardens. There were countless motor bikes, mostly for two, and several youth groups were going afoot to a camp. We saw few churches in Bucharest but more in the country, and once we thought we saw a few people coming from a service, and at least one church door stood open.

Somebody whispered that we were to live in a castle, and the word went quickly around. We didn't believe it, but when we arrived, there they were, three great castles, summer palaces of former kings, to be our home for the next ten days. The first castle was now a museum and people were waiting to get in; it had been built by King Carol I. His son Ferdinand built the second castle, called Polishor, for himself and Queen Marie, and this is where most of us stayed. This palace was heavy, with a stone base, then stone covered with plaster and painted yellow with green trimmings. Turrets were tiled in red and there were plaster decorations on the outer walls and an occasional statue. My room had been Queen Marie's salon. It was large, with an oriental ceiling, casement windows, heavy dark furniture, and beautiful runners hand-worked in gay colours on bureau and tables. Water jugs and towels bore designs of royal crowns. At one side two steps led to an enclosure with pillars to the ceiling which puzzled me until someone suggested this might have been set aside for prayers. No two rooms were alike. An Hungarian monk had Queen Marie's bedroom, and an Italian couple named Nataletti had her boudoir, dining-room and bathroom. A secret stairway ran from Ferdinand's bathroom on the floor below to two entrances to the queen's chambers. One was through a cupboard, which seems an undignified way for a king to come to his queen, if indeed he did, and the other by way of her balcony. Miss Bartlett's room was the most imaginative. It was in a turret and had steps leading to a reclining or reading room with a delightful panoramic view. The chapel was used as a dormitory for young women of the staff. It was lined with gold. To be in this extraordinary setting was like living a fairy tale until we were brought to reality by the sound of soldiers drilling outside and occasional gun practice in the distance.

As we climbed the hill to the next palace, my thoughts went back to December 1920 when I had met Klondyke Boyle in New York and heard of his association with Prince Carol. Little did I think then I would ever be in one of his palaces. The modern building we next came to, which Carol had built for Madame Lupescu whom he had met a few years later, was to be the setting for our conference and I could roam through this building at leisure. A beautiful winding staircase carpeted in red with a long landing and large window midway led to Madame Lupescu's spacious bedroom, now occupied by Miss Karpeles. However, it was the conference room that impressed us most. It must have been the drawing room originally, but was set up like a small United Nations. We sat on gold chairs and there was a head table from which four tables branched and at each place there were headphones that could be plugged in to receive any of six languages. At each table two microphones were attached to long cords so that any member wishing to comment could do so without moving. When the head table speaker stopped, the side table microphones were freed and could be switched on at will. Most papers had been translated in advance and we were given copies in our own language.

Meetings were well attended because there were no distractions in this rural setting, and we were not permitted to stray further than the village of Sinaia. We were seated alphabetically according to countries, and our badges had our country's name beneath our own. Twenty-six were represented, and we listened to one another's music in an atmosphere of mutual regard. Surely friendships that blossomed under these circumstances must help to establish world peace. (When I came home I made this statement in a speech which a Halifax paper put in an editorial shared with Ed Sullivan who was then bringing Russian dancers to his television programs for this very purpose.)

The outstanding theme was instrumental music, and most speakers were highly trained musicologists and active collectors of folk music. Papers were illustrated by the playing and displaying of instruments, tape recordings, and films, and it was a relief when a gifted speaker could sing the illustrations as Ruth Rubin did when talking about Yiddish songs from Montreal. Helène Baillargeon, Montreal folk singer, was there and illustrated my Acadian songs. When my National Film Board picture was shown, the Rumanians asked for more Canadian films which opened a new exchange between our countries.

What little French I knew was painfully inadequate where people slipped easily from one language to another, and I worried until I realized that if I'd been brought up in Europe I would be doing the same. And as I listened to other papers, I realized the one I had prepared needed to be livened up. That could be done with a tape I'd brought along which had been recorded a few years before with Ken Homer for the CBC. This meant employing the services of Rumanian technicians. My dubbing session began after an evening meeting and went on until 12.30, and these young men, trained to show no sign of fatigue, continued that night with another delegate until 2 a.m. As Ken Homer's voice came through one technician said, "What a nice voice," and another said, "I know that voice; he's CBC." Listening to programs on our international radio service was one way they learned our language. They also served us well by having interpreters give instantaneous translations of all papers which we picked up on our receiving sets. In another room there were more interpreters as well as typewriters and all the manuscript paper a delegate might need. These interpreters were all women and they were always within call.

Excitement rippled as we approached the terrace at King Carol's palace for the first evening performance of Rumanian talent. Peasants from the plains wore gayly embroidered blouses, kerchiefs, and there were aprons over their full skirts. Men wore long smocks to their knees, white trousers, and sometimes a fancy headdress. Delegates with flash bulbs for their cameras and battery-run tape recorders were kept busy. The music of the older women was most interesting, and they sang old style lyric songs pitched high. A most unusual performance was given on a fish scale from the carp. It was held unseen in the mouth and the player stood with hands at his side. The music was sweet and different from anything most of us had heard. The performer is considered a great artist and can be heard on commercial records. At first the performers seemed sullen, but as they sensed our appreciation they were pleased.

In Rumania when talented folk singers are discovered, their names are put on a list and they may be called at any time to entertain visiting conferences. We had two evenings of native song and dance and two films, one entirely folk and the other almost entirely propaganda. We had several trips to outside points on one of which I heard a Dane on our bus singing one of Erica Deichmann's songs. It was thrilling to hum along with her in these Transylvanian hills so different from the New Brunswick setting where I'd learned it.

Each meal was a banquet and dinner might last from eight to ten p.m. The food, especially the delicious cakes and desserts, was rich, and, knowing we would be sick from our change in diet, there was always a doctor on hand with proper medication. We had an expedition to the plains to see village life, but there was no chance to roam, and villagers were brought to the hall to perform. Since we could walk to Sinaia, I attended a service in the Greek Orthodox Church. The music, which came from the back, was beautiful. With few exceptions the congregation stood, for there were neither pews nor chairs. An exception was an aristocratic lady with the sort of headdress associated with pictures of Queen Marie, and as I looked at her, the only one of her kind, I wondered what her story was. The church was filled, but mostly with women, and I was told men could attend, but they would advance no further in the Party. In all our contacts folklore was stressed, and we were told how it was changing so that in place of the old love and romance in song and story, it now was the Party that had precedence.

In Bucharest on our two last days our hosts were so anxious to entertain us that they left no time for meals. Lunch was dispensed with entirely and dinner was at eleven-thirty or midnight. One of the delights here was to look out on the wide streets where groups in costume practised their dances for their great folk competition then being held. At concerts many of their most strenuous dances were performed by men over seventy. One of the best embraced three generations, and the emphasis was on their footwork. We were told this was possible because their new way of life made them strong. As foreigners we were openly stared at on the streets of Bucharest, and at Sinaia when the mayor entertained us we came out to find peasants standing five feet deep just to look at us. No matter where we wanted to go there was always someone to escort us, which we soon realized was a precaution to keep us from talking to people on the streets. When we left, Bucharest was preparing to celebrate its relief from Nazi domination. Flags of red, yellow, and dark blue were everywhere, and huge pictures of their leaders had been erected along the streets. We met scores of armed soldiers being driven into the city and regretted this military scene after the peace of Sinaia. My return home was not the end of my contact with Rumania because ever since I have been receiving their official folklore publication, *Revista de Ethnografie Şi Folclor.*

Why the Rumanians wouldn't allow me to travel with Mrs. Vicky McLain, an American living in Cairo who was going to meet her husband in West Berlin, neither of us understood, and my only course seemed to be to go by way of East Berlin alone, a thing my new European friends said they wouldn't want to do. However this had been mapped out by my travel agent, and it was fortunate that Mr. Myklebust of the Norwegian radio station was on board and could deliver me to the East Berlin airport and secure an interpreter. After that I was on my own and without their currency as we couldn't get it in advance, so my first act was to get some change. Canadian money was valued higher than American money at that time, so I presented one American Express bill and one Canadian five-dollar bill which the banker accepted with relish. This gave me my transit visa, bus fare to the terminal, and taxi to West Berlin. The airport staff was most helpful, and as a foreigner with a problem I was, of course, conspicuous. It was not surprising then that a middle-aged man called out that I could drive with him, that he was going to the West Berlin airport. I looked at him gratefully and said thank you very much, but I think I'll go by bus. I can only speak kindly of these people including the bus driver who kept his eyes open for a taxi, a rarity in East Berlin. The wall wasn't up then, but there were still signs of devastation. Sentries asked for my passport at the border, and it was a great relief when that part of my trip was over.

It was nine p.m. when I arrived at Kiel, and I was surprised when my taxi driver there spoke English with the same accent as our Lunenburg County's German descendants in Nova Scotia, and I learned that their Lüneburg is just south of Kiel. As we drove up to the place where a room had been reserved, it looked dark and forbidding, but it turned out to be a youth hostel run by nuns, one of whom took me to a room on the third floor which I was to share. I asked if I could have a room to myself and on a lower floor, and my pleading eyes which by now must have looked like two burnt holes in a blanket, must have touched her because she gave me a room on the ground floor. She asked if she could get me tea or coffee and then said, "I know what you need, a bottle of beer." Well, I thought, to be served beer by a nun in Kiel will be a new experience. The bed sagged badly in the middle, there was a hen yard outside my window, and many people passed my door in the early morning, but I slept soundly, awaking in time for breakfast. I went back to bed then and slept till noon and after lunch slept again. When dinner was over I thought I couldn't possibly sleep all night but mercifully did and by Monday morning I was ready for anything.

Suddenly life changed. In Rumania I had known few people and, as my country's representative, had been on my dignity. At Kiel I was on my own and as I entered the building where the Folk Tale Congress was

214

being held I heard, "Hi, Helen!" This was Professor War-
ren Roberts from Indiana University who was followed
by Professor Wayland Hand, whom I had also met at
Indiana. Most of the papers here were in foreign languages and there were no translations, which I didn't regret
since I'd been concentrating on so many papers. The
real benefit came from meeting the world's great folklore scholars, and it was no small satisfaction to hear
renowned professors from Norway and France quoting
from my books with which they were familiar. Luc Lacourcière had given his paper which included references
to our Acadian tales from Pubnico, and he had made
many friends. At the banquet that night I sat at his table
with such notables as Hamish Henderson and Calum
McLean from Scotland, as merry a pair as I ever saw;
Dr. Thelma James and Mrs. Hicks from Detroit; Miss
Genevieve Massignon from Paris; and the Richard Dor-
sons from Indiana. While conversation flowed gayly,
Hamish sang Scottish ballads in my ear. I'd heard of
Professor Archer Taylor for years and now met him. Dr.
Delargy from Ireland was there as well as the dean of
folk tale study on this continent and perhaps in the
world, my old friend Stith Thompson. Thirty countries
were represented.

Before I took this trip, Lloyd McInnes had interviewed me for radio and television in Sydney and Halifax and had asked about a tale he'd heard from an old
man at Sugar Loaf in northern Cape Breton. It had been
told in the first person, but he thought it was traditional
and so did I. I would never have a better opportunity to
find out, and it was a surprise that the greatest folk tale
scholars had never heard it. One day on a bus I sat next
to Dr. Linda Dégh from Hungary, and when I mentioned
the story she said she had taken it down many times,
but the Hungarian tale was much longer than ours. This
had a sequel. In 1962 in Edmonton I was fascinated by
the variety of foreign accents, and one day asked a taxi
driver where he had lived before, and he said Hungary.

I said, "I have a folk tale that has been found nowhere in the world but in your country and my province of Nova Scotia." "What is it?" he asked, so I told my story. He said, "I know a story something like that my grandmother told me," so I said, "What is yours?" and as we sped through the city streets I committed it to memory.

After my return to Canada I gave talks on radio, television, and in person at home and as far afield as Old Sturbridge, Maine, Ottawa, and the University of New Brunswick in Fredericton. A Rumanian government gift of recorded folk music made welcome illustrations.

I have mentioned various unexplainable things that have happened in my life. In 1960 my dear friend Mrs. Stanley Walker (Ella) was having her first visit in Halifax since her husband's death five years before, and I suggested she join me on a trip. On our second night in a beautiful new motel in Middleton I awoke to see Dr. Walker standing as though on guard at the foot of her bed, and I was struck by the nobility of his appearance. Usually I thought of him with his scholar's stoop and glasses slightly tilted downward on his nose. He had died in the fullness of health, and I had taken his sons to the funeral home to see him. There, as I saw him laid out, I had also been startled by this appearance of nobility. I have concluded that a person who wants to be seen after death will appear in some way that will startle the observer into instant recognition. In a moment the vision was over, and I went back to sleep. In the morning I told Ella rather hesitantly and wasn't surprised when she looked doubtful. For months I wondered why he would guard his wife when she was in one of the safest places in the world and with one of her closest friends so near her. I decided if he had appeared to her she would have been frightened, but if I saw him she might think, "Oh that's just some of Helen's nonsense," but in time might come to accept it and be pleased, and that is what happened. I told this to Dr. Puxley, Dr. Walker's successor at King's who was not at all surprised because he had often felt him in the office looking over his shoulder. His presence brought no sensation of fear to either of us.

A merit award came that June which almost missed me. The envelope looked like an advertisement, and I nearly consigned it to the wastebasket without opening it. Inside was a hundred dollar cheque from the late Henry Munro fund and I think perhaps this good friend who had started me off would have been pleased.

Television played an important part in the summer of 1960, first with an interview on "Open House" now known as "Take Thirty." Anna Cameron did the interview after which I took her to the Nova Scotia Yacht Squadron where the secretary, Colonel Sircom, welcomed her, and Mr. and Mrs. Gerald Dwyer, members, told about interesting events there in the past. Later we were dining together at her hotel when a middle-aged man came to our table and said to her, "I couldn't leave without telling you that you are much more beautiful off the screen than on," a gracious impulse.

"Open House" though live, was short and easy to do, but "Land of the Old Songs" was to take a full hour. Thom Benson, executive producer and Bob Barclay, film producer, both from Toronto, and Ken Homer from Woodstock, New Brunswick, came to discuss it with me, and I realized I was expected to be as professional as if this were my regular business. We met in the CBC's board room, and the longer we talked the more enthused we became. After Thom and Ken left, I gave Bob names of people to see and the specific songs they should sing, a necessary precaution. I wasn't needed for these excursions, but before returning to field work on Grand Manan I was taken to Herring Cove where I was filmed as I sat on a rock and poured coffee from a thermos as though at the end of the day. As I looked pensively towards the open sea the rising sun would give the effect of moonlight on the water. Through the summer there were occasional telephone calls to report progress and ask for suggestions, and in August I was flown back to Halifax. Ed McCurdy and Joyce Sullivan were here to present some of the music professionally. There were many high spots in the final release. The show opened with a scene of Fred Little at Terence Bay rowing his boat and singing the ballad "Lord Bateman." Then there was Mrs. Gallagher's voice coming from the tape while Ed McCurdy looked heavenward in rapt attention and picked the song up where she left off, Freeman Young singing to two small boys in his fish house and at the end smiling into the camera, the Owens family sitting on a bank beyond a lily pond singing their jubilee songs, Mrs. McNeil in a rocking chair sewing a patchwork quilt with her daughter, Marie Catherine, ironing beside her and joining her in an Acadian lullaby, and Fred Redden chopping a tree as he sang a beautiful love ballad, "She's Like a Swan." Between these numbers Ken Homer and I talked, weaving the story together. I loved it all, but what a challenge. It was sprung on me at my busiest season and I had to memorize a long script in a few hours.

This film was seen by Dr. A. C. Gluek of Michigan State University, and as a result Finvola, also in the film, and I were invited to give a program at one of their Canadian-American seminars. Alan Mills and Jean Carignon, Quebec fiddler, joined us, and our two hours on stage went all too quickly. Alan knew my collection so well he could alternate with Finvola in making illustrations, and occasionally he and Finvola would do a question and answer song. The evening ended with a showing of the film and the house was filled to overflowing.

Since we were going as far as East Lansing, this seemed a good opportunity to meet folklore students and staff at Indiana University, so I suggested this to their Dr. Richard Dorson and immediately received an invitation. We arrived tired out and were told there had been a mistake in the dates, and could we do it that evening? We did, of course, for an hour and a half, but they mercifully postponed the question period until the morning. Indiana gives a Ph.D. in folklore, and that year had a class of thirty-five. One or two were dressed as beatniks, for it was that era, and they must have been surprised when I stated that a collector should never dress down while working; that informants are flattered when you arrive clean and neatly dressed and are therefore more prone to make friends.

On the way home we stopped in Toronto to see Dr. Richard Johnston who had arranged Finvola's "Boat Song" for piano, and to see my publishers who arrranged for me to go on the interview program known as "701." Joyce Davidson, who did the interviewing, had probably never heard of me before, but when she found I had written a book of ghosts stories, she confided that twice in Hamilton quite recently she had met herself walking towards herself. She didn't know this was a bad omen, yet it had distressed her. I mention it because no dire consequences followed to explain it. Finvola and I thought the universities had paid us well, but, as one of my singers would put it, the profits ate up all the expenses, and we about broke even.

Through the years I had taken many trips to Cape Breton, and I always came back with a few Gaelic songs. By 1961 I decided it was time to do something with them, so I made a suggestion to the National Museum. As a result, Major Calum MacLeod of St. Francis Xavier University agreed to collaborate with me on a book for which he would be Gaelic editor. He was an Old Country Scot who knew everything published there but who had travelled extensively through Cape Breton so that he also knew the situation here. This meant taking my duplicate tapes to him in Antigonish where we could go over them together and he could transcribe the words of those we considered most suitable. Tunes had already been transcribed by Kenneth Peacock.

Until then I knew Major MacLeod only through his adjudications of Scottish dancing, and when I found him loving our work I discovered I'd selected a poet, piper, and scholar. It was he, not I, who, after a coffee break with his charming wife Iona, would say, "Back to the salt mines," and as we played the tapes over and over again, our enthusiasm grew for we knew that what we had was good. After he had typed the words in Gaelic he made an English translation and this perhaps for me was the most interesting part. I'd often said, "What is this song about?" and a singer would reply off-handedly, "Oh, it's about a fellow and his girl." I thought then in English terms. In that tradition, folk songs seldom elaborate on a lady's charms nor do they become ecstatic over the beauty of the homeland. English songs are mostly action songs but translations from the Gaelic would run like this:

"Your virtues are without number. You are a beauteous young maiden, handsome, elegant, pure, and of even disposition. Your cheeks are like apples in an orchard; your voice is sweeter than the music of harpstrings." And of their countryside: "Cape Breton is the land of my love, the land of trees and high mountains. Cape Breton is the land of my love; we deem it the most beautiful land on earth." Now at last I understood why they look enchanted when they sing.

If I jump in my narrative from one activity to another, it is because life has been like that, and I suspect its variety has kept me going. When an invitation came to speak to the Canadian Authors Convention in Toronto that summer, I knew I must go whereas I had felt I must refuse a similar invitation a year or two before. I accepted wondering what new thing would be woven into my life's pattern. Don Thomson was then president, and it was up to him to find a successor. Would I take over? I was appalled by his request, knowing I hadn't the health for it, but when I talked to my friends Richard Johnston and George Coutts, both of the Royal Conservatory of Music, they both felt the Museum would be proud to have one of their staff in this high

office. I knew that I was in for it, but put off asking the
Museum until August when the Director, Dr. L. S. Russell, came to the Miramichi Folk Song Festival. By that
time I had another item for him, a letter from the Rector
of Laval University which read, "The authorities of our
University are anxious to convey to you a testimony of
their high esteem and to emphasize your brilliant
achievements in the field of Folklore. So I have the
honour, on behalf of the Senate of Laval University, to
offer you the honorary degree of Doctor of Letters. I can
assure you that we should be very happy to receive you
in the College of our Doctors." This would be conferred
at the Conference of the International Folk Music Council in Quebec on September 1st. The letter's arrival was
most timely for I was surrounded by friends in folklore,
all of whom shared my delight.

Plans for the Quebec conference had been made in
Ottawa and I was to prepare a program from Nova
Scotia. I thought a Scottish group would provide the
most variety and asked Major MacLeod to assemble one.
Then I asked the provincial government for money to
transport them, but was too modest in my request. The
problem was finally solved when the group agreed to go
by train, and I was told they started singing at Sydney
and didn't stop until they reached Quebec. They en-
deared themselves to everybody, practising first thing in
the morning, then visiting churches and museums all
day and arriving at the university in the evening, foot-
sore but full of the enjoyment of their trip. Our Society
had little money, but when I asked our President, Dr.
Barbeau, if something could be found so they would not
be out of pocket, he produced a cheque for one hundred
and fifty dollars. Their appreciation was shown in the
extra effort they put into their performance, and I was
told they set the whole tone for that side of our conference. Shy and reserved when approached individually,
here in this assemblage of scholars, they were completely at ease, so much so that the soloist in the milling

frolic sprang a new verse on them which resulted in spontaneous merriment. The following morning Major MacLeod was up early to pipe us into breakfast, his kilt swinging gracefully with his rhythmic stride.

Five of us were given honorary degrees, and we represented England, France, the United States, and English and French Canada. Despite my resolve to enjoy it and not be nervous, especially when Maud Karpeles was to give the address, my knees shook as I donned cap and gown, and when I had to sit and sign the Golden Book my hand refused to move. I felt as you do in a dream when you want to run and your legs won't move. Somehow I pushed the pen ahead, but it must be a shaky signature. Then I stood while my citation was read in French and tried to catch what was being said. The diploma was presented in a scarlet roll by the Chancellor of the university, now Cardinal Maurice Roy. Also, we received an *épitoge*, a scarf of scarlet and gold silk with bands of white fur and a red rosette where it fits at the top of the shoulder. This was in a scarlet box lined with white moire silk and bore an inscription in gold letters which read: "Mlle Helen Creighton, Docteur *Honoris Causa* De L'Université Laval, Le Ier Septembre 1961." Then we were toasted in champagne. I was told that in any academic procession I should wear my épitoge along with any other hood, and I do so proudly. As Dr. Lorne Pierce, then editor-in-chief of Ryerson Press, wrote, having been similarly honoured here, "I felt I had reached the ultimate."

The American recipient was Dr. Bertrand Harris Bronson, University of California, author of a monumental series of books, *The Traditional Tunes of the Child Ballads*. He had used every ballad tune I had published, and I was glad to see our music taking its place in this great world study, even though any financial compensation was impossible. A few months later an enormous box arrived with a complimentary copy of Volume II. I went through it eagerly, but it was not until six years later that I needed to consult it. As I did, I thought, "I wish I had Volume III." Then I told myself not to be silly, I wouldn't be spending twenty-five dollars for it. The next day I sighed again and wished for Volume III. Almost immediately the doorbell rang and I was handed a large package. What was it? Volume III, of course. I kept blinking all day in wonderment for things don't happen like that. But this time it did.

My ghosts were put to a new use in October of '61. Animated drawings were made by the CBC's gifted staff artist, Harry Orenstein. The story was called *The Box* and dealt with a duel. To anyone not accustomed to ghost stories it must have been spine-chilling. They had written a script which I read as the story unfolded. I find the use of my material exciting and inspiring, especially when it takes such a variety of forms. But CBC Halifax did us a great disservice where our songs were concerned. When the sort I was collecting were at their height of popularity, they ran many programs of folk songs "from here there and everywhere." Indeed they were from there and everywhere, but never from here except for "The Cherry Tree Carol" and "Farewell to Nova Scotia." I never felt there was anything personal in this, but why were they so short-sighted as to ignore their own heritage, especially when many of our songs are of equal merit to, if not better than, most? It was hard to work at times under such discouragement.

Many of our singers lived to a great age, with Charles Owens of Bridgetown heading the list at 101 or 102 years. I kept a number of obituaries but neglected to put down the dates. Mrs. Morse of Aylesford and Mrs. Duncan of Dartmouth were in their nineties when they died, and so were Isaac Doyle of West Jeddore and Dennis Smith of East Chezzetcook. Richard Hartlan was never sick in his life, but while probably in his seventies, he was run into by a motor car and killed. When Walter Roast died I went to his funeral and found that fairly late in life he had married a genial wife, and I rejoiced that his latter years had been so happy. Some to whom I had sent Christmas cards after our first meeting kept this exchange up for the rest of their lives, and indeed I still hear from Mrs. Clergy whose husband has been dead for years. For those few still living there will always be a cherished bond between us. We meet occasionally.

Chapter 11

On my way to Edmonton in 1962 to be inducted as Authors president, I stopped in Toronto where Georgeanna Smith, now Hamilton, of the Ryerson Press wanted to give publicity to my forthcoming book, *Maritime Folk Songs*. In her charming and youthful enthusiasm she had planned three television interviews, two on radio, and two with the press, not to mention luncheon with Dr. Grant, the editor. It was a whirl and reminded me of Martha Banning Thomas who often said in these days, "I don't see how you can buzz and whiz so much." I enjoyed it, mainly because Georgeanna was gay and made it all such fun. When my plane finally took off I thought, "I can't feel any worse because if I do, I'll die, so I must soon start to feel better." After an hour or so of sitting on the plane, life began to return to my weary limbs. I had foreseen my fatigue and had arrived a day early so I could go straight to a hotel and sleep the clock around.

A president is supposed to visit every branch at least once during the two-year term of office. I began by attending a dinner of the Montreal branch in honour of Mr. Leslie Roberts, and I had the pleasure of sitting next to Mayor Jean Drapeau. There were tape-recorded tributes from many of Mr. Roberts' friends, which must have been a moving experience for him. My talk in Montreal I thought stiff for I was trying to say all the things

225

a president ought to say. When I repeated it in Ottawa I made it more personal and felt happier about it. Ottawa was a challenge because in addition to their own branch members, Mr. Walter Herbert of the Canada Foundation was there, and Dr. Carmen Roy, Chief of the Folklore Division of the National Museum, arrived just as we were starting. I shared the spotlight with the Ukrainian poet, Alexandre Pidsuka who was on a goodwill tour of Canada. Mr. Herbert had asked our association to look after his hospitality. We had never been asked for such a service before, and with its Unesco sponsoring, we felt our participation was important. I had written all the regional presidents, and the result was that in every city where we had branches, he was taken under our wing. I now have a piece of Ukrainian pottery in token of his appreciation.

Don Thomson, my predecessor, was my adviser through two eventful and happy years. There was excitement when Mrs. Vicky Metcalf offered a thousand-dollar prize which we decided to give for writing works inspirational to Canadian youth, and it was a joy to write Kerry Wood one year and John Hayes the next to tell them they were our winners. In Toronto there was a memorable luncheon given by the branch president, Cynewulf Robbins, when he, Lyn Harrington, Arthur Hailey and I talked from twelve-thirty until three. Arthur was just beginning his rise to fame, and it was thrilling to sit for a moment on the threshold with him. Robert Fontaine, author of *The Happy Time*, a book dramatized by the CBC in which Alan Mills had starred as Uncle Louis, was a special guest at the 1963 banquet. In Winnipeg I spoke to the authors as their president, and to the Maritime Club for the National Museum, and the following day the Honourable and Mrs. Errick Willis had a small luncheon for me. In Ottawa the Honourable Arthur Laing and I sent invitations jointly to the unveiling of a monument commemorating the poet Duncan Campbell Scott. From a reception given at the home of the Prime Minister, I have a picture of Mrs. Lester Pearson with Dr. Marius Barbeau's arm linked in hers on one side, and mine on the other. At a civic luncheon given the Authors in Halifax, the city presented me with earrings bearing the Halifax crest, and on my retirement as president I was given the usual silver and labradorite paperweight facetiously referred to as "the coffin." Executive members attended meetings faithfully at great sacrifice of time and money, and I am particularly indebted to two who have since died, Allan Sangster and Gordon Thompson.

Some writers, and I am one, need an association like this where we can mingle with other writers and learn from one another. Writing is a lonely profession, for we shut ourselves up within our own four walls and are entirely dependent upon ourselves for whatever success we achieve. My desire was to stimulate the branches so that they would inspire their members as I had so often been inspired when I was young, and to this end I worked by correspondence and through meetings, and travelled from coast to coast, speaking as in Winnipeg for both the Authors and the National Museum. I would like to be remembered as an inspiring president, but have been cited for my success with public relations. Perhaps that is not so different after all.

One day Gordon Thompson brought the national executive an idea. He felt that the song our generation had grown up with, *The Maple Leaf Forever*, was too good to be discarded just because a few of the words now gave offence in some parts of Canada. He therefore suggested a contest for new lyrics. He offered a prize of one thousand dollars and said his music company would publish the winning song. We accepted his proposal realizing that remarks from the public would not all be complimentary, made our announcement and waited for the results. Dr. Roy Fenwick, Sir Ernest MacMillan, Allan Sangster, Helmut Blume and I were judges. Columnists had great amusement at our expense and composed

227

verses themselves making the dandelion the emblem, or northern wheat. They referred to the old words as "The May-pul Leaf, our em-blum dear," which is what it used to sound like when we sang in at top volume in school. Somebody thought the popular television show, "Front Page Challenge" should join in the fun. Consequently I found myself one day being met at the Toronto airport by a charming Mr. McKeen from the CBC and being whisked to the hotel where they usually house their challengers. Here I stayed in hiding until the next afternoon when he called for us. We were put through our paces with a practice panel, and one of them got very excited because he had just been working on a tape of ghost stories he had made at my home a few weeks before, and hadn't recognized my voice. We were taken to an exotic restaurant for dinner to put us in a relaxed and mellow mood, and then we were smuggled into the studio by a side door lest one of the evening panel see us. Two shows were done. Mr. Innes Taylor and Mr. Mendes France were televised live, and Mr. Norman Thomas, American socialist, and I were video-taped to be shown the following week. Panelist Pierre Berton guessed my name just in time and then surprised us all by singing his own composed version. Their first questions dealt with the contest and took a light tone. They then turned to the question of the Canadian flag, a subject of hot debate at that time, and panelist Gordon Sinclair was rude as I had expected.

Before we began, he had asked one of the afternoon panel what this show would be like and had been told, "We think it will be one of the best we've ever done." Gordon, who cherishes his pennies, bet a dollar it wouldn't, but at its conclusion handed over his dollar. There were some comical reactions. My charwoman said, "If I didn't know it was going to be you I wouldn't have known you, you looked so lovely," and another person said, "You looked so nice; much nicer than in real life." Many friends protested Gordon Sinclair's manner of speaking to me and wanted to punch his nose. I didn't feel quite that way because I'd said to him after the show, "I've been holding conversations with you all week trying to anticipate your questions," and he said with unexpected solicitude, "I wasn't too hard on you was I?" The nicest of the many fan letters came from a stranger and ended, "Thank you for my lovely meeting of you."

I knew I'd been pushing too hard, but how else could I do my job as president and keep up my work for the Museum? I suppose it is because I accomplish so much that nobody realizes the long hours I have always had to spend resting, and how limited my strength is. A new director had come to the Museum who left all folklore decisions in the capable hands of Dr. Roy. She has built up the Archives splendidly, and to her the Museum comes first; I knew she wasn't happy that I was giving it limited attention. I was not too surprised then when the surgical axe fell, but before coming to that, let us go back a year.

On my way to the Miramichi Folk Song Festival in 1963, I had stopped off for a night's rest at Marshlands Inn, the nicest place of its kind in the Maritime Provinces, and more of a club than an inn. I decided to sleep in the early evening and go downstairs later for cocoa which is always served at bedtime, and where there are always interesting people to be met. I had wakened and was getting out of bed when I saw a vision of myself coming towards me, but as a child of ten with a very sweet and welcoming expression on my face. I recognized this immediately as the worst omen I could have and put my hands out as though pushing it away. It faded but returned almost immediately but not quite so vividly. Again I made the gesture of pushing it away. It came a third time, but by then was quite faint. I got up and went downstairs as planned, determined to forget it as I always react when anything supernatural occurs. I met the other guests as though nothing had happened and afterwards had a good night's rest.

In the morning it began to bother me and I felt I must drive with extra caution. I had kept especially alert when going through a wooded section and had come to a clearing when suddenly, directly in front of my car, I saw a deer. It seemed to have come from nowhere. Isn't it extraordinary how much the mind can think of in a split second of time? I said to myself, "There's a deer; I can't miss it." Then I prayed fervently, "Oh God, *please* help me," and because I believed this possible, I took my hands off the steering wheel. There was a crash —that was inevitable—but I was not propelled forward as I would expect after colliding with a heavy object at fifty miles an hour, nor did the car swerve off the road, but came to a gentle stop. With shaking knees I got out to survey the damage for I had heard the sound of glass being shattered. The right headlight and lens were broken in many pieces and the metal below the light was pierced. I looked for the deer but it had disappeared, and even though I backed up there was no sign of it. Were it not for the evidence, I would have thought the whole thing an illusion. I concluded that the vision coming as a child and not an adult, had not been a death omen but a warning. The conclusion was strengthened the following spring when on the train between Toronto and Winnipeg I heard the porter singing and talked to him about Negro songs. We then got around to folklore, and among other things he mentioned that his mother had said a person born with a caul would always have a warning before danger. He of course had no idea I was born with a caul, so it is odd that he mentioned it.

In June of '63 I told my experience in a speech at the Canadian Authors convention and afterwards a young woman came to me trembling and said she had experienced a similar vision. In her case her father had died within a week. Another author, Frances Shelly Wees, threw further light on it. She said the vision's proper name is *Doppelgänger*, and she gave me this note: "Every individual has a 'spiritual' or non-physical double. This double never appears, nor can it be seen by anyone else. It is in a sense the 'guard,' the archon, the protector of the physical person. To see the *Doppelgänger* (the double-goer) is supposed to be dangerous because obviously at this point strong protection is going to be needed. It is only when the *Doppelgänger* comes *too* close that death is imminent—the *two* cannot merge on this earth."

The next odd occurrence came in March 1964 as I was writing a cheque for my Northeast Folklore Society dues. It was a small amount, so I thought I might pay for the next year as well. Then I changed my mind and thought, "No, I'll be seeing Sandy Ives at the Miramichi Folk Song Festival in August, and can pay him in person," but a voice inside me objected and said, "You won't be alive by then." I replied, again inside my head, "What?" and the message was repeated. "Don't be silly," I objected, or words to that effect, and sat down to complete my letter, but found I couldn't do it. I knew then that something bad in a physical sense would happen before the middle of August, and therefore I hastened a trip to England to visit my nephew Peter in his home as he and his family had so happily visited me in mine the year before.

My term as Authors president drew to a close in 1964 with the annual convention held that year in Halifax, and I was thankful to be able to preside and enjoy my office to the end. I felt as well as I ever do, and if I was more tired than I knew was wise, excitement carried me through. Nature will take so much, and, I suppose, this time nature rebelled. At any rate, a week later there were sudden indications of a growth, and it was thought to be malignant. I fully expected the operation to be successful, but was prepared to be told the cancer had spread. As I lay in my hospital bed awaiting the doctor's verdict, my Doppelgänger reappeared. This time I seemed to be about thirty-eight years of age. I had a board which I was holding at waist height and I was paddling my way through heavy water and making slow but steady progress. The important thing was that I paid no attention to myself but passed by without so much as a glance.

"I've had a reprieve," I thought, and so it turned out. In 1966 I saw myself again, this time walking away in the opposite direction with one shoulder drooped as in age or from a heavy burden. My fishermen friends have told me that walking away means a long life, so I expect to be around for a while yet. Nonetheless, I had reached a turning point. Whether or not it is true an ailing daughter improves in health when her mother dies, I was much stronger in my forties, fifties, and early sixties than I'd been in the hard twenties and thirties. I had been aware of the passing years, but didn't need to cater to them. I could do that no longer. However I was far from through yet.

In the spring of 1966 a telephone call came from Glenn Sarty, a Nova Scotian in Toronto producing the interview show, "Telescope" for the CBC. He had bought *Bluenose Ghosts* for his son but had read it himself and could see that a number of stories would work well on camera. Would I be interested in doing a show in which I would make occasional appearances, but most of the stories would be told by those who had contributed them in the book? I would indeed, for that summer I was not doing field work. I had concluded I was not getting any younger and it would be much better to make material on hand available rather than to keep accumulating it for someone else to publish. Fortuitously, Dr. Wayland Hand had written to know if I would do a book on the popular beliefs and superstitions of Nova Scotia. It was to be a documentary requiring long hours of detailed work. The show appealed to me as being creative and stimulating, a welcome relief from assembling these notes and making an index.

The country had never looked more fresh and lovely than on the June day when we first set out, and as we drove over the familiar roads, I realized what a lot of time had elapsed since my collecting began. We paused at the Eastern Passage bridge where in the old days they used to hold dances. The Osborne house where we had met so often, with the little hand-pumped organ, had disappeared. The road that used to fill up with sand was now paved. As for the Hartlan estate, all the spruce trees had gone, and the ground was now a golf course. What had become of Enos Hartlan's ghostesses and witches? And on Devil's Island would we find any dwelling habitable except that of the lightkeeper? We made a few contacts and then Glenn went off on his own, armed with a list I had given him. What surprised him was the ease with which people talked about the supernatural. After a few minutes conversation he would say, "Have you ever seen a ghost?" and they would answer as naturally as if he had said, "Have you ever caught a salmon?"

Except for a script assistant, Halifax CBC provided the whole crew. Glenn is known as a hard driver, but nobody seemed to mind because he drove himself even harder, and this job was much more imaginative than the usual run of programs. There were ten in the crew when I was with them, and I loved to watch the fishermen when Vaunda Crozier made them up with daubs of powder and rouge. They adored it.

An odd thing happened on our first filming day. We had gone to Freeman Young's, whom you will remember as one of the Petpeswick singers who had given me "Farewell to Nova Scotia." Now when he sang it he repeated the last line of the chorus, something he had never done before. He had picked it up from Catherine McKinnon's rendition on television. A collector today would have to be constantly aware of these outside influences. Freeman at ninety could still acquire new tricks.

When we went to Devil's Island I wondered how I would feel after all I'd heard of its effect upon my friends. From the time Edmund Henneberry and his son met me with their boat I felt exhilarated. As we approached land Edmund said, "See where the breakwater used to be? That's all that's left," and, "The old man's store (Mr. Ben's fishhouse) was over there," and "That's all that's left of the Edwards' house." And Aunt Jane's house? Not a stick to be seen. We strolled along the path where I used to push the wheelbarrow with the melodeon. Memories were of kindness, music, and the Islanders gathering around to help, and I felt I was missing a lot now that I was retired and working with words instead of people.

It seemed odd to find Cape Bretoners in the lightkeeper's house, and living in a modern dwelling even to hardwood floors. Their greetings were as warm as the Faulkners' had been thirty-eight years before. The island's new owner, Mr. Mont, had heard we were there and had come to see what was going on, and he told me he hoped to explore for treasure. I told about the barrel two boys had seen long before my first visit. Edmund added that it had disappeared from sight and although a sluice was made and the lake drained, it was never seen again. He also said you could put a pole down fifteen feet at that spot and not touch bottom.

The keeper, Mr. MacDonald, spoke about the lighthouse. "There's something there," he declared. "There's one thing I won't tell anybody until I leave the island, but when you go up to the light a depression comes over you and stays with you till you come down again. I've kept other lights and never felt anything like this in any of them." Glenn video-taped this storytelling and they took innumerable pictures of waves beating against the rocky shore and of deserted houses that looked inviting for spectral visitations. The fishermen of my day still surviving live and work on the mainland now and only a few fish.

My most gruelling day lasted for twelve hours and when everything was set up, I found that my voice was husky. It often is in the morning, especially if I'm tired. "I'm not going to ruin it all by not having a voice!" Then

I remembered Nathan Hatt's solution and put salt on my tongue. That did it.

When the network presentation came on, CBC Halifax, at their own suggestion, put a colour set in their conference room where I could take a dozen guests. Scenic shots, especially of surf, were spectacular. When tales were tragic, the sea was grey and boiling; in peaceful scenes, as when the old man's heaven was to come back and see the view, the water was calm and serene. Shadows were used to give ghostly effects, and the horse-drawn hearse driven over a rough country road was proof of Glenn's ingenuity—to unearth such a vehicle and driver in this day and age! Best of all were the storytellers with their sincerity and implicit belief in their tales. He had managed to fit everybody in that he had filmed, "But," he wrote, "don't blink an eyelash or you might miss someone." It was called "Lady of the Legends."

In the summer of 1967 Glenn was producing the afternoon television show, "Take Thirty." To use up material that couldn't be fitted into the previous production, he suggested putting it on "Take Thirty," which meant a little additional video-taping. This time at Eastern Passage, interviewer Paul Soles and I walked towards the bridge and I explained how this had come to be my path of destiny. There was also a short interview in my home, and there Paul sat on an antique chair that had been mended. The house was then one hundred years old so it was natural for him to ask, "Has anything supernatural ever happened here?" and then lean back to await my reply. At that moment the mended back broke and the top half crashed to the floor. Poor Paul!

A few weeks after my work on the "Telescope" show was finished and long before it was on the air, I dreamed that two people had been given a present and then I was given one much more important than the other two. All that day I puzzled, wondering what it could mean. In the late afternoon the doorbell rang and a delivery man handed me a box containing a dozen red roses. Who had sent such a lovely gift? They were from Glenn with a note to say he had just screened the show and was delighted. The following day the Halifax script assistant came to record a few missing words and I told her my dream. She said, "I can tell you who the others were." He had sent the two script writers one rose each.

In 1967 the Canadian Folk Music Society sponsored a Workshop on Ethnomusicology at the University of British Columbia. I was then a vice president and chairman of the scholars' committee. (I am now honorary president.) Our president, Graham George, was having a sabbatical in France, and it was my good luck to take his place. This meant giving the address of welcome, chairing two sessions, presenting some of our Micmac Indian music, and finally summing up the deliberations. Nine participants from as far away as Denmark and Hawaii presented hour-long papers with ample time for discussions, and with their high scholarly standing and diversity of backgrounds it was a centennial project to remember. Mr. Crossley-Holland, known to many through England's radio broadcast, Third Programme, kept notes and later wrote it up in detail for the British Columbia government. I felt greatly privileged to be there.

Indeed this was my university year, because a month before the Vancouver trip I'd been given my third honorary degree, a D.C.L. from the University of King's College. Later in the year I was asked to speak to their Haliburton Club, the oldest literary club on the continent. They made me a Fellow, the first woman to be so honoured, and then I was given a two-year term on King's Board of Governors.

That same year I was asked to make a November tour of the universities of Saskatchewan, Alberta, Winnipeg and Manitoba. They were to be informal gatherings with small groups so nothing need be prepared in advance. Fortunately I was too experienced not to know that one should always be prepared in advance. I took along a centennial record of Canadian folk music that

236

had just been published by the CBC and RCA Victor, and twenty-six of the songs were from my collection. I also took along my two ethnic (Folkways) records and a few slides. The first two classes were small and informal, but I found myself early in the tour facing Professor Murray Adaskin's class of one hundred and seventy-five, and I had to fill an hour. There would be questions at the end, but students needed something on which to base them. I hastily listed records and slides in the order wanted and with Professor Adaskin and Dr. Kaplan, head of the Music Department expecting a rare treat, I rose to the challenge greatly helped by a technician who always had the right needle in the right groove at the right moment. The tour ended with a two-hour lecture at the University of Manitoba after which thirty music students took me to lunch. Two escorted me back to the beautiful guest suite I was occupying. Then I came down with flu. I mentioned to Mrs. Leathers as she and Mrs. Swayze, wives of professors, drove me to the airport in the morning how calamitous it would have been if the attack had come on before the lecture and she replied with an old saying, "The body accommodates itself to its need." Hospitality was overwhelming, some official and some personal as in the case of composer Violet Archer at Edmonton whom I'd met before.

I had arranged to take in meetings of the American Folklore Society in Toronto on my way back. I did, but managed only a few sessions, and tried not to look too bedraggled when my "Lady of the Legends" film was shown. At its conclusion a member said I was the most televised folklorist on the continent. He was probably right, with Dr. Barbeau a close runner-up. This Society has now made me a Fellow. With its membership of eight hundred individuals, or two thousand if we include universities and organizations, and less than forty-five Fellows, this for a folklorist must be the ultimate honour. In 1969 I attended a Fellows' luncheon at their Atlanta, Georgia meetings. It was a great moment when I took my place and received my certificate.

Like so many things, that had come as a surprise. It had also been a surprise when in 1963 the Dartmouth Academy, a new school for boys, asked me to serve on its Board of Governors. I would be a liaison with the town, or city as we are now, and also, as a non-parent, would have no personal involvement. Through this connection I have met a whole new set of people, mostly newcomers to this area, and enjoyed this new interest, so different from other things I had done. I served in this capacity for ten years.

Another surprise came in 1966 when the Dartmouth Kiwanis Club invited me to speak at their December dinner. With the demands of compiling *Bluenose Magic*, preparations for Christmas, chronic fatigue, and the fact that I'd been refusing such invitations right and left, I surprised even myself by accepting. A few days before the event Mayor Zatzman phoned for biographical notes, and it didn't occur to me that there was anything unusual in having the introduction given by our senior official. When dinner was over two photographers appeared and I supposed this had something to do with the club's own activities and paid no attention. When Mr. Zatzman rose I was interested to see what he would make of what I'd told him. Suddenly it was borne upon my stupid head that this was no ordinary occasion and that I was being presented with a beautiful bronze plaque and declared Citizen of the Year, here in my own home town. My hand shook as I accepted their tribute and my voice did too as I began my speech. The plaque has since hung proudly in my sitting-room.

Another honour had a strange forerunner. On a December morning in 1967 I looked towards the sunrise which was red and beautiful, but a cross stood above it. I'd never seen this before, but it didn't strike me as an ill omen. That morning the postman brought a registered parcel, a centennial medal given (as declared to 49,999 other recipients) "in recognition of valuable service to the nation." A ribbon and bow accompanied the medal, and when put in place, these formed just such a cross as I had seen.

I could mention many odd things that have happened through the years—like the time I leaned down to get a log of wood for the fire in the grate. When I straightened up my eyes were level with a picture of my father in an oval frame. In the same oval shape there was a mist or cloud about three inches thick enclosing the picture. I presume it was his aura. I had no particular worry at the time nor did anything occur to account for it.

When my sister Lilian died in 1968, I had the most amazing experience, and one that still gives me comfort and joy. Usually when I was worried about her I could feel my parents around, but when I held my lonely vigil in the Tatamagouche hospital, I had no feeling of their presence and missed them. I had gone to church myself to say special prayers for her, but as the moment of death approached, I realized no clergyman had been asked to visit her in hospital. I must have looked stricken as I rushed to the nurse on duty.

Reverend James Fraser came quickly, and as he stood on one side of the bed and I on the other, the two attendant nurses left. He read a passage from Scripture, said a prayer for the dying and one for me. I didn't realize until later that she had probably stopped breathing during his prayer for me. She was certainly alive when he started. When he was through we sat for a moment in conversation until I realized that the shoulder which had been pulsating with her rapid breathing had ceased its motion.

What happened during the prayer for me was an inflow of strength so vigorous that I knew it would sustain me through the days ahead. In fact it sustained me for most of the following year. I learned later that this is known as the gift of grace. The theological meaning is "strengthening influence" or "divine regenerating." It uplifted me in a way I had never known, like a benediction, and I was in a state almost of ecstasy. Since then I have never thought of her with relief as at the dropping of a heavy burden, but always with love and affection, and usually I find myself smiling. At first I used to feel her close as though things were reversed now and she was looking after me, and one time in that period between waking and sleeping, I saw her. It was just her head. She looked happy and seemed to be flying slowly through the air at the centre of a little group I can only think of as a heavenly host.

For years I have thought that one day I would lead a more social life and see more of my friends, but things keep turning up with my work and the people I see most are connected with it in one way or another. I've been consulting with music educators at Dalhousie University and in the Halifax school system on songs suitable for teaching in our schools. Also, with Mrs. Kaye Dimock to direct the singing, I have had a small choir, and we have given many programs locally. We also performed on July 1st, 1971 on Ottawa's Parliament Hill and at the National Library. There have been other radio and television shows, an article in the magazine *Ethnomusicology* entitled "An Ethnomusicological Survey of the Maritime Provinces," and I now serve on the Board of the *Encyclopedia of Music in Canada*.

A high point came in May, 1974. Plans began with the Kodaly International Symposium at Oakland, California in the summer of 1973, to which perhaps I should have gone. However my brother Mac and nephew Peter were coming from England, and they had priority. At the symposium, Kaye Dimock heard from my old friend, Richard Johnston, now of the University of Alberta, that the Canadian Music Council meetings were to be in Halifax the following summer and that folklore would be their theme. They then began to get ideas. Snippets of information were fed to me from time to time, but I had no idea the coming events would be so stupendous, even though in the spring I was visited by Mr. Ronald Napier, President of the Canadian Music Council and Mr. Keith Bissell, a director and composer.

On the morning of May 3rd I took part in a panel discussion on Maritime Folk Music chaired by Professor George Proctor, head of the Mount Allison Music Department, and Father Chiasson of the University of Moncton, a collector of Acadian folk music. I took as my theme the advantages of being a pioneer. In 1967 Cape Breton miners had formed a singing group called Men of the Deeps, and I had helped Mrs. Harry Cohen in its establishment. They were performing that afternoon, which meant I must be there but it left little time for a trip home to change for the evening and no time for a rest.

Before leaving, I had a short conversation with Mr. Hugh Davidson of the Canada Council. He remarked, "And this evening they're giving you a medal." He was astonished when I said, "So that's what it is!" I told him I hadn't wanted to know and that I had a little story to tell after the presentation and he hadn't told me anything, had he? To which he obligingly replied, "No, I didn't say a word."

Dr. Roxane Carlisle, Head Ethnomusicologist at the National Museum was my house guest, and at dinner we sat at a table with Dr. Kolinsky and other prominent musicians. At the conclusion of the dinner Richard Johnston read my citation and did it in French which took me back to the day I got my honorary degree at Laval and wondered what they were saying about me. My little story was that I didn't know whether this was the end of my first childhood or the beginning of my second, but when I was told some weeks before that there would be a presentation I had asked not to be told what it would be so I could enjoy the anticipation to the end. It had never occurred to me that it would be a medal.

After the presentation people crowded around. The singing miners were dinner guests and most shook hands. One or two more daring than the rest kissed me, one saying "I just wanted to be able to go home and tell my wife I did it." The medal is of highly polished bronze with the Council's name in English and French on one side and my name and the date on the other. It has a white leather case and is a new design. I treasure it with pride. But there was more to come.

When I drove Roxane to the morning meetings next day, I had thought of taking one in but decided there was only one place for me, and that was resting in bed. Invitations for the dinner that evening to be given by the Nova Scotia Government said that the affair would be in my honour, so I felt I must be at my best. The Olives, my tenants from upstairs, presented me with a beautiful red rose, and this was followed by a bouquet of spring flowers from the John Scotts of Pickering. (Mrs. Scott is Joyce Sullivan who is still singing from my collection.) My gown was of pink brocaded satin with long sleeves and a plain matching sleeveless coat, and when we arrived at the hotel Mrs. Gillis, Director of Protocol, pinned a beautiful orchid on the coat. I had felt that a dinner given in my honour was sufficient, but it was possible they might also present a gift, and if so I would have to be prepared with a few words of appreciation. I had asked Mrs. Olive if she knew what was planned. Poor Nesta—Hugh Conrod, Deputy Minister of Recreation, had sworn her to secrecy, but the expression on her face was sufficient, and as we entered the hotel we saw our host, the Honourable A. Garnet Brown, followed by a man carrying a large square box wrapped in festive paper, so I said to her, "There it is."

At the reception I was agreeably surprised to see many local guests and to realize that this was not just a dinner for visiting musicians, but a full-sized banquet. After head table names were called out and the others had taken their places, a piper in full regalia piped us in, observing the usual custom here at government dinners. Following the dinner, Mr. Brown, Minister of Recreation, spoke briefly on his department's interest in cultural affairs and then referred to the contribution I had made. The large square box I had already seen was then presented, but when I started to rise he said, "Not yet," and his wife presented me with two dozen red roses. Still I was not allowed to rise, and this time I was given a framed Award of Recognition. And as if that were not enough, the Mayor of Dartmouth, Mrs. Eileen Stubbs, also made a little speech and presented me with a gold brooch bearing the crest of my home city. It was overwhelming, especially as at the two banquets when the awards were made the whole room had stood and applauded. In my words of thanks when I said that when I get old I will have many wonderful things to look upon, some of my friends rocked with laughter, which of course I intended. I also told them that my greatest happiness in the last two days had been that the music was being recognized, that I was known mostly for ghosts, but music had been my first love. To be honoured nationally, provincially, and even by my own home town in the course of two days was a little heady, and I wondered at one point if I had died and this was what heaven is like.

So many kisses! But we were already late for the concert which Kaye Dimock had so diligently arranged with all the music taken from my collection. Some new arrangements had been made, and the thought behind it was to show our visitors the quality of music in Halifax today. On the stage's left from the view of the audience, were a choral group composed of some of the city's finest singers. At the extreme right there were some thirty students in the thirteen-to-fifteen age group from the Halifax Schools String Ensemble. In the centre were Gary Karr, world-renowned player of the double bass who had cancelled a New York engagement in order to be here, his accompanist Harmon Lewis, Stephen Pedersen, flutist, and Phyllis Ensher, harpist with the Atlantic Symphony Orchestra. My part was a short introduction of each number.

When the last song was started, with everyone on stage taking part, two figures emerged from the opposite wings dressed in sheets and having large blue noses and bright shining eyes. They made their stealthy way towards me through the strings and choral sections and then picked me up, chair and all, and carried me off the stage whereupon Gary Karr stepped forward and remarked, "We always knew Bluenose Ghosts would get her in the end."

What was in the large square box? A replica of the schooner *Bluenose* carved in walnut from the wrecked bark *Aurora* lost off Brier Island in 1908. It stands about a foot high with all sails set. A brass plate bears my name and records the occasion. Now when it all seems like a gorgeous dream I look at my mementoes which testify to the reality of it all.

Now in 1975 I see our songs used in text books in Canada and abroad. Many have been arranged for solo and choral singing and appear in sheet music; others are combined with melodies from Newfoundland for orchestral playing. I am especially pleased that locally we have a band number composed by Kenneth Elloway, choral arrangements by Mona Maund, Eunice Sircom and others, and harp arrangements by Phyllis Ensher. We have two symphonies by Klaro Mizirit, conductor of the Atlantic Symphony Orchestra, and one by Alex Tilley as well as a mini-opera by Steven Freygood. Dave Woods and Dennis Farrell have made compositions from our melodies for Gary Karr which he plays on his extensive travels, and when the Men of the Deeps perform in China this year, our songs will be in their repertoire. From *Bluenose Ghosts*, the Nova Scotia Photographic Department has just released a twenty minute film using the title of the book and having stories performed by Neptune Theatre actors and actresses. It will be distributed by the Nova Scotia Tourist Bureau. At the St. Francis Xavier spring convocation I was given the honorary degree of Doctor of Letters, and at Dartmouth's Natal Day celebrations there was a presentation of a gold medal. Now, mindful of a rich, full life I can say in the words of the Psalmist, "The lines are fallen unto me in pleasant places; yea, I have a goodly heritage."